QUEEN VICTORIA'S SECRETS

QUEEN VICTORIA'S SECRETS

ADRIENNE MUNICH

Columbia University Press
New York

Columbia University Press
New York   Chichester, West Sussex
Copyright © 1996 Columbia University Press
All rights reserved

∞

Library of Congress Cataloging-in-Publication Data
Munich, Adrienne.
    Queen Victoria's secrets / Adrienne Munich.
        p.   cm.
    Includes bibliographical references (p. 237) and index.
    ISBN 0-231-10480-4 (cloth) 0-231-10481-2 (paper)
        1. Victoria, Queen of Great Britain. 1819–1901.   2. Great Britain—
    Social life and customs—19th century.   3. Great Britain—History—
    Victoria, 1837–1901   4. Women—Great Britain—History—19th
    century.   5. Queens—Great Britain—Biography.   I. Title.
    DA554.M86   1996
    941.081—dc20   95-43737

Printed in the United States of America
c 10 9 8 7 6 5 4 3 2 1
p 10 9 8 7 6 5 4 3 2

FOR DICK AND PAT,

who share some of

Queen Victoria's best virtues

CONTENTS

ILLUSTRATIONS

ACKNOWLEDGMENTS

Upon the completion of Sir Robert Martin's five-volume biography of Prince Albert—a fourteen-year project—Queen Victoria thanked the author but characteristically acknowledged her awareness of more mixed emotions: "She feels too a sadness that it should be finished." I recognize her feeling as my own much shorter and more modest project comes to an end. The queen has been great company. Hospitable libraries and curious librarians have helped me uncover odd and dusty parts of her history: at Stony Brook, Yale, Cornell, the New York Public Library, the Boston Public Library, the Sydney Public Library, the New York Botanical Gardens, the British Library, the Victoria and Albert Museum, the Yale Center for British Art, the Harry Ransom Collection at the University of Texas, the White Plains Public Library, the Fashion Institute of Technology, the Library of Congress, and the Royal Archives at Windsor Castle.

Fifteen years ago I gave my first paper on Queen Victoria to a spirited gathering of colleagues at the Northeast Victorian Studies Association, many of whom have lingered for the finale. Without Margaret Homans's ideas for a collaborative venture and our exchanges over the years, my ideas might slowly be turning to mist. The

Humanities Institute at Stony Brook under the direction of Ann Kaplan encouraged intellectual exchange of the best sort. Warm thanks to Stony Brook colleagues Helen Cooper, Lou Deutsch, Temma Kaplan, Steve Larese, Ira Livingston, Bill Miller, Sandy Petrey, Mary Rawlinson, Jim Rubin, and Kathleen Wilson and to Stony Brook graduate students in a seminar on Victorian Gender and Authority. Audiences at the Center for Independent Study in New Haven, at the Australasian Victorian Studies Association, the Modern Language Association, the CUNY Victorian Seminar, and the Armstrong Browning Library, Baylor University, asked good questions. Jessica Benjamin, Miriam Brody, Susan Brown, Susan Casteras, Veneta and Robert Colby, Mandy Frisken, Barbara and Harry Garlick, Barbara Gates, Helen Grace, Rachel Jacoff, Isaac Kramnick, Jonathan Kramnick, Rusty Shteir, Betsy Sledge, Kay Staniland, and Marjorie Stone are all in this book in one way or another. Dorothy Thompson's hospitality and generosity to a stranger amazes me even now.

Those who read this book in earlier versions—Carole Silver, Carolyn Williams, Nina Auerbach, Pat Spacks, and Carole Woods—and those who read bits of it—Helen Cooper, Lou Deutsch, Diana Diamond, Ann Kaplan, Bernie Kendler, Eva Kittay, Susan Squier, and Susan Walsh—make me feel fortunate to have friends smarter than I, although I reluctantly excuse them from not being able to make me smarter. Research assistants Donesse Champeau, Martha Heller, Matthew Munich, and Fran O'Connor found Queen Victorias in many odd places. The Victoria list on the Internet gave more prolonged answers than I thought possible. Jennifer Crewe's editorial capabilities once again receive my affectionate praise; she and the others at Columbia University Press, Anne McCoy and Susan Heath, manuscript editor extraordinary, in particular, turn me into a fortunate coworker. My coeditors at The Munich Express, Dick, Edwin, and Matthew, provide an ethical and loving center in this postmodern world.

CHRONOLOGY

1818 MARRIAGE OF EDWARD AUGUSTUS, DUKE OF KENT, FOURTH SON
     OF GEORGE III, AND VICTOIRE OF LEININGEN, MAY 29

1819 BIRTH OF PRINCESS ALEXANDRINA VICTORIA, MAY 24
     BIRTH OF PRINCE ALBERT OF SAXE-COBURG, AUGUST 26

1820 DEATH OF DUKE OF KENT, JANUARY 23
     DEATH OF GEORGE III
     ACCESSION OF GEORGE IV

1824 LOUISE LEHZEN (LATER BARONESS) BECOMES VICTORIA'S
     GOVERNESS

1830 DEATH OF GEORGE IV
     ACCESSION OF WILLIAM IV
     LEOPOLD BECOMES KING OF THE BELGIANS

1832 FIRST REFORM BILL PASSED
     MARRIAGE OF KING LEOPOLD TO LOUISE MARIE OF ORLÉANS,
      DAUGHTER OF KING LOUIS PHILIPPE OF FRANCE, AUGUST 9

1835 LORD MELBOURNE (WHIG) BECOMES PRIME MINISTER
     PRINCESS VICTORIA AND THE DUCHESS OF KENT BECOME
      PATRONS OF THE SOCIETY FOR THE PREVENTION OF
      CRUELTY TO ANIMALS

1836 FIRST VISIT TO ENGLAND OF PRINCE ALBERT, MAY 22–JUNE 7

1837 DEATH OF WILLIAM IV
     ACCESSION OF QUEEN VICTORIA, JUNE 20

1838 CORONATION OF QUEEN VICTORIA, JUNE 28
     ELIZABETH BARRETT [BROWNING], "VICTORIA'S TEARS,"
      "THE YOUNG QUEEN"

1839 PRINCE ALBERT'S SECOND VISIT TO ENGLAND, OCTOBER 10

QUEEN VICTORIA PROPOSES MARRIAGE TO PRINCE ALBERT,
OCTOBER 15
ACT OF PARLIAMENT AGAINST CRUELTY TO DOGS

1840   MARRIAGE OF QUEEN VICTORIA AND PRINCE ALBERT,
FEBRUARY 10
ELIZABETH BARRETT [BROWNING], "CROWNED AND WEDDED"
FIRST ASSASSINATION ATTEMPT, JUNE 10
BIRTH OF THE PRINCESS ROYAL, VICTORIA ADELAIDE MARY
LOUISE "VICKY," NOVEMBER 21

1841   SIR ROBERT PEEL (TORY) BECOMES PRIME MINISTER,
SEPTEMBER
BIRTH OF PRINCE OF WALES, ALBERT EDWARD "BERTIE"
(KING EDWARD VII), NOVEMBER 9
GEORGE RUSSELL FRENCH, *The Ancestry of Her Majesty Queen
Victoria and of His Royal Highness Prince Albert*
SIR EDWIN LANDSEER, *Windsor Castle in Modern Times*

1842   CHARTIST PROCESSION TO PARLIMENT, MAY 2
PLANTAGENET BALL, MAY 12
SECOND ASSASSINATION ATTEMPT, MAY 29
THIRD ASSASSINATION ATTEMPT, JULY 3
FIRST VISIT TO SCOTLAND, AUGUST 29–SEPTEMBER 17
EDWIN LANDSEER, *The Sanctuary*, PURCHASED BY VICTORIA
FOR ALBERT
BARONESS LEHZEN IS RETIRED, SEPTEMBER 30

1843   BIRTH OF PRINCESS ALICE MARY MAUD, APRIL 23
PURCHASE OF OSBORNE HOUSE, ISLE OF WIGHT

1844   DEATH OF ERNEST I OF COBURG (ALBERT'S FATHER),
JANUARY 29
BIRTH OF PRINCE ALFRED ERNEST ALBERT "AFFIE," DUKE OF
EDINBURGH AND DUKE OF COBURG, AUGUST 6
VISIT OF KING LOUIS PHILIPPE OF FRANCE, SEPTEMBER

1846   BIRTH OF PRINCESS HELENA AUGUSTA VICTORIA "LENCHEN,"
MAY 25
LORD JOHN RUSSELL (WHIG) BECOMES PRIME MINISTER

1847   PURCHASE OF BALMORAL CASTLE IN THE SCOTTISH HIGHLANDS

1848   BIRTH OF PRINCESS LOUISE CAROLINE ALBERTA "LOOSY,"
         MARCH 18
       CHARTIST MEETING
       FIRST VISIT TO BALMORAL CASTLE
       DEATH OF LORD MELBOURNE, NOVEMBER 24

1849   FOURTH ASSASSINATION ATTEMPT, MAY
       VISIT TO IRELAND WITH CHILDREN, AUGUST 3–10

1850   DUKE OF WELLINGTON RESIGNS AS COMMANDER OF THE ARMY
       BIRTH OF PRINCE ARTHUR WILLIAM PATRICK ALBERT, DUKE OF
         CONNAUGHT, MAY 1
       FIFTH ASSASSINATION ATTEMPT, JUNE
       ALFRED TENNYSON, *In Memoriam* PUBLISHED; TENNYSON NAMED
         POET LAUREATE

1851   OPENING OF THE GREAT EXHIBITION OF THE WORKS OF
         INDUSTRY OF ALL NATIONS AT THE CRYSTAL PALACE
       JOHN BROWN ENTERS ROYAL SERVICE
       COUP D'ÉTAT OF LOUIS-NAPOLÉON
       JOHN KENNEDY, *The Natural History of Man*
       EDWIN LANDSEER, *The Monarch of the Glen*

1852   LORD DERBY (TORY) BECOMES PRIME MINISTER
       DEATH OF THE DUKE OF WELLINGTON
       LOUIS NAPOLEON DECLARES HIMSELF EMPEROR
         (SECOND EMPIRE)
       LORD ABERDEEN (WHIG/PEELITE) BECOMES PRIME MINISTER

1853   BIRTH OF PRINCE LEOPOLD GEORGE DUNCAN ALBERT, DUKE OF
         ALBANY, APRIL 7

1854   ENGLAND DECLARES WAR ON RUSSIA (CRIMEAN WAR)

1855   RECIPROCAL VISITS BETWEEN LOUIS-NAPOLÉON AND EUGÉNIE
         AND VICTORIA AND ALBERT, FIRST VISIT TO PARIS BY AN
         ENGLISH SOVEREIGN SINCE 1431
       LORD PALMERSTON (WHIG) BECOMES PRIME MINISTER
       FALL OF SEBASTOPOL, BEGINNING OF TREATY, SEPTEMBER 8
       PRINCE FREDERICK OF PRUSSIA, "FRITZ," PROPOSES TO VICKY

1856   PEACE TREATY SIGNED IN PARIS

1857   BIRTH OF PRINCESS BEATRICE MARY VICTORIA FEODORA
        "BABY," APRIL 14
        INDIAN MUTINY
        PRINCE ALBERT GRANTED TITLE OF PRINCE CONSORT

1858   MARRIAGE OF CROWN PRINCESS VICTORIA AND PRINCE
        FREDERICK OF PRUSSIA, JANUARY 25
        LORD DERBY (TORY) BECOMES PRIME MINISTER
        GOVERNMENT OF INDIA TRANSFERRED TO THE CROWN

1859   BIRTH OF VICKY'S FIRST CHILD, CROWN PRINCE WILLIAM
        OF PRUSSIA, "WILLIE," GERMAN EMPEROR, KAISER
        WILHELM II, FEBRUARY
        LORD PALMERSTON (WHIG) BECOMES PRIME MINISTER

1860   GEORGE ELIOT, *The Mill on the Floss*
        CHARLES DICKENS, *Great Expectations* (SERIALIZED TO 1861)
        CHARLES KINGSLEY, INAUGURAL LECTURE, EVENTUALLY
        PUBLISHED AS *The Roman and the Teuton*, CAMBRIDGE,
        NOVEMBER

1861   DEATH OF DUCHESS OF KENT, MARCH 16
        TRENT EPISODE BETWEEN UNITED STATES AND ENGLAND
        DURING WAR BETWEEN THE STATES
        T. JONES BARKER, *The Secret of Her Greatness* (BEGUN?)
        DEATH OF PRINCE ALBERT IN BLUE ROOM, WINDSOR CASTLE,
        DECEMBER 14

1862   MARRIAGE OF PRINCESS ALICE AND PRINCE LOUIS OF HESSE-
        DARMSTADT, JULY 1
        PRINCESS ALEXANDRA "ALIX" OF DENMARK, VISITS QUEEN
        VICTORIA AT OSBORNE AS FIANCÉE OF THE PRINCE OF
        WALES, NOVEMBER
        TENNYSON'S FIRST AUDIENCE WITH QUEEN VICTORIA AFTER
        DEDICATION FOR A NEW EDITION OF *Idylls of the King*, IN
        MEMORY OF THE PRINCE CONSORT, APRIL

1863   WEDDING OF BERTIE AND ALIX

1864   JOHN BROWN BECOMES VICTORIA'S SERVANT IN WINDSOR AS
        WELL AS BALMORAL
        CHARLES DICKENS, *Our Mutual Friend* (SERIALIZED TO 1865)

1865   LORD RUSSELL (WHIG) BECOMES PRIME MINISTER
DEATH OF KING LEOPOLD
BIRTH OF PRINCE GEORGE (GEORGE V)
JOHN RUSKIN, "OF QUEEN'S GARDENS" PUBLISHED THE
    FOLLOWING YEAR
CHARLES KINGSLEY, *Hereward the Wake: "Last of the English"*
LEWIS CARROLL, *Alice in Wonderland*

1866   QUEEN VICTORIA OPENS PARLIAMENT FOR THE FIRST TIME
    SINCE PRINCE ALBERT'S DEATH, FEBRUARY 6
LORD DERBY (TORY) BECOMES PRIME MINISTER
PRUSSIA DECLARES WAR ON AUSTRIA
MARRIAGE OF PRINCESS HELENA TO PRINCE CHRISTIAN OF
    SCHLESWIG-HOLSTEIN-SONDERBURG-AUGUSTENBURG, JULY 5
GEORGE ELIOT, *Felix Holt, The Radical*
ALGERNON CHARLES SWINBURNE, *Poems and Ballads*

1867   SUPPOSED FENIAN CONSPIRACIES TO ASSASSINATE THE QUEEN
SECOND REFORM BILL PASSED, ENGINEERED BY DISRAELI
PUBLICATION OF *The Early Years of the Prince Consort*, COMPILED
    BY LORD GREY, UNDER QUEEN VICTORIA'S DIRECTION
WILLIAM THEED, *Queen Victoria and Prince Albert in Anglo-
    Saxon Dress*

1868   PUBLICATION OF *Leaves from a Journal of Our Life in the Highlands*
BENJAMIN DISRAELI (TORY) BECOMES PRIME MINISTER,
    FEBRUARY
WILLIAM EWART GLADSTONE (LIBERAL) BECOMES PRIME
    MINISTER, NOVEMBER

1870   HENRY PONSONBY BECOMES THE QUEEN'S PRIVATE SECRETARY
FRANCO-PRUSSIAN WAR
THIRD REPUBLIC PROCLAIMED

1871   EXILE IN ENGLAND OF LOUIS-NAPOLÉON AND EUGÉNIE
PROCLAMATION OF GERMAN EMPIRE
MARRIAGE OF PRINCESS LOUISE AND THE MARQUIS OF LORNE,
    MARCH 21
PRINCE OF WALES DANGEROUSLY ILL WITH TYPHOID

1872   SIXTH ASSASSINATION ATTEMPT, FEBRUARY
LEWIS CARROLL, *Through the Looking-Glass*

1873   DEATH OF LOUIS-NAPOLÉON
      SHAH OF PERSIA VISITS ENGLAND

1874   MARRIAGE OF PRINCE ALFRED AND MARIE, GRAND DUCHESS
       OF RUSSIA, JANUARY 23
      DISRAELI BECOMES PRIME MINISTER

1875   DISRAELI'S COUP TO CONTROL THE SUEZ CANAL, WITH
       BORROWED MONEY FROM BARON ROTHSCHILD TO BUY
       CONTROLLING SHARES FOR BRITAIN
      PRINCE OF WALES VISITS INDIA
      GILBERT AND SULLIVAN, *Trial by Jury*, THEIR FIRST
       SAVOY OPERA

1876   ROYAL TITLES BILL, DECLARING VICTORIA EMPRESS OF INDIA
      VIVISECTION ACT, REGULATING VIVISECTION
      DISRAELI GRANTED TITLE OF EARL OF BEACONSFIELD
      SULTAN OF TURKEY MASSACRES THOUSANDS IN UPRISINGS IN
       BOSNIA-HERZEGOVINA, SERBIA, AND BULGARIA

1877   TSAR DECLARES WAR ON TURKEY

1878   DEATH OF PRINCESS ALICE OF DIPHTHERIA (CAUGHT FROM
       NURSING HER CHILDREN), DECEMBER 14, THE ANNIVERSARY
       OF ALBERT'S DEATH

1879   DEFEAT AND MASSACRE OF ENGLISH TROOPS BY ZULUS UNDER
       CHIEF CETEWAYO AT ISANDHLWANA
      MARRIAGE OF PRINCE ARTHUR AND LOUISE OF PRUSSIA,
       MARCH 13
      WAR IN AFGHANISTAN

1880   GLADSTONE (LIBERAL) BECOMES PRIME MINISTER
      GILBERT AND SULLIVAN, *The Pirates of Penzance*

1881   BOERS KILL BRITISH COMMANDER, FEBRUARY
      MARRIAGE OF PRINCE WILLIAM AND PRINCESS AUGUSTA OF
       SCHLESWIG-SONDERBURG-AUGUSTENBURG, FEBRUARY
      TRANSVAAL GIVEN INDEPENDENCE, AUGUST
      WAR IN EGYPT, SEPTEMBER
      DEATH OF DISRAELI, APRIL 6

1882   SEVENTH ASSASSINATION ATTEMPT, MARCH 2; RUDYARD
          KIPLING, "AVE IMPERATRIX," A POEM OF THANKSGIVING
       MARRIAGE OF PRINCE LEOPOLD TO HELEN OF WALDECK,
          APRIL 27
       PHOENIX PARK MURDERS
       GENERAL WOOLSEY WINS BATTLE AT TEL-EL-KEBIR
       JOHN BROWN GRANTED TITLE OF "ESQUIRE"

1883   DEATH OF JOHN BROWN

1884   GENERAL GORDON SENT TO EGYPT
       PUBLICATION OF *More Leaves from a Journal of Our Life in the
          Highlands,* DEDICATED TO JOHN BROWN
       DEATH OF PRINCE LEOPOLD, SUFFERING FROM HEMOPHILIA

1885   GENERAL GORDON KILLED AT KHARTOUM, JANUARY
       MARRIAGE OF PRINCESS BEATRICE AND PRINCE HENRY OF
          BATTENBURG, JULY 23
       LORD SALISBURY (CONSERVATIVE) BECOMES PRIME
          MINISTER
       JOHN BEDDOE, *The Races of Britain*
       GILBERT AND SULLIVAN, *The Mikado*

1886   GLADSTONE BECOMES PRIME MINISTER
       HOME RULE FOR IRISH DEFEATED
       LORD SALISBURY BECOMES PRIME MINISTER

1887   QUEEN VICTORIA'S GOLDEN JUBILEE
       ABDUL KARIM AND OTHER INDIAN SERVANTS BEGIN WAITING
          ON QUEEN VICTORIA
       MARIE MALLET BECOMES MAID OF HONOUR
       H. RYDER HAGGARD, *She: A History of Adventure*
       ALFRED GILBERT, JUBILEE STATUE OF QUEEN VICTORIA FOR
          HAMPSHIRE COUNTY COUNCIL
       GILBERT AND SULLIVAN, *Ruddigore*

1888   ACCESSION OF EMPEROR AND EMPRESS FREDERICK III
          (VICKY AND FRITZ)
       DEATH OF FREDERICK III OF THROAT CANCER
       ACCESSION OF KAISER WILHELM II
       ABDUL KARIM CONFERRED TITLE OF MUNSHI

1891   QUEEN VISITS GRASSE

1892   GLADSTONE BECOMES PRIME MINISTER
            ABDUL KARIM CONFERRED TITLE OF MUNSHI HAFIZ

1893   LORD ROSEBERY (LIBERAL) BECOMES PRIME MINISTER
            BIRTH OF PRINCE EDWARD (EDWARD VIII)
            OPENING OF THE IMPERIAL INSTITUTE, MAY 10
            MARRIAGE OF DUKE AND DUCHESS OF YORK (KING GEORGE V
                AND QUEEN MARY, QUEEN ELIZABETH II'S GRANDPARENTS)
                JULY 6
            JULIAN ROBINSON (PSEUD.), *Gynecocracy*
            GEORGE GISSING, *In the Year of Jubilee*

1894   ABDUL KARIM RECEIVES COMPANION OF THE ORDER OF THE
                INDIAN EMPIRE
            MARY AUGUSTA (MRS. HUMPHRY) WARD, *Marcella*
            JEMADAR ABDUR RAZZAK, *The Native Officer's Diary*

1895   LORD SALISBURY (CONSERVATIVE) BECOMES PRIME MINISTER
            DEATH OF HENRY PONSONBY
            MARIE MALLET APPOINTED EXTRA WOMAN OF THE
                BEDCHAMBER
            BIRTH OF PRINCE GEORGE (GEORGE VI)

1897   QUEEN VICTORIA'S DIAMOND JUBILEE
            T. MULLET ELLIS, *The Fairies' Favourite*
            HAVELOCK ELLIS, *Studies in the Psychology of Sex*

1898   DEATH OF GLADSTONE

1899   BOER WAR

1900   DEATH OF DUKE OF EDINBURGH (AFFIE) OF TONGUE CANCER,
                JULY 30

1901   DEATH OF QUEEN VICTORIA, JANUARY 22

QUEEN VICTORIA'S SECRETS

1

ELEMENTS OF POWER

The King of the Belgians to Queen Victoria, January 16, 1838:
Monarchy to be carried on requires certain elements, and the
occupation of the Sovereign must be constantly to preserve these
elements, or should they have been too much weakened by
untoward circumstances, to contrive by every means to strengthen
them again. You are too clever not to know, that it is not the being
called Queen or King, which can be of the least consequence, when
to the title there is not also annexed the power indispensable for the
exercise of those functions. All trades must be learned, and
nowadays the trade of a constitutional Sovereign, to do it well,
is a very difficult one.
—Letters of Queen Victoria

A visitor to Bryce Canyon National Park in Utah, a state founded the year before Queen Victoria's Diamond Jubilee in 1897, might be sufficiently intrigued by its name to consider a hike down the three-quarter mile, self-guided Queen's Garden Trail. What queen would have a garden in the far reaches of a democratic republic? Catching a possible allusion to John Ruskin's "Of Queen's Gardens," a student of the Victorian age might guess that the royalty honored was not a person of royal blood but womanhood itself at its most nurturant and domesticated. The student would be wrong. At the end of the trail, Queen Victoria, a "lovely natural limestone sculpture" in the words of the guidebook, dominates the horizon. Crowned, her monumental body unmistakable in the bright, un-British light, the craggy queen presides over a garden of stone pinnacles, ridges, and spires in a land that her grandfather, King George III, neither claimed nor ceded. Shaped by elemental forces, the massive stone lump imparts a seeming inevitability to Victoria's awesome queenliness.

Taking accident for artifact, the travel writer calls the formation a "statue," as if it were wrought by a reverential human subject rather than by wind and rain. The configuration is in fact a "hoodoo," a word meaning both a pillar of rock eroded into a fantastic shape and a person or thing that brings bad luck. Removed in time and space from its model's geographic realm, the Victoria hoodoo bears witness to the queen's imperial conquest of the imagination. Within that symbolic empire, her solid form rules as a totemic figure, gathering together different peoples of the world under the sign of her clan. Or, on a smaller scale, her image bears talismanic power for good as well as evil. Her name or image—evoked like a charm—conjures powers beyond those accorded by any constitutional monarchy.

To assess the Victoria totem's meanings would not be easy. Years must pass after her death, so the writer Edmund Gosse insisted, before the "bewildering radiance" surrounding Victoria died down. Only then might more dispassionate eyes see "what were the elements, and what the evolution of her character," and what influences she might have had on history.[1] No one would argue against Gosse's confidence in time's moderating virtues. Yet new kinds of dazzlement may bewilder an earnest seeker after the "real" Victoria. Currently, the glare shining on Victoria's descendants casts a softer but not necessarily a clearer light on Queen Elizabeth II's great-great-grandmother. Nostalgia over the Victorians in general constitutes our version of bewildering radiance, one that includes Victoria in its nimbus. Rather than engage in a further effort to uncover a real Victoria, *Queen Victoria's Secrets* examines malicious as well as pious distortions, cultural fantasies as well as literature, painting, memoirs, and letters to explore some of the ways in which Victorian culture accommodated ideas of Victoria to represent its self-interested moment. Many traditional powers of the monarchy were transferred to Parliament during Victoria's reign, although the publication of her letters after her death challenged the public perception of a powerless queen. The myth of Queen Victoria's historical insignificance is slow to die however; recent social and political histories rarely mention her.[2] In contrast to the attention Elizabeth I receives as a shaper of her culture, Victoria is usually regarded as a nineteenth-century curiosity—a fascinating subject for frequent biographies but not an essential object for the analysis of Victorian culture. Unlike Elizabethan scholars, Victorianists do not regard Victoria as central to her era, though no one denies her function as a cultural icon. Not simply passive or static symbol, however, Victoria performed cultural work for her age. The following chapters explore the various kinds of work she performed, some of the expected and unexpected places where she performed it, and how those kinds of work blend invisibly into the Victorian period.

Culture adjusts facts—of individual lives and social events—to

Queen Victoria, the hoodoo in Bryce Canyon National Park, Utah, a limestone shape formed by erosion. *English Illustrated Magazine, vol. 17, 1897.*

accord with its ideologies, frequently in paradoxical ways. Queen Victoria was considered as the quintessential domestic figure but also a ruler of exotic lands; she was loved as a mother, though she claimed not to enjoy her own children's company; she was viewed as a prudish moral arbiter yet was ridiculed or feared as a woman hungry for sex; in her veins flowed the bluest blood, but in her heart she felt akin to the common people. What secrets permitted the culture to accommodate Queen Victoria's contradictory meanings?

In posing that question, I draw on three slightly different but related senses of *secrets.* Regarding her office, *secret* applies to the mystery enshrouding all monarchical authority. Walter Bagehot, who lived in Victoria's realm for thirty years before writing *The English Constitution,* accepted both the "mystic obligation" governing an English monarch's sacred right to rule and the mystery surrounding the monarch herself as essential elements of royal power.[3] Pointing out that in a constitutional government a "secrecy prerogative is an anomaly," he found just that anomaly inherent in royalty: "That secrecy is, however, essential to the utility of English royalty as it now is. Above all things our royalty is to be reverenced and if you begin to poke about it you cannot reverence it. When there is a select committee on the Queen, the charm of royalty will be gone. Its mystery is its life."[4] Victoria's anointment gave her a "secrecy prerogative" that she exercised to enhance her image. That prerogative enabled her to represent what was ordinary and common, precisely what could seem least secretive—and least regal.

Secret not only means "covert" but also "a method or formula upon which success is based"—my second use of the word. The secrets explored in this book, not at all hidden, are observable methods or formulas defining and authorizing Queen Victoria's power; they are "open secrets" about the Victorian age that have heretofore been unacknowledged as enabling methods of Queen Victoria's monarchy. To consider Queen Victoria as the quintessential Victorian requires a recognition that she had a hand in defining that category and in fitting herself to it. The reign's extraordinary success in representing itself as if it were simply what it represented itself as being is one of its secrets.

Finally, *secret* in its more familiar meaning as *mysterious* not only conjures up Bagehot's secrecy prerogative possessed by all kings and queens but also applies to Victoria's gender. The age's notions about woman's mysterious power adds a special aura to Victoria's monarchy. In reference to women, *secret* connotes what has been taken to be an unknown female essence. Far more mystery surrounds the notion of a queen, not only a woman but also a sovereign. For a Victorian queen to rule might itself imply that she employed secret methods. Victoria and her image makers could depend on the power that made a social problem and a psychological mystery of the Victorian woman. Victoria's success in permeating the cultural imagination suggests a mysterious womanly formula, made all the more secret because possessed by a queen.

Queen Victoria's secrets became felt as a visceral part of her age. How did that happen? The cultural anthropologist Victor Turner proposes a concept he calls "public reflexivity" to describe performative processes whereby a culture "seeks to portray, understand, and then act on itself."[5] Selected individuals, he thinks, perform a culture's codes and thereby adjust them. As a useful model for understanding how Victoria manipulated her power, public reflexivity allows for a dynamic interchange between the performers of cultural codes and those who receive and understand the performances. The persons performing a culture's codes can transform how they are understood. Seeming to "'hold the mirror up to nature,' they do this with 'magic mirrors' which make ugly or beautiful events or relationships which cannot be recognized as such in the continuous flow of quotidian life in which we are embedded. The mirrors themselves are not mechanical, but consist of reflecting consciousness and the products of such consciousness formed into vocabularies and rules . . . by means of which new unprecedented performances may be generated."[6] Queen Victoria, by all reports a gifted performer, reinterpreted her era's cultural codes to fit her self-identity, writing her culture, to use Turner's linguistic metaphor, in her own idiom. Further, she set the stage for performances not of her own contrivance.

Anointed to a liminal or sacred space reserved for sovereigns, the queen reflected cultural codes while marking them with her particular sensibility. Like all representation, her performances did not merely reflect those cultural codes; they also substituted, replaced, adjusted, and altered them. Queen Victoria gave back to her culture her own stamp on its sense of itself. Guided by her tutors in queenship, she held up magic mirrors to the Victorian age to reflect images in which it could believe. Her performances centered cultural meaning on herself, so that by the time of her death in 1901 she named her age, seeming synonymous with it. Indeed, sometimes she seemed transparent—as if she were not a mirror but a window.

Marshaling unique monarchical resources, Queen Victoria acted out an imagined or ideal Victorian life in the privileged stage reserved for a monarch, by position the *one* representing the nation.[7] She made her luxurious spaces seem both marvelous and ordinary, telling of her exalted position while promising an emotional stability available to all. Within her various dwellings Queen Victoria performed her quotidian life as if she were everywoman. The spectacle of the queen—supported by a cast of characters drawn from her family and Household—mourning, housekeeping, dancing, traveling, and marrying places her as the locus of cultural meanings. The audiences for these performances interpret them, often discovering the connotations they desire in order to make sense of their own lives. In that reciprocity, such "manly" activities in the nation as imperial exploration, to use one example, seem to serve the sovereign's liminal domicile and also to fulfill her personal desires. Because of the way she represented herself, subjects could think that they were doing whatever they did for their queen.

Victoria's reflexive performances centered herself in the age's self-image. Ultimately she became iconic: a figure of benevolent, maternal imperialism to some, a virago of chaotic desires to others; a homely middle-class folk heroine to most or, as many think of her today, a figure of somber repression who, denied pleasure, denied it to others by not being amused.

Advertisement for Monarch Cycles, *Life*, vol. 30, 1897. "It was while taking her favourite drive . . . in the Isle of Wight that she for the first time saw a lady riding a tricycle, and she was so much pleased that she ordered two machines . . . for some of her ladies to ride upon. When the . . . bicycle came into use, Her Majesty looked askance for a time at ladies using it; but now she takes the greatest delight in watching the merry cycling parties of princesses which start daily from Balmoral." *The Personal Life of Queen Victoria*, by Sarah Tooley, 1897.

⇥ The Monarchical Trade ⇤

The queen's gender marks her as an unconventional figure in an age excluding women from government. Although England lacked Salic law forbidding female monarchs, the relative rarity of English female sovereigns grants a queen a prominence unavailable to a king. Particularly for her times, Victoria's presence on the throne highlighted controversies, debates, concerns, and anxieties about differences between men and women.[8] The following chapters address the concerns governing a Victorian woman's life—family alliances, fashion, entertainments, domesticity, sexual behavior, mourning, and motherhood—to demonstrate how the queen mobilized them to sovereign service. Rather than attempt a seamless narrative that would show Victoria and the Victorians from a single vantage point, *Queen Victoria's Secrets* focuses on sometimes contradictory interpretations of her cultural images. I am concerned with what different people make of their given world, a process exemplified by the anonymous walker in Utah who discovered a ruler of the century's imagination in a fortuitous stone shape.

Victoria's image could not have traveled westward had its lineaments not been commonplace. New technology fashioned it into familiarity. Formed during an age that began to exploit mechanical reproduction, her image became a media event, not only through such traditional arts as painting and statuary but also through photographs and prints, through broadside ballads and advertisements, through souvenir plates, parian statues, buttons, and other bric-a-brac. Especially in their cheap editions, her best-selling illustrated journals revealing her simple life in the Scottish Highlands sold millions. Printed on the label of a Bombay gin bottle, her regal head associated her rich empire with genteel imbibing, selling spirits by superimposing a quintessentially respectable Victoria over gin's earlier reputation as the sop of the lowest masses. Her image on the first penny postage stamp traveled through the mails.

Those aspects of Victoria's image produced by calculation anticipate the media techniques of today. The queen relied on personal managers of great skill, among the most adroit of them being her first prime minister, Lord Melbourne; her husband, Prince Albert; and Benjamin Disraeli, the prime minister who contrived to add Empress of India to her titles. Well before her accession in 1837, her uncle Leopold, her mother's brother and widower of Princess Charlotte, had coached her. He was particularly qualified to do so because, as husband to Princess Charlotte when she was next in line to the English throne, he had studied the English system. When, after Charlotte's death, Leopold was pen-

sioned off, he gave Victoria the advice he had been hoping to use himself as royal consort. By the time Victoria came to the throne, Leopold
had become King of the Belgians. Along with his ability to calculate and
evaluate, he drew on his English experience to advise his niece.
Thinking about how to do the royal work of his particular moment,
Leopold developed principles of sovereignty for his own kingdom that
he believed were exportable. The year before her accession, Princess
Victoria read with attention and admiration *The Directions and Advices*
that Leopold wrote for his nephew and Victoria's cousin Ferdinand
upon his marriage to the queen of Portugal. Finding its principles
"most valuable, important and sage," she continued to read it, beyond
its specific information about the Portuguese to the "*Observations
Générales*, about the rules of sovereignty in general."[9]

Leopold had also observed his in-laws in their undignified waste of
English monarchical capital; he wrote avuncular cautions from his
Belgian throne, one (quoted in the epigraph to this chapter) discussing those same "elements" about monarchy that Gosse employed
in describing the queen. Believing that a constitutional monarch
required constant vigilance to protect her "elements of power,"
Leopold warned Victoria to guard her present powers and even regain
the power lost by her predecessors.[10] But to do so, he thought, a
monarch must move with the times. Leopold reconceptualized monarchy for the nineteenth century in bourgeois terms, imagining the
monarch as being "in trade." The royal tradesperson, like those in
other occupations, must do the job well to secure the highest payoff. It
was an inspired concept, one that Victoria extended to perform her
domestic life, emphasizing the ways in which it, too, harmonized with
values of a entrepreneurial society.

Victoria's husband, Prince Albert of Saxe-Coburg and Gotha, shaped
her image. After Leopold provided a text and Melbourne outlined a
model, Albert became Victoria's queenmaker. With a temperament
unlike that of the headstrong, sometimes impetuous Victoria, the
prince planned and strategized. He loved to organize and to employ
such new technologies as the camera.[11] He knew how to capitalize on
assets. Pondering his role in maintaining a strong monarchy, the prince
calculated the profits to be derived from the age's gender arrangements. Since the conventional gender hierarchy was reversed by a
female monarch, there would be nothing to do, he recognized, but to
make a virtue of necessity.

Albert set down the responsibilities of the queen's consort in 1843
and then revised and submitted them in a memorandum to the Duke
of Wellington in 1850 when the duke suggested Albert take command

of the army. Although the prince recognized potential conflicts of interest in his assuming a public position, his letters to Wellington indicate that the two had discussed the political limitations posed by Victoria's gender that tempted Albert to consider the post. "The present Sovereign, as a lady, was not able at all times to perform the many duties imposed upon her," they decided.[12] Ignoring Queen Boadicea's militaristic precedent, both apparently agreed that commanding an army would not be ladylike. After discussing with Victoria his proper role as her husband, Albert then formulated a method whereby he might exercise power by exploiting the considerable attributes unique to a sovereign queen: "Whilst a female sovereign has a great many disadvantages in comparison with a king, yet, if she is married, and her husband understands and does his duty, her position, on the other hand, has many compensating advantages, and, in the long run will be found to be even stronger than that of a male sovereign."[13] Despite its frustrating vagueness at crucial points—for instance, what did Albert consider "compensating advantages"?—his phrase indicates that he appreciated that the age's formulation of what it called "true womanhood" might enhance the monarchy and consolidate its power. Qualities associated with true womanhood—domesticity, motherhood, and sympathy—transmitted in images of Victoria and her happy home life—were to prove advantageous in securing the powers of a strong constitutional sovereign.

Albert's idea of using Victoria's womanhood to advantage depended for its success, however, on a strong husband manager who did not compete for attention with his wife. In order to work, this formula, he thought, "requires that the husband should entirely sink his *own individual existence* in that of his wife—that he should aim at no power by himself or for himself . . . but make his position entirely part of hers, . . . continually and anxiously watch every part of the public business in order to be able to advise and assist her."[14] Albert's program entailed the considerable task of making an already strong independent person follow his lead and as a consequence change her assumptions and her behavior.

By sinking his existence into hers, Albert did *not* mean that he would accept Victoria as he found her. Being an only child with no companions her own age and no father to observe as head of household, the queen did not immediately appreciate her subservient status as a Victorian wife. Moreover, she had enjoyed three independent years as an unmarried queen. First Albert needed to make his will master of hers, in the words of the prince consort's private secretary, George Anson, by "reforming her mind—& drawing out her Powers."[15] Only

Opening of the Crystal Palace, May 1, 1851. Queen Victoria, Prince Albert, the Duchess of Kent, the Crown Princess, and the Prince of Wales were portrayed in the front of the dais, barely discernible in this print. Victoria wrote to Uncle Leopold: "I wish you *could* have witnessed the *1st May* 1851, the *greatest* day in our history, the *most beautiful* and *imposing* and *touching* spectacle ever seen, and the triumph of my beloved Albert."

then, when she had appreciated her feminine place, could Albert disappear behind the newly subordinated Victoria.

By 1850, when Albert declined the offer to command the army, Victoria's mind had been reformed. The following year, the prince unveiled his next monument to sovereign management. The Great Exhibition of the Works of Industry of All Nations exemplifies a way Albert managed Queen Victoria's "trade" as sovereign. The exhibition conformed to his sense of a good international show, one enhancing his adopted country and not incidentally placing the royal family as the force from which such national power emanated. For the queen and the prince to open the exhibition as a family emphasized one of the secrets of Queen Victoria's reign. What might appear as "family secrets" secluded from public gaze were revealed for all to see in a glass house.

By means of a ritual performance, the royal family became identified with Great Britain's position as a leader in new industry, new technologies, new sciences. As if they were holding a great reception in their own palace, the hostess queen, her husband, mother, and two children received all nations.

The monarchy depended upon skillful exhibitions and heartfelt performances. Victoria and Albert's devotion to duty and their sincerity contributed to their success. Albert paid a high price. He exhausted himself attending not simply to details of official business but to family matters as well: domestic architecture, interior decoration, home finances, personal attire, children's education, model farms—no detail escaped his management. The price was also high for Victoria but, blessed with an iron constitution (thanks, some believed, to maternal breast-feeding), she endured, even embraced, her transformation. Since Albert and she wrought a combined image, his death in 1861, when they were both forty-two years old, threatened their monarchical formula. Once she had subordinated herself to Albert, Victoria thought herself unable to perform even the public official acts she had seemed to enjoy before her marriage. Albert died one year before the midpoint of her life. Convincing herself that she could not live without him, she spent a disappointing but productive decade after his death eagerly awaiting her imminent demise. During her years in seclusion, however, she gradually reformulated herself, exploiting the advantages accruing to a widowed mother. Although Victoria often referred to her widowed years as a dreary living out of her "angel's" projects for her, the queen's life as a cultural icon took on more various—even more lively—forms after her prince consort's death.

At her own death, when her womanly aura was at its fullest and her influence was at its most global, Washington Gladden, minister of the First Congregational Church in Columbus, Ohio, preached a memorial sermon eulogizing the British queen as a model for his woman congregants: "Finally, it must be said of Victoria that her greatness was that of a true womanhood. It was her pure womanliness that drew to her the hearts of her people, with a strength of affection that no English monarch has ever called forth. There was no sufferer anywhere in her realm who was not sure of the queen's sympathy; the neediest and lowliest felt that her heart was with them. And it was her womanliness that made her a great ruler."[16] The Reverend Gladden's opinion confirmed Albert's strategy of focusing on Victoria's gender to strengthen the monarchy.

Queen Victoria's symbolic images collect and collide during her long reign and beyond it to our own moment. Fascination with Queen

Victoria's life continues to produce new biographies, each one claiming to capture an essential truth.[17] This Victoria industry thrives in part because the queen presented herself in many different guises, a quality contemporaries noticed. Gosse regarded Victoria's character "to an unusual degree, a composite one. . . . It presented itself to the observer a kind of mosaic, smoothed and harmonized by circumstances into a marvelously even surface." Although Gosse wants to find a harmonious whole in Victoria's character, he does acknowledge potentially discordant elements: "Her character was built up of elements which are usually antagonistic, but in her case were so nicely balanced that they held one another in check, and facilitated . . . that directness of purpose and instinct for going straight to the mark, which were indispensable to success in her sovereign career."[18] Though many agreed that Victoria's character contained antagonistic elements, not all found that her inner system of checks and balances operated effectively. More vehemently than most, Victoria espoused opposite sides of the same questions; more composite than many, her character displayed its incompatible elements. Multiple aspects of her nature produced contradictory impressions of the queen but so, too, did various cultural vantages. Institutions, individuals, and ideologies construct from different data, weighted differently, the Victoria of their desires and beliefs. Whatever portrait of Queen Victoria emerges from the chapters that follow, it allows for unmatched edges, bumps, and fissures; if the whole produces a kind of harmony built from discordances, it contains the self-interested notes of Gosse and many of his contemporaries.

Even in her time, the queen's contrariness defied efforts to characterize her. Henry Ponsonby, particularly suited to his job as private secretary to Victoria by virtue of his fine sense of the absurd, obeyed her wishes to the letter while solemnly enjoying his participation in their farcical aspects. From an attitude of affectionate tolerance, he appreciated how his employer defied simple categorization:

> Queen Victoria did not belong to any conceivable category
> of monarchs or of women. She bore no resemblance to an
> aristocratic English lady, she bore no resemblance to a
> wealthy middle-class Englishwoman, nor to any typical
> princess of a German court. She was not in the least like the
> three queens regnant (omitting Mary Stuart who was just the
> wife of William III) her predecessors. Mary Tudor was a
> fanatic, Queen Elizabeth was an autocrat and Queen Anne
> in her harassed and ramshackle way was occupied in coping
> with the intrigues around her. . . . Moreover she reigned

longer than all the three other queens put together. Never in her life could she be confused with anyone else, nor will she be in history. Such expressions as "people like Queen Victoria" or "that sort of woman" could not be used about her.[19]

Ponsonby's claim that Victoria belonged to a unique category supports my contention that she blended into her age while standing apart from it. Her uniqueness enabled those of differing interests and needs to create the Victoria of their particular dreams. To characterize the queen in one way or another would distort Victoria's multiple significations. Further, to the extent that Victoria shaped her own image, she could not control many of its cultural meanings. The power of fixing the meanings given even to one's own carefully managed self-representations escapes everyone—even a monarch. No matter how brilliant the script and the performance, both unconscious revelations and cultural interpretations exceed any performer's control. This book takes account of those excesses of meaning.

Victoria's methods of rule gave her historical moment what it demanded and thereby strengthened her monarchy's elements of power. *Secret*—in the wording of the *OED*: "that which accounts for something surprising or extraordinary; the essential thing[s] to be observed to achieve some end"—provides me with a concept that moves from the mysterious to the surprising, both unexpected notions to apply to a queen some regard as powerless, stodgy, prudish, even humorless, while at the same time the appetite for new information about her fills new books and daily newspapers alike.

✤ Dream Queens ✦

It might be hazarded, as a paradox, that her originality lay in her very lack of originality.
—Edmund Gosse

One imperfectly kept household secret governed Victoria's earliest years. Her destiny to be queen of England was not mentioned to the carefully guarded Princess "Drina," as Alexandrina Victoria was called in her girlhood. Not until she was eleven did she learn explicitly of her fate, and then only indirectly from a genealogical table slipped into her history book. "I will be good," she promised when she absorbed its message. Her mother, the widowed Duchess of Kent, tried to guarantee that oath in its

Idealized image, "The Queen in the Year of Her Accession," from a painting by Eugenio Latilla, published in "The Glorious Reign of Queen Victoria," *English Illustrated Magazine,* vol. 17, 1897.

narrowest sense. Boys older than six were forbidden her presence; George IV, busy with his mistress and other bodily indulgences, entertained her only a few times, once on a fishing barge with musicians following behind. She rarely visited King William IV, due in large part to her mother's petty feuds with the court in her eagerness to reign as regent. From her thirteenth birthday on, she traveled the country once a year, staying in great country seats and becoming familiar with her realm. She was not entirely secluded, but except for regular Carleton House visits to her Uncle Leopold, the walls of Kensington Palace circumscribed the princess's daily life. At night she slept in her mother's bedroom.

Shielded from public as well as royal eyes, the eighteen-year-old girl was a national mystery when, in the early hours of June 20, 1837, King William IV died and Victoria awakened to the news that she was queen.

Encouraged by lack of evidence, many hailed a creature constructed from hearsay, hope, and novelty. Assessing his sovereign during the last months of her life, Gosse pointed out that the "fierce light which beats upon the throne . . . produces a dazzlement, a glare of glory . . . a bewildering radiance" from which there can come no measured portrait.[20] For two periods during Queen Victoria's sixty-two-and-a-half-year reign that glare produced adulation: for a few early years and for fifteen or twenty years at its end. The cult of the young queen attracted male literary figures such as Charles Dickens, who used the language of valentines to express his admiration. Less smitten but hardly more accurate, the poet Elizabeth Barrett [Browning] read news reports, discussed the new queen in letters to her good friend, Mary Russell Mitford, and wrote a series of poems that construct a Victoria out of her age's idea of a perfect young woman who also happened to wear a crown of her own.

Written for Queen Victoria's accession, Barrett's, "The Young Queen," and "Victoria's Tears," published in 1838, employ devotional conventions to interpret what it meant at that moment to have a chit of a girl assume a position fit for a king. The poems' assumptions about Victoria's life and feelings bear little relation to historical record. "The Young Queen" begins with a quotation from the well-publicized scene when Victoria delivered her first official address, her Declaration in Council, on the morning of William IV's death. In graceful words, written by Lord Melbourne, Victoria took power, with humility in face of "this awful responsibility . . . sustained by the hope that Divine Providence, which has called me to this work, will give me strength for the performance of it." Evoking first the queen's clear voice, the poet turns to lugubrious images of the dead king and the grieving city, whose listening heart is smitten by the death knell, a sound "confusing sepulchre and throne." Barrett makes much from little. The death of one monarch always proclaims not an end of monarchy but its continuity, the more abstract institution substituting in "The Young Queen" for particular allusions to the late William IV. Few felt awestruck at the close of the short reign of a monarch some knew as Silly Billy. And although Victoria was apparently fond of the doddering sailor-king, there is no evidence that she believed herself unready or felt unhappy to take the throne. She entered in her journal the phrases that her biographers choose to characterize a confident yet modest young women: "Since it has pleased Providence to place me in this station, I shall do my utmost to fulfil my duty towards my country; I am very young and perhaps in many, though not in all things, inexperienced, but I am sure, that very few have more real good will and more real desire to do what is fit and right than I have."[21]

Many Victorian maidens—characters in novels, such as Dorothea Brooke in George Eliot's *Middlemarch,* and real women, such as Florence Nightingale—voiced such desires. Providence, however, had ordained Victoria, unlike them, to useful employment. On the eve of the king's death, when Victoria's half brother, Charles Leiningen, brought the news of William's decline, she cried briefly, leading him to assume falsely that his sister had not been apprised of the king's dire condition. On the contrary, Victoria was ready. Her first mentor, Uncle Leopold, had prepared her for this day.

Stanza by stanza, Barrett's poem evokes the Hanoverian family figures over which Victoria prevailed. Had Princess Charlotte, daughter of George IV, survived childbearing and incompetent doctors, she would have been queen. "The Young Queen" portrays Charlotte exchanging her "throne on earth" for "Jehovah's throne," eternally smiling to the angels. Had not the royal physicians persisted in their ability to kill their patients, Victoria's father, the Duke of Kent, weakened by cupping and leeching at age fifty-two, might have survived his cold to produce a son. Rather than evoke what Victoria herself viewed as a sad, isolated childhood spent among dolls and dogs, Barrett imagines Victoria wrenched from the small pleasures of youth for a cold throne room and a "deathly scented crown" that "weighs her shining ringlets down." Barrett's vision of a weighty crown reeking of the charnel house and bending the neck of a ringleted child produces a melodramatic scene, where the sweet victim walks throneward on the graves of relatives, most tellingly on her father's grave, her thoughts dwelling on death, her heart calling on God:

> Her thoughts are deep within her:
> No outward pageants win her
> From memories that in her soul are rolling wave on wave
> Her palace walls enring
> The dust that was a king—
> And very cold beneath her feet, she feels her father's grave.[22]

To fit the poetics of maidenly monarchy being constructed not only by Barrett but by general public sentiment, convention alters fact. Except for Princess Charlotte, the cast of other royal characters was not esteemed. George III, pathetic, ill, and lunatic, had, as readers of English Romantic poetry or American history know, lost a promising half of North America; in that war and against the French, he had emptied the coffers and mortgaged his country. Not one of his seven sons gave hope to the nation. As for the fourth son, the Duke of Kent,

Victoria's father, whose brutality cost him an army post, few could consider his death a serious national loss. True, he had been kind to his new wife, Victoire, princess of Saxe-Coburg-Saalfield, for whom he had abandoned a twenty-seven-year relationship, comfortable, though debt-encumbered, with Julie, Madame St. Laurent, in pursuit of legitimate progeny and a generous pension. His unexpected death inspired a cruel but just eulogy from Princess Lieven, wife of the Russian diplomat to the English court, to her lover, Count Metternich: "That Hercules of a man is no more. . . . No-one in England will mourn the Duke. He was false, hard and greedy. His so-called good qualities were only for show, and his last public appeal to the charity of the nation had lost him the support of the only friends he had—prisoners and City men."[23] Whatever his actual character, Victoria could draw only on hearsay and perhaps somatic traces, the memories of an eight-month infant. She thought of her father as a soldier and translated an idea of his strength to her lifelong attachments to male mentors, some unlikely ones drawn from the servant and colonized classes. But her first prime minister, Lord Melbourne—handsome, courtly, sophisticated, and naughty— provided both a substitute for a shadowy father and a capable guide to the intricacies of her new role. The official but uniquely intimate relationship where *he* was sworn to serve *her* might well seem the answer to any young maiden-queen's prayers.[24]

Of her mother, again the complex reality bears little on the conventions Barrett drew on for her poem. In "The Young Queen," Victoria seems a child weaned too soon from the maternal bosom to the obligations of a queen; from being made happy by one's mother to making others happy by one's rule. In fact, Victoria immediately severed the maternal cord, moving her bed out of her mother's room the day of her succession. Adding to that separation, the queen banned her mother, except upon petition, from her royal presence and also considered sending "Mamma" abroad on a long family visit. Her pleasure at her newfound independence can be gauged by her proud use of the word *alone* in her journal to describe her official acts. Moreover, the poem's charge to the queen that she rejoice in her people as her mother "joys in thee" can only be a purely positive wish for the nation, were one to ignore ambition as a component of the duchess's maternal joy. She unsuccessfully maneuvered to be named regent until Victoria was twenty-one years old.

Rather than portray a Victoria released from enforced intimacy, verging at times upon solitary confinement, the poem evokes a child of nature expelled from blissful union with her mother. Alluding to a familiar description of the toddler Victoria in the Kensington Palace

A pastoral image, "The Queen at the Age of Eleven," from a picture by Richard Westall, R.A., published in "The Glorious Reign of Queen Victoria," *English Illustrated Magazine*, vol. 17, 1897.

garden in "her childhood's rest by loving heart, and sport on grassy sod," the poem takes a report of Princess Victoria playing in a garden and superimposes a romantic convention in which the young princess turns into a Wordsworthian Lucy, a child of nature who emerges from literature to cleanse the polluted realms of male monarchs.[25]

The muse governing Barrett's pen offered no convention for a chaste, yet unfeminine eagerness to rule. Rather than recognize Victoria's pleasure in her new powers, Barrett, in "Victoria's Tears," portrays the young queen weeping in sorrowful humility. The refrain "She wept, to wear a crown!" rings the changes of a constant theme: the burden of rule makes Victoria weep. Those of Victoria's biographers who mention Barrett's poem agree that it misreads those tears. The poem commemorates the Queen's Proclamation, when she stood between Lord Melbourne and Lord Lansdowne at the open window of the Privy Council chamber. At the crowd's cheers evoked by the heralds, an observer noted, "the colour faded from the queen's cheeks and her eyes filled with tears. The emotion thus called forth imparted an additional charm to the winning courtesy with which the girl sovereign accepted the proffered homage." These charmingly brimming eyes spilled over extravagantly in the *Times* of the next day (June 22, 1837) to influence the imagery of Barrett's poem: "The spectacle presented . . . was one of a singularly beautiful and affecting description. In the centre stood a female monarch of tender years suddenly summoned to assume the difficult and perilous office of earthly ruler and preserver of the interests of a great nation—in this position stood a youthful Queen bathed in tears, and nearly over-whelmed by . . . the warm and heartfelt outpourings of a willing and devoted people."

No doubt the crowds of subjects paying loud homage moved Victoria to tears. Flanked by imposing male bodies representative of the state, she received her nation's affection. That she embraced her role and that overbrimming eyes might also signify fulfillment, independence, sovereignty in all its meanings, escaped the accessible cultural vocabulary. Ordinary girls might dream of queenship, but to tell that secret of a real queen violated Victorian convention. Instead, Barrett turns female ambition into womanly service:

> The young Queen is very interesting to me—& those tears, wept not only amidst the multitudes at the proclamation, but in the silence of the dead midnight—(we heard that she cried all night before holding her first privy council, notwith-standing the stateliness & composure with which she received her councillors) are beautiful & touching to think upon. . . . There is something hardening, I fear, in power— even if there is not in pomp! and the coldnesses of state eti-quette gather too nearly round the heart, not to chill it, often! But our young Queen wears still a very tender heart! and long may its natural emotions lie warm within it![26]

For Barrett, the gender-inflected tears signify the sympathy with com-mon people that would be a renewing source of popularity throughout Victoria's reign, though in fact she failed to support large-scale social reforms for the poor. Yet the volume of tears seems in excess of their meaning. From a bath in the newspaper report, tears gather in Barrett's letter to a minor deluge, flooding Princess Victoria's pillow. According to her journal, Victoria was sleeping when her mother awakened her to receive her ministers as queen, although a few momentary tears fell when she heard their expected news. But the poem's quantity of *mournful* tears justifies a new kind of monarchy, one protecting the new industrial order from Mammon and immorality. For this image, a tearful prayerful girl fits the bill. Barrett heralds a new kind of rule, one liberating the nation from imbeciles, debt, and profligacy by means of feminine sympathy, piety, and chastity. A saintly Victoria absorbs the nation's sorrows so that it can smile, as in the lines of "The Young Queen": "Make room within thy bright clear eyes for all its gathered tears."

Reigning as virginal martyr for her people, weeping for them, her reign prepares Victoria for "that heavenly crown," the last words of "Victoria's Tears." To end the poem among the heavenly hosts blurs the ordinary stages in a woman's life, unless the queen were to emulate Princess Charlotte in an early maternal death. Almost miraculously vigorous and seemingly immune to death by childbirth, Victoria outlived the conventional plot that rids novels and households of Victorian mothers. To function simultaneously as wife, mother, and queen fitted no Victorian conventions—for those place women either on a domestic or a heavenly throne.

The first two of Barrett's Victoria poems place the queen on the celestial throne, while the third enshrines her on the domestic one. When, in 1840, Victoria married Albert, Barrett's title for her poem on that occasion, "Crowned and Wedded," alludes to a particular Victorian ideological conflict between queen, wife, and mother. The poem confronts anomaly by replacing a real monarchical crown with a figurative one. For Barrett the Victorian ideology of womanhood takes precedence over monarchy. Based upon a feudal model, monarchy depends on a hierarchy allowing for a woman only courtly, not court, rule. In marriage, woman rules the heart while man rules the kingdom or home. Shifting actual rule for domestic sentiment, "Crowned and Wedded" parallels two scenes in which Victoria bowed her head before "her people's face" to take a vow: the coronation and the wedding. The poem clearly demonstrates the trouble Victorians had conceptualizing a happily married female sovereign. It struggles to replace the crown with the ring, while the country had to live with the fact that even after marrying, Victoria remained queen. Barrett's poem celebrates the bride while denying the queen:

> She vows to love who vowed to rule—(the chosen at her side)
> Let none say, God preserve the queen! but rather, Bless the bride.

Placing ruling and loving as incompatible states for a woman, the poem suggests that Victoria's earlier vows "to rule" need to be moderated, if not replaced conceptually with her "vow to love."[27] "Love" covers here for the vow that Victoria herself allowed to be kept in the marriage ceremony. When the archbishop asked whether the queen wished any adjustments in the marriage vows, she distinguished her position as sovereign from her role as wife, requiring no alteration in her vow "to obey" and stating that she wished "to be married as a woman, not as Queen."[28] The poem enjoins Albert to value Victoria not as a queen but as a woman:

> Esteem that wedded hand less dear for sceptre than for ring,
> And hold her uncrowned womanhood to be the royal thing.

By the end of the poem, Barrett has transformed Victoria Regina into a wife, similar to any humble subject. The poem's final benediction levels all classes to common brideship: "The blessings happy PEASANTS have, be thine, O crowned queen." If Victoria does not quite become a peasant, she is likened to one. Democratized and domesticated—wedded *yet* crowned—Victoria upholds a romantic idea of the happily married folk, a characteristic associated with Victorian middle-class morality.

Barrett's "the royal thing," a wonderfully ambiguous phrase, signifies a cultural wish for Victorian middle-class wives. The poem reflects a construction of true womanhood that serves the real queen in representing her age. John Ruskin prepared an imaginary garden for all good women in which they could exercise the particularly Victorian royal thing. In his December 14, 1864, lecture, "Of Queen's Gardens," delivered in the Manchester Town Hall, then revised and published in 1865, Ruskin pleads with the women of England to live out their natural role as queens: "And whether consciously or not, you must be, in many a heart, enthroned: there is no putting by that crown; queens you must always be; queens to your lovers; queens to your husbands and your sons; queens of higher mystery to the world beyond, which bows itself, and will forever bow, before the myrtle crown, and the stainless sceptre, of womanhood." Ruskin stops just short of rhetorical hysteria in placing womanhood on the "throne that is founded on the rock of justice," where she will act as the "centre of order, the balm of distress, and the mirror of beauty,"[29] both within her gates and in the public sphere, where she secures "the world's order, comfort, and loveliness."[30]

"Of Queen's Gardens" attempts to ennoble a process consolidated during Victoria's reign of bringing the queen to the level of the middle classes while it exhorted middle-class women to aspire to the level of queens. Whereas Barrett's poem likens Victoria's happiness to a similar feeling of the most simple people, Ruskin's lecture raises well-trained middle-class women to queendom. He tells them, in essence, that if they are good women, they cannot avoid being queens. Multiplied by legions of her like, Victoria stands among them but alone, the part representing the whole. Crowning all good women of "benignant power," Ruskin denies the queen's singularity. He creates and reflects the age's construction of true womanhood as a replacement for religious faith, envisioning a host of regal heroines trained to rescue the age—though within the vantage of their walled gardens—from new versions of old sins. In Ruskin's lecture women/queens appear in the world to create soft laps, like those of the "Mother of the Son of Man," as he says. This Victorian Virgin Victoria practices a kind of public philanthropy as a way of influencing the world. Like the Manchester ladies who are supposed to emulate her, the virtuous queen provides a model imagined as indistinguishable from any respectable lady, mingling among her peoples, yet chosen among the many to represent their aggregate greatness. Victoria's position, both as representing the period's construction of the middle-class woman and apart from it as resembling no other woman in the world, constructs a queen with open secrets, much of whose power derives from her unique ordinariness.

2

GENEALOGIES IN HER CLOSET

*A Briton may feel some pride in recollecting that in the veins
of his Queen there runs the blood of those who have helped to raise
England to her pitch of greatness; . . . circumstances have brought
about a union of several currents into one stream, in a manner
more remarkable than was ever seen in the pedigree of other
royal houses.*

—George Russell French

Prince Albert's gifts for party giving have been unappreciated. Teutonic
in disposition, he is usually portrayed as preferring the study to the ball-
room, the conversation of intellectual men to social chat. Yet, in addition to orchestrating imaginative family birthday parties, he liked playing games with a historical theme. A biography "compiled under the
direction of Her Majesty the Queen" portrays the ten-year-old Albert
with his friends "assuming the characters of the most distinguished wor-
thies of old times, and of making the most remarkable incidents in by-
gone German history the subject of their games."[1] At least through the
first five years of his marriage to Victoria, Albert—still in his early twenties—continued to enjoy such games, now played on a more elaborate
scale, staging them as entertainments at fancy dress, or costume, balls.

Victoria, who could dance the night away, declared herself mystified
by her husband's elaborate pretexts for parties. In 1842, two years and
two children after their nuptials, Victoria wrote Uncle Leopold with
strange delight at the extensive plans for a fancy dress ball: "I am quite
bewildered with all the arrangements for our *bal costumé*, which I wish
you could see; we are to be Edward III and Queen Philippa, and a great
number of our Court to be dressed like the people in those times, and

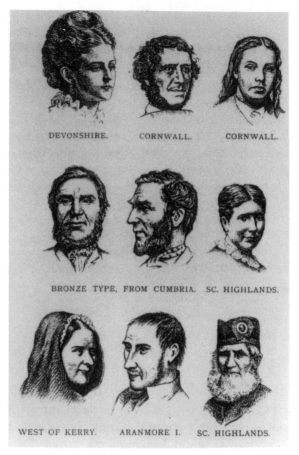

Illustration from *The Races of Britain*, John Beddoe,
1885. Beddoe's photographs were used in later ethnographic books.

very correctly, so as to make a grand *Aufzug*; but there is such asking,
and so many silks and drawings and crowns, and God knows what, to
look at, that I, who hate being troubled about dress, am quite *confusé*."[2]
Bewildered and confused, Victoria nonetheless dressed up for balls that
identify her and her prince with particular "racial" strains in the British
Isles.[3] Along with the ancient practice of genealogy, the developing profession of ethnology provides a context for understanding some possible meanings in Victoria and Albert's choices for their masquerades.
They dressed in clothes that were identified with British "races." Their
costumes constructed nationalistic mythologies, with the couple performing a selective royal genealogy as a way of declaring their sovereignty over the "races" of Britain.

In using clothes to identify races, the royal couple reflected contemporary scientific thinking. In their study of the human race, British ethnographers distinguished one race from another not only by measuring components of the physical frame but by judging how that frame was covered. Not only were clothes deemed essential to human survival, but ethnographers rated the wearing of clothes as proof of human superiority over all other species. "The human animal is the only one which is naked, and the only one which can clothe itself," John Kennedy boasted in his 1851 book *The Natural History of Man; or, Popular Chapters on Ethnography*.[4] Victorian ethnographers classified humans according to exacting, though arbitrary, scales. Color of hair, eyes, skin; measure of skull angle and size signified not only difference among the races of man but also differences of quality: "The idea of stupidity is associated, even by the vulgar, with the elongation of the snout, which necessarily lowers the facial line," Kennedy asserted, whereas, "an elevated facial angle indicates intellectual advancement and nobleness."[5] Ethnographers used human bodily shapes for racial and class typologies and to explain such characteristics as criminality, amativeness, and intelligence. Calipers measured skull size to assess race, but hairstyle, hats, and other fashioning were also considered as racial characteristics. John Beddoe, author of *The Races of Britain*, took many photographs to illustrate racial differences, photographs widely used by subsequent ethnographers throughout the century. His "evidence" indicates that bodily enhancements aided him in his racial typing.

Complementing ethnology's study of racial differences, genealogy, the study of family bloodlines, also characterized a person's abilities. In contrast to ethnology, genealogy focused on the upper classes, those people, who according to Beddoe, could not be charted ethnographically because of their frequent migratory and miscegenating practices. Royalty mingled so many noble blood groups that ethnographic particularity was lost. "As a rule, I take no note of persons who apparently belong to the upper classes, as these are more migratory and more often mixed in blood," explained Beddoe in regard to his fieldwork delineating British races.[6] Genealogy served for those with "blood" what ethnography explained for the purer but more lowly classes. If Queen Victoria was "born to succeed," as one biography suggests,[7] that success signified blood and racial lines whose meanings the ethnographer and the genealogist attempted to chart with scientific authority. While Victoria gradually learned of her genealogy, Albert was born into full genealogical consciousness. The *Almanach de Gotha*, in which European royalty and nobility were rated according to their relative blue-bloodedness, issued from Albert's birthplace. Queen Victoria's let-

Title page from *Discent of Her Majesty Victoria* . . .

ters to her family indicate that they paid close, sometimes disapproving, attention to its rankings. Throughout her reign genealogies of Victoria were published, some with an explicitly political purpose, such as the *Discent of Her Majesty Victoria Queen of England from the Arsacid Kings of Armenia.*[8] An enormous illuminated genealogical chart hand-painted for Christmas 1884, *Coronation Stone*, traced "an unbroken descent of Her Majesty Queen Victoria by an unbroken series of 124 generations from our FIRST PARENTS."[9] The kings of Armenia allied themselves with a powerful nation, while Adam and Eve wrote in stone Albert and Victoria's right to rule.

During the twenty years of their marriage, Victoria and Albert masqueraded as different racial strains on their family tree—races that also occupied the attentions of the ethnographer and the genealogist. Their costumes build an imaginative sovereign identity. Like other Victorian exhibitions, royal costume proclaimed national values composed of mutually constitutive commercial, colonial, and imperial ideas. Costumes actually worn or—in my final example—worn in effigy, perform Victoria and Albert's royal lineage; the couple's dress enacts the pedigree signifying their particular license to practice the British monarchical trade. Although her bloodlines were for the most part foreign, the queen dresses as if she were indigenous, even homegrown.

↷ Genealogical Galas ↶

In Spitalfields the Weavers worked with joy, in former ages,
But they're tired out of asking for a better scale of wages.
— *"Striking Times," street ballad*

In the forties and fifties Victoria and Albert gave a series of fancy dress balls with themes based on English history. In 1842 six months after the birth of Albert Edward, second child and heir to the throne, the couple held the most elaborate of these productions, the Plantagenet Ball. In 1845 the Powder Ball required that celebrants wear powdered wigs of the ball's period theme—between 1740 and 1750. Sarah Tooley, publishing a gossipy book during 1897, the year of the Diamond Jubilee, scanned contemporary newspaper articles as well as private recollections of this ball and observed great latitude in matters of accuracy: "The time (1740–50) was not one at which the dress was very becoming, and when the royal fiat went forth ladies were horrified. . . . The Queen, dressed as the Lady of the Feast, wore a magnificent brocade covered with point lace drawn from the hoards of her grandmother, Queen Charlotte; while Prince Albert looked bravely in a scarlet velvet coat and gold waistcoat."[10] Victoria's lace confirms her pedigree while glossing over less admirable details of her grandparents' reign.

In 1851 the Stuart (or Restoration) Ball honored Charles II, the "Merry Monarch," and allowed Victoria and Albert to play out their inheritance of the Scottish throne. Even William Gladstone entered into the festivities, clad as Sir Leoline Jenkins, judge in the High Court of Admiralty.[11] This ball heralded the monarchy's restoration from its previous reputation for profligacy, irresponsibility, and low moral tone, while showing that it could have fun. At the same time, the costumes promoted Victoria and Albert as an integral genealogical part of English history.

The most significant of these balls, however, was the Plantagenet Ball, whose theme may have been inspired by George Russell French, an architect who was also an amateur but exacting genealogist.

Appearing the year before the ball and focusing almost exclusively on Victoria, his book, *The Ancestry of Her Majesty Queen Victoria and of his Royal Highness Prince Albert*, traces her lineage back through Noah to Adam, creating a genealogy superior to that of any European monarch. According to French, the blood of six ninth-century princes, each of whom formed a dynasty, flowed through Victoria's veins. Her marriage to Prince Albert confirmed the queen's racial superiority by reinforcing strong genealogical ties to the great Saxon chief Witikind II, Count of Wettin. The "new" dynasty, initiated by Victoria and Albert, thus draws on a biblical pedigree while at the same time establishing the royal couple in English history and presenting genealogical justification for their imperial pretensions.

The royal couple affirmed their genealogy by reconstructing history. Not content simply to render an approximation of medieval display, Victoria and Albert hired James Planché, an expert on historical dress, to construct convincing details of costume and decor for their ball. Accuracy testified to authenticity, as if performance itself made visible an actual past. As the *Times* remarked, the pageant "presented as it were the descriptions of the ancient chroniclers bodily before us."[12] The reporter was dazzled not only by the magnificence that served to display the great wealth and superiority of the British monarchy but also by the illusion that "fantasy became reality" (May 14, 1842) and turned the ball into history's truth. Given Edward and Philippa's reputation in the nineteenth century for enjoying a mutually supportive, forty-year relationship, their reincarnation at the Plantagenet Ball might suggest a similarly auspicious future for the current monarchs. Their realm might prosper as well. Under the influence of his intelligent, kind, and cultivated queen, Edward studied architecture, patronized the arts, protected the English wool industry, and founded the Order of the Garter. Unusually conscious of his image, he staged displays of majesty, during which he healed hundreds of supplicants. Together, Edward and Philippa revived the monarchy.

Building on the precedent of Victoria's English-made wedding gown and lace, Victoria and Albert promoted the ball as a benefit for the foundering Spitalfields silk-weaving industry. The queen's awareness of the East London weavers dates at least to 1837, her first public appearance at an Opera House Ball for their benefit, an event reported in the *Lady's Magazine and Museum*:

> This fête took place on the 1st ultimo, and was perhaps, in every respect, the most court-like of meetings out of the precincts of a palace. . . . Our present young and gracious

> Queen was a great object of interest, it being her first appear-
> ance in common with the public. Her head-tire was a simple
> wreath of white flowers; her hair was parted equally on either
> side of the face, and her dress most simple. . . . General and
> ardent plaudits followed her parting footsteps. She withdrew
> doubtless much gratified at the public affection for her
> house.[13]

Gratifying memories may enhance the object of charity's worthiness, while the contrast between Victoria's simple attire at the earlier ball and her fabulous bejeweled dress in the later Plantagenet affair speaks to a change in purpose, values, and methods of self-presentation.

The elaborate costumes provided the opportunity to display the specialized skills of the Spitalfields hand weavers while also bolstering other trades associated with producing the fête. As the *London Illustrated News* reported: "The purpose of this splendid gathering of the brave and beautiful, it is known, was to give stimulus to trade in all the various departments that could be affected by the enormous outlay it would necessarily involve, and we have no doubt that many thousands are this day grateful for the temporary aid which this right royal entertainment has been the means of affording them." For the pleasure of the more than two thousand who danced at the ball, throngs of workers gained employment. But to what end and with what implications for the year 1842?

Eighteen forty-two was the year of Chartist strikes; the ball on May 12 followed by ten days the Chartists' enormous procession on May 2, accompanying the second National Petition to the House of Commons.[14] Apart from the royal couple's isolation from working-class privations and given their possible youthful ignorance, the fear of Chartism provides a context for their decision to stage the sumptuous ball as a way of employing starving workers. Since Victoria was convinced that Chartists were ruffians who posed a danger to the monarchy and to the nation, it may not be accidental that her masque travesties the Chartist procession, its charity also exhibiting monarchical power.

The ritual processions forming part of the queen's festivities act as a counterpart to the Chartist's solemn procession to deliver their petition with its alleged 3,317,702 signatures to Parliament:

> At the very early hours of that morning detachments of
> Chartists assembled in various parts of London, and
> marched to the rendezvous in Lincoln's Inn Fields. At noon
> the Petition arrived, mounted on a huge wooden frame, on

the front of which were painted the figures "3,317,702"
above the legend "The Charter." At the back appeared the
same figures and "Liberty." On the sides were set forth the
"six points" of the Charter. The Petition was just over six
miles long. The great bobbin-like frame was mounted on
poles for the thirty bearers. The journey to the House
began.[15]

A detailed argument for full franchise as part of a democracy with representation of those taxed, the charter delineated the discrepancy of
wealth between the productive classes and those "whose comparative
usefulness ought to be questioned." In that last category the charter
mentioned the queen, Prince Albert, the king of Hanover, and the archbishop of Canterbury.[16]

At the Plantagenet Ball sovereign power performed its claims for
authority against an organized English labor movement whose procession was supplicating not royalty but Parliament. Some of the daily journals drew attention to the contrast between the sumptuous royal fête and
the privations of the workers. Reporting the ball's excesses with some
irony, the *Times* remarked: "Her Gracious Sovereign has gradually
stretched her hospitality to the enormous extent of 2.000 invitations. . . .
The expenditure for this one night's entertainment will be enormous.
One noble lord, we hear of who is to pay £150 for the hire of diaments
and ladies of rank will expend a far greater sum." All the "Great Jewellers
of London . . . even down to the Jew diamond merchants" had exhausted
their store by the day of the event.[17] Queen Victoria's stomacher alone
was festooned with jewels reputedly worth £60,000. Written in the context of Chartist agitation, such reportage uses awe to editorialize.

Tooley reported that the queen's charitable "motives were misun-
derstood and much called in question at the time, and there were
papers which printed the cost of the Court pageants in one column,
and gave the list of those who were dying from starvation in another."[18]
Six years later, in the face of a feared Chartist revolution, Victoria and
Albert, decreeing that Court Ladies should wear only British clothes at
her drawing rooms, threw another great ball to benefit Spitalfields; this
time, however, more than half the money raised went toward
expenses.[19] This later ball indicates that Victoria and Albert responded
consciously to the workers' distress by producing charity galas.

By means of historical allusion, the Plantagenet masquerade played
out royalty's historic ties to the English cloth industry. As courtly lover,
Edward III paid obeisance to his lady, being influenced by her gentle
sympathies in her intercession for the burghers of Calais, a subject

painted by Benjamin West as part of a series for the audience room in Windsor Castle. In the fourteenth century Queen Philippa had protected the French burghers from the sentence of death her husband had pronounced upon them. As a proper chatelaine, Philippa appealed to Edward's mercy, and as a proper courtly lover, Edward acceded. The story offers parallels to Victoria and Albert's staged reaction to the Chartists. As Philippa and Edward showed mercy to the French during a triumphant moment in the Hundred Years War, so Victoria and Albert could be understood as interceding on behalf of the Huguenot-descended silk weavers, whose ancestors had settled in London when they escaped from France in the seventeenth century.[20] If actual connections with Spitalfields were impressionistic, they nevertheless tell about the kind of monarchy constructed by the Plantagenet Ball. For it is not simply that the medieval garb disguises a bourgeois family narrative, as Simon Schama in his insightful study of royal portraiture claims,[21] but that such costumes reveal a regressive historical identification with "medieval" versions of monarchy.

The Spitalfields weavers fit nicely into a medieval model. As part of an industry that began with the immigration of the Huguenots but was in decline by 1832, Spitalfields weavers remained loyal to ancient technology. They did not adopt new inventions, even within the hand loom. Unlike provincial weavers from Manchester, Lancashire, and Yorkshire, for example, Spitalfields weavers did not employ the Jacquard machine or the fly shuttle, eighteenth-century inventions that came to England around 1820.[22] In the very weave of their silken dress, Victoria and Albert announced that their monarchy drew its sustenance from a feudal model, where hierarchical rights differed radically from the Chartists' democratic ideal.

While the Plantagenet disguise "answers" the class uprising in the political sphere, it also addresses the irregularity in the domestic sphere. Clad in their costumes, the prince no longer seems to be subservient to Victoria. In the chivalric code, as the Victorians imagined it, the lady rules by courtesy, but the king forms the apex of the feudal hierarchy, ruling both his lady and his realm. Edwin Landseer painted the couple in their Plantagenet garb, attending to the details of a courtly love first delineated in the elegant fashions and protocol of another age, then transferred to Victoria's life story by means of a theatrical set. Albert holds his lady's hand, honoring yet ruling her: the sword prominently at his side replicates the jeweled sword of state—part of the king's coronation regalia, as is the jeweled crown on his head: real jewels connote the genuineness of a role that Albert could never perform.

To complicate the simple gender reversal, in which the male reasserts his dominance by means of masquerading as a king, Queen Philippa was not the ordinary courtly lady that her intercession on behalf of the condemned Calais burghers might seem to make of her. In that story, she uses her influence nonaggressively, as is meet and properly feminine. In other stories, though, the fiercely bellicose Edward III met his match in his lady Philippa. While he was winning the Battle of Crécy against the French, Philippa, commanding twelve thousand troops, won the Battle of Nevill's Cross against fifty thousand Scots, taking King David of Scotland prisoner on October 17, 1346. West's series for the Audience Room in Windsor Castle included a painting of Philippa at Nevill's Cross.

In addition to redressing a gender anomaly, the Plantagenet costumes also smooth over ethnological and genealogical difficulties by muting Albert's problematic German bloodline. The Plantagenet connection lent an ancient patina to contemporary suspicions concerning Prince Albert's continuing allegiances to his native land. Landseer's painting shows Victoria and Albert dressed as if they are medieval English, harking back both to Norman and Norse racial lines. As Edward Plantagenet, Prince Albert of Saxe-Coburg and Gotha (with no official English title at this time) elides his German ancestry. And as Philippa of Hainault, Victoria, too, seems less Hanoverian and less the child of a controlling German mother who did not speak English when her daughter was born. Ethnographically and through the power of costume, Victoria's blue blood wears a trace of stalwart fighters, a quality that could be passed on to the newly born heir to the throne. Taking appearance for reality, the couple dress in what the newspaper called "the costume of their race" (*Times*, May 13, 1842). Announced in bejeweled raiment, Victoria's selective genealogy reminds her people of a race constructed through creative anachronism.

The renovated throne room at Buckingham Palace "copied from an authentic source," was hung with shields bearing the arms of England and France, the main scene of the ball being a portrayal of the meeting between the Plantagenet court and the French court of Anne of Brittany. In addition to this masque, quadrilles, organized according to each nation in its turn, offered homage to the "Plantagenets": France, Germany, Spain, Italy, and Scotland, all in accurate costume for period and locale. The ball's rituals thus introduced Plantagenet Victoria and Albert representing England as the pinnacle of Western civilization.

The ball provoked controversy, and Victoria learned that it was not universally admired. One minister took as his sermon's text, "When Charity took to dancing it ceased to be Charity and became a wan-

Queen Victoria and Prince Albert at the Bal Costumé, May 1842, by Sir Edwin Landseer, 1842–1846. *Illustration from the Royal Archives, by permission of The Royal Collection © Her Majesty Queen Elizabeth II.*

ton."[23] A spoof reported a debate in the French Chamber of Deputies alleging that the ball was thrown to remind France of the disasters of Crécy and Poitiers and the loss of Calais. The article speculated that the French ambassador, M. de St. Aulaire, accompanied by his attachés, planned to attend as the unfortunate burghers, with bare feet and halters around their necks as Edward III had demanded. Many French believed the article, and the ball became a diplomatic embarrassment.

PRINCE ALBERT'S OWN NATIVE INFANTRY.

"We understand that the Prince of Wales has already been appointed a colonel," reported *Punch*, vol. 3, 1842, p. 221.

Lord Melbourne found it necessary to assure Victoria that her party "was the most magnificent and beautiful spectacle that he ever beheld. . . . Lord Melbourne also believes it to be very popular, for the reasons which your Majesty mentions."[24] A letter to the *Times* questioned the taste of "people coming as Lucretia and Caesar Borgia" (May 19, 1842, p. 5). When crowds came to view Victoria's sumptuous Philippa costume displayed in Hanover Square, many judged it to be a concrete reminder of centuries of royal callousness to human misery.[25]

Others mocked the couple's choice. An anonymous satire, published the month of the ball, entitled *The Queen's Masque*, portrayed Victoria and Albert as weak imitations of a far hardier stock. The satirist contrasts valiant Edward and effeminate Albert as an indication of a "happy" change from the ferocity of former days. Questioning Albert's "curious choice of character," the author proceeds to point out its anomalies:

> But why he chose King Edward's part,
> Heaven and Victoria only know;
> Perhaps because the dress was smart,
> Or Philippa would have it so.
> For from his prototype, our youth
> His German Highness varies much,
> Ned was a valiant man, in sooth,
> But Albert is by no means such.
> The former through strange lands to roam
> Rejoiced, in search of glorious strife;

The latter loves to sit at home,
And nurse the lapdog of his wife.

. . . .

Why then does Albert now assume
The semblance of that gallant Prince?

. . . .

Hush, let irreverence cease to jeer—
Mark those two babes in smiling charms,
To England's love and pocket dear—
Those are *our* Prince's *deeds in arms!*[26]

The Queen's Masque accuses Prince Albert of insufficient manliness to battle the foe. His role more closely approximates a lackey, even a gigolo. As royal inseminator to the queen, his advantageous marriage gives him the purse to gratify his grandiose self-presentation.

Disapproval of sumptuous displays did not necessarily mean that those finding them morally lacking rejected the gender and economic values enacted in the masque of chivalric marriage. One might object to the medium while absorbing its messages. Other costumes, different rituals, dressed the monarchy in other ethnicities and combined to imprint the monarchy within its territories. The fancy dress balls responded to a series of problems by playing at them. Their staging performed cultural work, not as a coherent narrative but as a message that, when repeated in other guises, presented possibilities for representing monarchy in the Victorian age. From a perspective that allows certain patterns to emerge and certain messages to be decoded, the *bal masqué* proves to be an epitome of later ethnic impersonations. Parts of the performance needed restaging, different dialogues, and different props. But to a remarkable extent the simple royal folly of a fancy dress ball reveals how Victoria's monarchy performed sovereign and national agendas by reimagining old ways.

⇥ Highland Progresses ⇤

I feel a sort of reverence in going over these scenes in this most beautiful country, which I am proud to call my own, . . . for Stuart blood is in my veins, and I am now their representative.
—More Leaves from the Journal of Our Life in the Highlands

Several months after the Plantagenet Ball, Victoria and Albert set out for Scotland for the first time. They traveled by water, fearing possible Chartist riots in the north. The trip to Scotland could also be regarded as an elaborate genealogical performance, resembling some rituals of the Plantagenet masque. Like the fête, the Scottish venture made concrete a kind of British imperial rule based upon a feudal model of patrician activity. It surveyed a territory joined to England by the Act of Union of 1707.[27] Victoria's uncle, George IV, set a precedent for her trip by visiting Scotland in 1822, when bagpipes played and the king adopted the Royal Stuart tartans. Victoria published a description of a ritual, affirming her place on the Scottish family tree:

> September 7: We walked out, and saw the mound where the ancient Scotch kings were always crowned; also the old arch with James VI.'s arms, and the old cross, which is very interesting.
>
> Before our windows stands a sycamore-tree planted by James VI. A curious old book was brought to us from *Perth*, in which the last signatures are those of James I (of England) and of Charles I., and we were asked to write our names in it, and we did so.[28]

Writing in the curious old book inscribes the couple in a lineage based on an ancient presence in Scotland. The trip to the northern reaches of the British Isles harkened to an earlier time, where ancient chronicles blurred distinctions between literature and life. Victoria confided to her journal: "Lord Mansfield told me yesterday that there were some people in the town who wore the identical dresses that had been worn in Charles I.'s time" (84). The much-publicized journey itself and the subsequent publication of the queen's journal in 1868 made their first visit to Scotland seem like a homecoming.

The trip combined elements of a royal progress, a fancy dress ball, and a scouting mission. After passing the battlefield where the Highlanders defeated the Danes, the queen's entourage passed through Birnam, renowned, Victoria tells us, in *Macbeth*. On to "*Dunkeld* [where] . . . before a triumphal arch, Lord Glenlyon's Highlanders, with halberds, met us, and formed our guard—a piper playing before us . . . in the midst of their encampments. . . . We walked down the ranks of the Highlanders, and then partook of luncheon; the piper played, and one of the Highlanders danced the 'sword dance.' . . . Some of the others danced a reel"(26). They continued to Taymouth, Lord Breadalbane's territory, met again by a guard of Highlanders who would ultimately dance reels ("which they do to perfection") to the "sound of the pipes, by torchlight." Victoria's theatrical sense saw the "scene" not only as Scott but as operatic Scott, Donizetti's *Lucia di Lammermoor* (1836):

The house is a kind of castle, built of granite. The *coup-d'œil* was indescribable. There were a number of Lord Breadalbane's Highlanders, all in the Campbell tartan, drawn up in front of the house, with Lord Breadalbane himself in a Highland dress at their head, a few of Sir Neil Menzies' men (in the Menzies red and white tartan), a number of pipers playing, and a company of the 92d Highlanders, also in kilts. The firing of the guns, the cheering of the great crowd, the picturesqueness of the dresses, the beauty of the surrounding country, with its rich background of wooded hills, altogether formed one of the finest scenes imaginable. It seemed as if a great chieftain in olden feudal times was receiving his sovereign. It was princely and romantic. . . . After dinner the gardens were most splendidly illuminated—a whole chain of lamps along the railings, and on the ground was written in lamps, "Welcome Victoria—Albert."

(38–39)

A ritual harkening back to "olden feudal times" sets Victoria and Albert in an amorphously defined feudal time, designated as "olden." Writing the royal couple's names on the earth, Lord Breadalbane and Sir Neil Menzies participate in a ritual act that the anthropologist Clifford Geertz describes as a sovereign's "marking" territory:

The very thing that the elaborate mystique of court ceremonial is supposed to conceal—that majesty is made, not born—is demonstrated by it. . . .

This comes out as clearly as anywhere else in the ceremonial forms by which kings take symbolic possession of their realm. In particular, royal progresses . . . locate the society's center and affirm its connection with transcendent things by stamping a territory with ritual signs of dominance. When kings journey around the countryside . . . they mark it, like some wolf or tiger spreading his scent through his territory, as almost physically part of them.[29]

Those creating pageantry construct the marking rituals, but those observing also participate in conveying its codes. Such observers usually remain anonymous, but Victoria and Albert were lucky in being accompanied by a physician who thought himself a poet. Transported by the honor, James D. Howie, M.D., set his impressions to epic verse, the very amateurishness of which exposes the medieval pretense behind the ceremonies, partly because Howie himself loves every minute of them.

In the preface to "The Queen in Scotland, A Descriptive Poem," Howie claims both literal and visionary truth: "the Author has only to say, that the scenes . . . are those only which came under his own observation. At the same time, . . . it embraces, with scarcely a single exception, every thing interesting connected with the Queen's visit to Scotland; and therefore, whatever may be thought of the production in a different respect, it will be found to possess the merit of a strict adherence to truth."[30] Admitting that his work may lack poetic genius, Howie claims its validity as historical truth. Poetic convention, such as the invocation to Victoria, appears to be the representation of actual queenly attributes:

> Ye soft gales, blow
> Heave, ye resplendent billows! They have borne,
> In days of old, to Caledonia's shores
> Queens young and beautiful, but never one
> Excelling thee in aught, Victoria dear!
> For thou art good as young, beauteous as meek,
> Modest as royal, merciful as just,
> Cheerful as dignified,—uniting all
> The qualities for which we most praise queens,
> Without their failings.
>
> *(4–5)*

In genealogical progression, Victoria arrives on the scene to fulfill the promise of earlier queens, wedding her to the Scots through their common literary deity, Sir Walter Scott:

> A sculptured column to her minstrel hoar,
> Whose Caledonian lyre entranced a world,
> She paused, and dropped a consecrated tear
> To genius, grandeur, and Sir Walter Scott!
>
> *(14)*

Perhaps Victoria remembered meeting Scott when she was about nine; Scott reported that the princess played too much at being a queen not to suspect her future.[31] Whatever her personal recollections, Victoria's tears for him bind her to her Scottish subjects through common reverence. While confirming that Scott created the Scotland of the tour, tears also bridge class and ethnological boundaries.

For Howie, as for Victoria, the Scottish scene evoked the Middle Ages, particularly in the relationship between Victoria and Albert:

> Leaning on Albert's arm, I saw our Queen,
> Our darling Queen, moving on Scottish soil
> A vision of light and beauty! (Such as made
> In days of olden chivalry the sword
> Of belted knight or plume-cap'd cavalier
> Instinctive from the scabbard leap, without
> The touch of human hand, to avenge the feared
> Approach of insult.)
>
> *(25–26)*

Allusions to chivalry transfer Victoria's rule to Albert's knightly protection. Howie is preparing for his later characterizations of the queen as wife and mother, describing her as a static maternal icon of monarchical authority, only moving when she leans on Albert's arm. The ending of the poem envisions her yearning for "home; most endearing word":

> The Queen thinks of her home: her babes are there,
> Her Albert and Maria. Ne'er till now,
> In full perfection had she felt the power
> Of strong parental love;
>
> *(90)*

Howie thus constructs a parental Victoria as an ordinary queen of a domestic home.

The royal couple eventually made a Scottish home, Balmoral, one that they promoted as ordinary in its domestic affections. Six years after their first visit, the royal couple had marked their territory, eventually encompassing a 30,000-acre estate, complete with a medievalized laird's castle, turreted and crenelated.[32] The couple's emotional embrace of the wild landscapes of the Scottish Highlands can be viewed as another colonizing masquerade, where territory retrospectively reaffirms their ancestry. Victoria records the couple's attire at a Torch Light Ball at Corriemulzie in 1852: "I wore a white bonnet, a gray watered silk, and (according to Highland fashion) my plaid scarf over my shoulder, and Albert his Highland dress, which he wears every evening" (130).

Long after "Balmorality" had established itself, Victoria's first volume of published memoirs, *Leaves from the Journal of Our Life in the*

Balmoral Castle, view from the southwest, from a photograph by G. W. Wilson and Co., Aberdeen.

Highlands from 1848 to 1861 (1868), disseminated news of the couple's Scottish ethnicity to an international audience, reflecting the kind of life associated with royal family pastimes rather than with sovereign responsibilities. As its capable editor, Arthur Helps, explained in the preface: "It will easily be seen that this little work does not make any pretension to be more than such a record of the impressions received by the Royal Author in the course of these journeys as might here after serve to recall to her own mind the scenes and circumstances which had been the source of so much pleasure. All references to political questions, or to the affairs of government, have, for obvious reasons, been studiously omitted" (vii). But in its conscious intention to focus on simple family pleasures, the book's publication affirmed the queen's manifest values, impressing on the reader that she recorded the substance of her life, not its trivialities. To omit the political made the political seem irrelevant.

Inevitably, *some* leaves from her life tended to be taken as the whole of it. A contemporary review notes the importance to history of *Leaves*, remarking on the value of its realistic detail: "our descendants will have the great figures of the historical portrait set before them with a minuteness of description, a completeness of detail, and a delicacy of touch, which will, after any lapse of time reproduce before them the real life of the present century in its best proportions."[33] Detail and verisimilitude present a portrait of the "real life" of a queen who never attends to business. In fact, while she wrote affectionately of Highland landscapes and its people who dance, sing wild songs, play games, and build cairns while Albert shoots and she sketches, visits ailing cottagers, and writes in her diary, Victoria Regina also sent daily dispatches to her ministers.[34] Queen Victoria's secret life in the Highlands was deeply involved in the affairs of state. Rather than only doing what a virtuous but rich wife does in her country place, Victoria worked hard at the monarchical trade.

She constructed a Highland landscape as filtered through Shakespeare's *Macbeth* and more directly through Sir Walter Scott and Sir Edwin Landseer. In her journal she invoked both writer and painter for inspiration and interpretation. In 1850: "I wished for Landseer's pencil" (127) and in 1860: "Then we came upon a most lovely spot—the scene of all Landseer's glory" (177). *Leaves*'s careful focus on such simple Scottish pleasures as family life, kirk, and shooting masks the political implications of such aesthetic tourism. The royal family's adoption of tartans performs the work of what Michael Hecter calls "internal colonization." Balmoral Castle resembles a colonial outpost, the *Leaves* a "simple record" of the kind of "matter of fact things" Victoria loved, by means of the recording of "personal joys and sorrows of our Sovereign" (vi).

Victoria publicized her husband's fictional Scottish heritage in her selections from her journal. As a genre, the memoir, as Virginia Woolf observed, "leaves out the person to whom things happened"; in the case of Victoria's journal this omission was strategic, allowing the journal to focus mainly on the recently dead Laird Albert. Its depiction of the Highlands as both a wild and hospitable place lent a crucial *masculine* aura to the prince, who was seen throughout his life in England as foreign and insufficiently manly to suit the Britons.[35] Substituting the Highland kilt for skintight gaiters or too impeccable clothes allowed Albert to display the legs Victoria admired, yet in a way associated with Celtic masculinity. Dr. Howie praised the effect of Taymouth entertainment described in *Leaves* by attributing its excitement specifically to masculine display, inherent in the "gorgeous tartans" on male bodies dancing to the "melodious pibrochs":

> There guardsmen too,
> With plumes and shouldered broadswords giving back
> The casements' gleaming light, in gay costume

> Of bold clan Campbell, shew their manly shapes
> To advantage.
>
> *(64)*

From at least as far back as the Union, the Celtic Highlander supplied militaristic fierceness crucial to an imperial image. According to Linda Colley's *The Britons*, the English seemed cowed by the stereotypical aggressive Scot; she explains English "obsession . . . with Scottish sexual potency" as a reaction to the Union, a kind of backlash where "the colonized become more potent than the colonizer."[36] In wearing the costume of the Highlander Albert puts on more than the kilt but also what proverbially is under it. Scottish Highlanders, so Lowland and English legend alleged, were "unusually well-endowed sexually."[37] Howie's Scotsmen, flinging themselves about in spangled kilts, stagily embody the fantasy of flamboyant manliness:

> Ten sturdy Gaels have mounted, gaily dressed
> In spangled tartans, flashing back the beams
> Flung from the illumined casement; boldly now
> They spread the active limb, they spring, they leap!
>
> *(66)*

The Gaels' military manliness resembles the Plantagenet Ball satirist's portrayal of Edward III. The warlike dances performed in 1842 transpose imaginatively into the legendary 42d Highlanders, the queen's famed regiment whose war exploits are captured in many contemporary paintings of the English colonial wars.[38]

In *Leaves* and in many renderings of the refurbished Scottish royalty, Albert, dressed in Highland attire, shoots the signature Scottish animal, the roebuck or stag. By association, Albert's clan animal, in the anthropological sense, becomes the royal or twelve-point stag delineated in Landseer's monumental painting *The Monarch of the Glen* (1851). In Landseer's depiction the mighty stag seems to dominate the world. Scott's *The Lady of the Lake* provides the context both for Landseer's picture and Albert's masculinization. Scott's monarch, pursued by hunters, finds a safe retreat in the wild heaths:

> The antler'd monarch of the waste
> Sprung from his heathery couch in haste.
> But, ere his fleet career he took,
> The dew-drops from his flanks he shook;
> Like crested leader proud and high,

Balmoral, Bringing Home the Stag, watercolor by Carl Haag, 1854. *Illustration from the Royal Archives, by permission of The Royal Collection © Her Majesty Queen Elizabeth II.*

> Toss'd his beam'd frontlet to the sky;
> A moment gazed adown the dale,
> A moment snuff'd the tainted gale,
> A moment listen'd to the cry,
> That thicken'd as the chase drew nigh;
> Then, as the headmost foes appear'd,
> With one brave bound the copse he clear'd,
> And, stretching forward free and far,
> Sought the wild heaths of Uam-Var.

(canto 1, stanza 2)

Scott's monarch seeks untainted, purer air, where he can be king. As in the Plantagenet Ball, the Scottish costumes gave Albert the authority he seemed to have lost by his marriage to a queen. Responding to the call of the wild, Victoria and Albert played out Scott's vision.

One painting in the royal collection, *Balmoral, Bringing Home the Stag* by Carl Haag (1854), demonstrates how the Scottish masquerade enhanced the prince's virility. In it, Albert displays a recently slain stag for his wife's admiration. Antlers dominate the painting; the prince holds up one side of a pair while the other side points to the sporran hanging between his legs at the virtual center of the composition. Other men in the painting are appropriately servile: three retainers hold torches aloft and another tends a horse bearing another stag car-

Balmoral Castle letterhead, by Sir Edwin Landseer. The stag assumes the noble pose, similar to Landseer's royal stag painting *The Monarch of the Glen*. He guards his resting mate. *Illustration from the Royal Archives, by permission of The Royal Collection © Her Majesty Queen Elizabeth II.*

cass next to Albert, while two men in the background, dressed in conventional black evening dress and standing in wooden poses, form a drab contrast to Albert's highlighted manliness. Albert thrusts his barely covered knee forward, while the Prince of Wales, also bekilted, points to the stag while looking up to his mother in mutual approval. Yet another pair of antlers, belonging to the dead beast in the right foreground, emphasizes Prince Albert's prowess.[39] Substituting stags and rifles for the satirist's babes in arms, a reinvented Albert steps forth as Monarch of the Glen. To reinforce the identification with the Highlands animal, Landseer designed the Balmoral writing paper with a pair of roebuck, the male in the commanding position and the doe lying at his feet.

During their first journey to Scotland, Victoria read Scott to the prince, primarily *The Lady of the Lake* and *The Lay of the Last Minstrel*. She also purchased a Landseer stag painting, *The Sanctuary* (1842) for Albert, in which a royal stag leads a party of birds and other wildlife into what might be imagined as the wilds of Uam Var. The painting could serve as a comment on Victoria and Albert's use of Balmoral, with its loyal servants, humble crofters, and distance from the Chartists. On their last evening aboard ship on the way to a train journey to Windsor Castle, Victoria bade farewell to Scotland by means of Scott's poetry:

"We went below at half past seven, and I read the fourth and fifth cantos of *The Lay of the Last Minstrel* to Albert, and then we played on the piano" (55).

Scott's poem, set in the sixteenth century, recounts the healing of a Highland feud, complicated by German mercenaries, English foes, and other races. Scott seems to invite the English to patronize Scotland when, in canto 5, stanza 30, he indicates that the Scots do not value their culture sufficiently to support its poets:

> After due pause, they bade him tell,
> Why he, who touch'd the harp so well,
> Should thus, with ill-rewarded toil,
> Wander a poor and thankless soil,
> When the more generous Southern land
> Would well requite his skillful hand.

Acting on Scott's invitation, Victoria thanked the Scottish soil by buying it up. Scott's immense popularity created an imaginative market for Scotland, taming its customs for increasingly eager consumers from the more generous South. Yet the effect of opening the Scottish market, some argue, was to sell the very ethnicity of the Scots to their conquerors. The royal occupation of Scotland occurred at a time when Scottish nationalists differentiated Scottish culture from English character if not from English rule. Magazines such as *Blackwood's* and *Fraser's* carried articles describing Scottish characteristics as well as the country's kirk, folklore, foods, and rites. According to Charles Oliver Ardersier-MacDonald, "Scotland and England are very different countries."[40] Another article lists the oppositions between Scots and English to distinguish their characters: "As a rule, every question for an Englishman is complex, every question for a Scotchman simple."[41]

Victoria and Albert no more invented the Scotland of *Leaves* and of the material fiefdom of their Balmoral estate than they invented the medievalism inspiring the Plantagenet Ball. They played in Scotland as well as in the renovated throne room at Buckingham Palace what the poet Gerard Manley Hopkins in another context called "charades of the Middle Ages." As Hugh Trevor-Roper argues, the nineteenth century invented the Scottish tradition, focusing on the tartan to the point of obsession. Victorian royalty participated in a known fiction: "No educated Englishman needs to be told nowadays that Scotchmen do not wear tartans—that figures one sees at the doors of tobacco-shops in London have no prototypes in the North,—that a kilt is seen just as frequently in Regent-street as on the Calton-hill," stated a correspondent

Drawing Room at Balmoral, watercolor by J. Roberts, 1857. The furniture is uphol-stered in the Victoria tartan. *Illustration from the Royal Archives, by permission of The Royal Collection © Her Majesty Queen Elizabeth II.*

to *Fraser's* in 1856.[42] Victoria and Albert designed their own signature tartans. Albert's, the Balmoral tartan of black, red, and lavender on a gray background, is still in use, while the queen's Victoria tartan was used mainly for furnishings.[43] The charade of "tartanitis,"[44] like the cos-tume balls, performs a genealogy.

Victoria's role in making meaning from contemporary discourses typically proceeded in contradictory, simultaneous, and paradoxical directions. Victoria validated the Scots in acts of mutual appropriation. Whether she genuinely loved Scotland is not in question. The cultural, political, and social meanings of her preferences locate a place for Scotland in the Victorian cultural imagination. Her patronage stimu-lated an enduring market where everyone could play at being a wee bit Scottish. One need only read Victoria's description of the honest Scots to encounter the paradigm for selling sports coats, whiskey, golf courses, and so on. In 1993 the elegant Texas department store, Neiman Marcus, emulated her majesty's creation of a signature tartan and offered a trip not essentially different from the queen's first voyage, complete with Scottish rituals.[45]

Royal tartanitis put Scotland on a particular kind of map, though many had reason to resent its wide publication. The queen's valuation

Queen Victoria wrote of Norman MacLeod in her journal:
"He was a complete type in its noblest sense of a Highlander
and a Celt." From *The Personal Life of Queen Victoria* by Sarah
Tooley, 1897.

of her life in the Highlands facilitated Scottish entrepreneurship and
acceptance on imperial missions to other parts of the globe. The eleva-
tion of the Scots character made speculations about its true nature popular—for instance, in Victorian periodical literature—while it gave the
Scotsman an acceptance in commercial, intellectual, and scientific ventures not equally open to others of the "Celtic fringe." [46] It was not only
Thomas Carlyle who made the English believe that sagacity could speak
in a Scots accent.

While Albert played the royal clansman, Victoria's way of ruling
became a secret, *the* secret of *Leaves from a Journal of Our Life in the Highlands*. Absenting herself as agent in the drama of the Highlands, she
generated the memoir while presenting herself as a kind of guardian
angel. So Howie represents her, when she makes a visitation to a dairy:

> The Queen! the Queen! they cried; and was it then
> Our own beloved Queen who smiled to us,
> And asked of churning and of dairy work,
> Content to learn the highland peasant's toil!

(68)

Although Albert was interested in bovine husbandry and designed a
model dairy, Victoria's particular Scottish attribute would not be a milk
pail but a spinning wheel. The queen had herself photographed and
sketched spinning and listening to the simple comforting words of her

Scottish minister, the Reverend Norman MacLeod, and she gave samples of her spinning skill as gifts.

Such an image complicates Victoria's self-representation. As a simple spinner of yarn, the fundamental stuff of human bodily covering, she could be seen as the faithful Penelope (the subject of a statue she bought for Albert), but she could also be seen as the spider, who, when Albert died, she was said to resemble. Like the spider, her appetites killed her mate, and when he was dead, so the story went, she turned to a more authentic and hardy Highlander, John Brown.[47] That story, taken up in chapter 7, develops later and represents a variation on a sexual myth involving Victoria and Albert's royal ability to costume themselves in the stuff of their realm. Covering themselves, their floors, sofas, and chairs with tartans, Victoria and Albert remade the Celtic race in their own image. Victoria's own tartan is an emblem of colonialist complexities, woven by her subjects into bolts of cloth.

⇥   Anglo-Saxon Heaven   ⇤

The Celt in all his variants from Builth to Ballyhoo
His mental processes are plain—one knows what he will do,
And can logically predicate his finish by his start;
But the English—ah, the English!—They are quite a race apart.

—Rudyard Kipling, "The Puzzler"

Charles Kingsley opens the prelude to his adventure story *Hereward the Wake:'Last of the English'* (1865) with an ethnological lesson that is also part of Queen Victoria's "genealogy." Kingsley (who was for a time the Prince of Wales's history tutor) turns from the Highlanders to tell the story of another, still more esteemed race, the Anglo-Saxons: "The heroic deeds of Highlanders, both in these islands and elsewhere, have been told in verse and prose, and not more often, nor more loudly, than they deserve."[48] Whereas the Highlands have preserved their hardy race, the lowlands and fens bred heroes who held out against the Norman foe. Lowlanders arose from the Vikings intermarrying with the Angles and Saxons to create the hardy, independent English race. So Kingsley's racial genealogy celebrates the last of the English as also the first among men.[49]

Influenced by Scott's delineation in *Ivanhoe* of the lowland Scot as Anglo-Saxon rather than Highland Celt, Kingsley's ethnology exalts the new breed as the "Anglo-Saxon," highest on the ethnic hierarchy, quintessentially as English as the oak tree. The ethnographer Kennedy found evidence of this amalgamated race's superiority in their brain size: "The Teutonic, or German race, embracing, as it does, the Anglo-Saxons, Anglo-Americans, Anglo-Irish, &c., possess the largest brain of any other people."[50] Anglo-Saxonizing, as a subset of Victorian racializing practices, ignored inconsistencies to create what were recognized as distinct characteristics. To be English was to be racially "Anglo-Saxon," a race notable for virility.[51]

Kingsley expanded on his racial theories in an influential but controversial series of university lectures (1860), later published as *The Roman and the Teuton*. In those lectures he described England's Saxon ancestors as boys to the superior English men they fathered. Their destiny, fulfilled by his Cambridge undergraduates, he implied, was to rule the world:

> To the strange and complicated education which God appointed for this race [he proclaimed to the Cambridge students] and by which he has fitted it to become, at least for many centuries henceforth, the ruling race of the world, . . . I wish to impress strongly on your minds this childishness of our forefathers. For good or for evil they were great boys; very noble boys; very often very naughty boys—as boys with the strength of men might well be.[52]

Naughty, perhaps, but Kingsley considered it an admirable primitive trait, associated with the origins of mighty genetic energies.

Charles Pearson discerned in the Anglo-Saxon male the primitive lineaments of an ideal man. In his *Early and Middle Ages of England*, first published in 1861, "The Saxon had the vices of a barbarian—gluttony, drunkenness, and the coarser sins of the flesh; but he was not immoral in light-heartedness or on principle; he respected marriage and womanly purity; he never sang the praises of illicit love."[53] Pearson summarized the racial theories of such scholars of English antiquity as John Kemble and Sir Francis Palgrave and popularized their views. On the basis of whatever manuscripts survived, Pearson contrived a barbaric Saxon to serve as a rough model for Victorian manhood. If not yet a Victorian gentleman, the Anglo-Saxon worshiped a true womanhood resembling Ruskin's queens.[54] With the Anglo-Saxon holding the place of honor in Victorian nation-building, it is not surprising that the royal family would include some Anglo-Saxon paraphernalia in its genealogy.

When Albert died in December 1861, his favorite child, Victoria, known in the family as Vicky, designed a memorial statue for him, *Queen Victoria and Prince Albert in Anglo-Saxon Dress*. Executed by William

Queen Victoria and Prince Albert in Anglo-Saxon Dress, by William
Theed, 1867. *Illustration from the Royal Archives, by permission of
The Royal Collection © Her Majesty Queen Elizabeth II.*

Theed and completed in 1867, the statue memorializes the couple who
sometimes declared their origins in costume. The statue crafts dress
into an ethnographic statement about Victoria and Albert's common
progenitor, Witikind II, Count of Wettin. It honors a race as well as a
dead prince, saying in effect of both: "we live on." For Vicky, who by
virtue of her marriage to Crown Prince Frederick of Prussia was inti-
mately aware of the problematics of ethnicity, dress fabricated genetic
ties between Germany and England, manifested in the continuity
between the blood of the Anglo-Saxons and the German Albert and
consummated by his marriage to Victoria. The costumes represent an
idea of manifest racial destiny while they forge the alliance between

England and Germany as ethnographic and genealogical, both racial and dynastic. This personal alliance inextricable from politics casts the Princess Royal's marriage backward in time to make it, too, seem incvitable. The statue eternalizes her parents' marriage by evoking an originary point in English nation-building and by linking that point with Albert and Victoria's union. By stressing the Saxon, the statue then extends its protective arm to Germany. This semiotic drawing together of Teuton and Saxon occurs at the threshold of the Franco-Prussian War, declared in 1870. Proclaiming Teutonic superiority over the Gallic French, the Prussians articulated their version of race by means of a nationalistic war. Although both mother and daughter would later repudiate Bismarck's nationalism, during the late 1860s they differentiated his boorish aggression from Albert's sturdy but honorable Saxon ethic. Victoria's 1867 biography of the prince's early years begins with his genealogy: "Prince Albert was descended from the Ernestine, or elder branch of the great Saxon Family."[55]

Theed's statue shows meticulously researched costuming, similar in intensity and racial importance to the antiquarian work for the Plantagenet Ball. Despite evident lack of material items, ancient manuscripts provided a fair idea of what royal Saxon ancestors wore. Pearson comments on the Saxon love of dress and describes their attire, citing as his authority an Aldhelm de Laud manuscript: "The Saxons seem to have adopted the Roman tunic, which reached to the knees, and to have completed it by long sleeves for the arms. A cloak over it, perhaps the chamys, was added for out of doors. The head-dress of an Anglo-Saxon lady was a hood with long pendants; her dress of course reached to the ground. Wool and flax, with silk for the lappets and the eyelet holes, were the common materials."[56] Recalling both a Roman legionnaire and the extent of the Roman Empire, Pearson's allusion imbues the Saxon with similar qualifications.

Theed's costume for Albert follows Pearson's description. Victoria's richly embroidered skirt, drawn up to reveal yards of underskirt, sweeps the ground, exposing only the toe of one slipper. Anglo-Saxon Victoria wears the crown, while her beloved remains bareheaded, like a noble Roman statue. Albert's bare sword beneath his feet indicates not merely fealty but perhaps loyalty beyond the grave, as his hand held aloft, finger pointing upward, indicates a benediction from heaven to his adoringly faithful lady. Both man and woman bear tokens of their mutual love in the form of armbands inscribed with the name of the beloved, Victoria's visible on her left arm above the elbow mirroring Albert's on his right. Victoria's closeness to Albert betokens her intimacy with him, but her position also requires her to crane her neck to look up at him.

In its spatial symbolism, her position represents devotion to his higher authority. The costume of an earlier time gives the couple a definitively English character as the racial slide from Ernestine Saxon to Anglo-Saxon performs semiotically, through the message of the marble.

The pedestal's inscription: "Allured to brighter worlds and led the way," taken from Oliver Goldsmith's poem, "The Deserted Village," alludes to a parson whose soul resembled Albert's in its purity and who also died leaving behind a desolated wife and offspring. Not only elegiac in tone, Goldsmith's line links the prince with a humble yet holy man. Using a notion of courtly love that overlooks its adulterous premise, Theed's statue linked a folk identity with knightly love to create a genealogical and ethnological myth of origins. While the myth directs Victoria's consummation heavenward, it also encourages "Anglo-Saxons" to dress for the project of empire.

Writing during the year of the Diamond Jubilee in 1897, Walter Besant meditated on the qualities of Englishness that made the empire inevitable. He linked the English people of his time through all its interminglings with hardy Anglo-Saxon blood: "I maintain that the modern Englishman is the same as King Alfred's Englishman, or King Edward the First's Englishman, or any other Englishman. The Anglo-Saxon, capable of purifying any other racial strain, sublimes it to its own Teutonic essence." Besant includes Anglo-Saxon Americans in his estimation; the genetic tracer resides in language as well as genes: "If then, we lay down the leading characteristics of the Englishman of to-day [by Englishman, once more, I include those of the Anglo-Saxon race who speak our tongue] we know those of the Englishman of the past."[57] Influenced by ethnographer-philologists such as Isaac Taylor, James Prichard, and John Beddoe, and echoing Charles Kingsley's vision of the English Teuton as having "conquered—one may almost say that they are—all nations which are alive upon the globe,"[58] Besant placed the English as the ablest in the human family to assimilate all racial Others, obliterating traces of weaker genetic elements.

In this opinion, Besant echoed other Anglo-Saxonists such as the influential John Kemble, who made a similar assertion: "The Englishman has inherited the noblest portion of his being from the Anglo-Saxons," he wrote in *The Saxons in England*, which appeared in 1849 with a dedication to the queen: "In spite of every influence, we bear a marvellous resemblance to our forefathers."[59] According to the Anglo-Saxonists, "English," a dominant trait, explained Anglo-Saxon world dominance. *Chambers's Edinburgh Journal* in 1848 gave this same trait a less admiring slant: "Saxons are a spreading, a stirring, an ambitious, and a conquering race."[60] The avatar of such destiny was King Alfred, to many antiquarians designated as "Ælfred." Victoria, through her daughter's design, dresses as his rightful heir, a genealogy emphasized by Besant: "The strong King Henry I. married a Saxon princess in order to make his title safer. By this marriage, our Queen is descended from King Alfred." [61]

In the iconography of Anglo-Saxon dress, the Saxon queen cleaves to her mate who, according to racial qualities, bears strong resemblances to the royal family's domestic ideals. Besant characterizes the Anglo-Saxon throughout history as a family man, "tender and even chivalrous towards women, he loves children, he sits at home with his wife and children and desires no other society." [62] Prince Albert receives an apotheosis as the English father; from the effete stud and baby-sitter to lapdog and infant alike in the satire of 1842, he now dominates as Ælbert, Anglo-Saxon and, though chivalrous, a bit barbaric.

✦ New Scene, Olden Costumes ✦

Marie [Mallet] asked the queen to satisfy a correspondent who wrote to H.M. what her surname would be. She said she thought Guelf D'Este of the House of Brunswick (not Hanover)
—Marie Mallet, Life with Queen Victoria

By means of ethnographic and genealogical concepts Victoria and Albert performed their pedigree for a Victorian reign. Royal ethnic dressing articulates what Domna Stanton, writing about the dandy, called "sartorial speech," [63] spelling out a monarchical role within new economic structures. Karl Marx also recognized costume's strategic messages. In reaction to Louis Napoleon's seizing power and proclaiming himself Emperor of France, Marx, in "The Eighteenth Brumaire of Louis Bonaparte," identified uses of conjuring up the past. "Men make their own history," he cautioned:

> But they do not make it just as they please; they do not make it under circumstances chosen by themselves, but under circumstances directly encountered, given and transmitted from the past. The tradition of all the dead generations weighs like a nightmare on the brain of the living. And just when they seem engaged in revolutionizing themselves and things, in creating something that has never yet existed, precisely in such periods of revolutionary crisis they anxiously conjure up the spirits of the past to their service and borrow from them names, battle cries and costumes in order to pre-

sent the new scene of world history in this time-honoured
disguise and this borrowed language.[64]

Marx commented in 1852 on the tactics of the man who charmed
Victoria from distrust of him into flirtatious admiration when he visited
England in 1854. Of Louis Napoleon, she wrote: "I am very glad to
know this wonderful and extraordinary man, whom it is certainly
impossible not to like when you live with him, and not, to a great extent,
to admire."[65] Marx's melodramatic scene of a French bourgeois revolution envisions the return of past generations as a nightmarish impediment to change. How can one imagine a future without falling back on
the past? Marx conjures the scene as if it were a farcical history play or
pantomime. The Chartist parades never erupted in the feared revolution; the Highland voyages neglected Ireland by default; yet Anglo-
Saxonizing eventually made imperial wars and genocide tolerable, even
biologically ordained, to many.

History records the nightmarish consequences of the kind of ethnographic and genealogical performances that may seem simply quaint or
fanciful when one looks at Victoria and Albert playing them. Marx's
observation about costuming covering over a new kind of regime—considering great differences between the situations in France and
England—gives meaning to Victoria and Albert's affirmation of English
monarchical authority by recourse to the past. When regarded as making a statement about the extent of their realm and their genealogical
sway over it, Victoria and Albert's costumes can be viewed as performing a kind of monarchy that would last in representation at least
another century. In an English empire of the imagination Victoria and
Albert masquerade as olden monarchs while ruling as new ones.
Sanctioning colonial practices and attitudes without articulating their
authorizing assumptions, they represent family, heaven, and the destiny
of the Anglo-Saxon to *absorb*, in the apt word of Tom Nairn, all the
Others into their person. The streams of blood merging in Victoria's
veins are more royal than any one of their noble sources. Royal ethnic
dressing unifies many peoples in a monarchical body. By means of the
genealogies in her closet, the royal couple's dressing up performs a way
of colonizing through clothes.

3

DRESSING THE BODY POLITIC

Ye lords of the creation.
Hide your diminish'd heads,
Since woman holds the sovereign sway
Our sex no tyrant dreads:
Be on your best behaviour,
Cast all your airs away,
And wear with grace the chains we weave,
For woman rules the day.
—*Street ballad on Queen Victoria's accession*

What should Queen Victoria wear? Given fashion's role in exposing what an 1846 magazine article called a woman's "leading qualities," the queen's choice of the right clothes entailed fundamental not frivolous matters: "With [women's] habitual delicacy of mind, and reserve of manner, dress becomes a sort of symbolical language—a kind of personal glossary—a species of body phrenology, the study of which it would be madness to neglect. Will Honeycomb says that he can tell the humour a woman is in by the colour of her hood. We go farther, and maintain that, to a proficient in the science, every woman walks about with a placard on which her leading qualities are advertised."[1] For early Victorian England noticeable attention to fashion branded a person as a member of the useless aristocracy or as a social climber. Edward Bulwer-Lytton pointed out in 1833: "The middle classes interest themselves in grave matters: the aggregate of their sentiments is called opinion. The great interest themselves in frivolities, and the aggregate of *their* sentiments is termed fashion."[2] C. Willet Cunnington, a late-nineteenth-century fashion historian, believed people disparaged fashion because of fear: "fear of society, fear of oneself, fear of the power of clothing; fear is the reason fashion is so often dismissed as flippant and foolish."[3] With so much riding on the image conveyed by clothes, no wonder Queen Victoria might fear fashion. Gender and class intersect in this discourse where the importance of what she wore to announce her virtues depended on her crafting a careful image through her not-too-fashionable clothes.

Clothes and their fabrics served the Victorians as a barometer of moral, mental, and economic health. Whereas the nineteenth-century ethnologists discussed in the previous chapter appreciated clothes' colonizing function, the age's fashion writers preached clothing's importance and touted its appeal to eros and to civilization.[4] Queen Victoria had to negotiate those extremes. Transforming Thomas Carlyle's assertion that "his Body and the Cloth are the site and materials whereon and whereby his beautified edifice, of a Person, is to be built,"[5] fashion writers stressed the personal meanings inherent in clothes. Carlyle drew on a fundamental denotation of "person" as a guise created rather than a thing born. Using the corporeal body as its site, clothes made a person—and for Victorian fashion writers, it was usually a female person. Writers recognized woman's increasing importance in conveying messages through clothes: while covering her bare skin, she revealed her morality, class, and taste in the cut, color, and fit of her dress. Whereas middle-class men wore clothes deemed "rational," fit for enterprise associated with the pursuit of an occupation, women wore their characters on their backs. They carried the culture's symbolic meaning not only, or perhaps not primarily, in their actions but in their attire.

By describing a woman's clothes as a "kind of body phrenology," the writer of "Art of Dress" attests to Carlyle's valuation of clothes; he also reveals, however, how clothes came to assume more symbolic meaning for women than for men. Their self-assertion suppressed ("delicacy of mind and reserve of manner"), women required the right clothes to speak their personhood. Proper sartorial language—cultivated and accurate—entailed both aesthetic and moral training. Bearing her soul on her wraps, the woman "advertises" her *self* to those acute to her idiom.

All the more signifying force bears on Queen Victoria's attire. Her clothes needed to communicate her properly feminine self and her thoroughly admirable monarchy, not only advertising her own leading womanly qualities but also purveying national values. In her ordinary dress, Queen Victoria was devising a part, if not from whole cloth then pieced from sources other than royal precedent.

Like theatricals, royal dress entailed performance and exhibition. Royal costume made statements about monarchical roles as Victoria played them in relation to commercial, colonial, and imperial ideas, as those concepts mutually constitute each other. Different forms of dressing and their cultural meanings provide the sovereign with apparent choices of using bodily embellishment to fashion the realm and her position in and over it. Clothes announced Victoria's role in Victorian culture. Her perceived bourgeois character derived partly from the advertisements that presented her as the queen of consumers, patronizing homely commodities, such as dress fabrics.[6] During their marriage Albert reportedly selected her overelaborate dresses, so that she seemed the dutiful wife, dressing for her man. In her widow's weeds, she appeared indistinguishable from her most humble subject. Excepting the opulent gowns of royal portraiture, unless she wore her robes of state, Victoria was rarely represented as dressing like a queen. Precisely in its seeming to deny Victoria any pretensions to sovereignty, the queen's dress enabled her to perform some of her age's most characteristic cultural codes.

⤞ A Symbolical Language ⤝

Sartor Resartus, Thomas Carlyle's analysis of early Victorian culture, considers clothes as an appropriate rubric for conceptualizing his century's spiritual and material questions. The work characterizes the Victorian age as a scientific one, where every conceivable subject, except for clothes, receives methodical scrutiny:

> Considering our present advanced state of culture, and how the Torch of Science has now been brandished and borne about, with more or less effect, for five thousand years and upwards; how, in these times especially, not only the Torch still burns, and perhaps more fiercely than ever, but innumerable Rush-lights, and Sulphur matches, kindled thereat, are also glancing in every direction, so that not the smallest cranny or doghole in Nature or Art can remain unilluminated,—it might strike the reflective mind with some surprise that hitherto little or nothing of a fundamental character, whether in the way of Philosophy or History, has been written on the subject of Clothes.   (*1*)

Much of *Sartor* shows how that opening sentence does not end in anti-climax. Clothes, as is true for all signs, can be misread. To guard against this danger, Carlyle insists upon historical specificity in decoding clothes' meaning. He calls history the "Time-Spirit," a concept that enables him to gauge moral temperatures by means of evidence within historical time.

When Carlyle published *Sartor Resartus* in *Fraser's Magazine* in 1833–34, he was not thinking of queens or even of the importance of clothes for women. The clad person subjected to the work's scientific analysis was male: "'To the eye of vulgar Logic,' says he, 'what is man?' An omnivorous Biped that wears Breeches" (56). *Sartor* does not mention the use of clothing as an increasingly significant marker of Victorian gender categories, as playing a part in placing women in a separate domestic sphere and constituting women as almost a separate species from men. Women's fashion does not interest Carlyle, for his sartorial attention fixes on a male fashion plate, the dandy. "*Clotha Virumque cano*" his motto, the dandy lives for clothes (242). Carlyle denounces the dandy as a person whose religion is "*self-worship*" and whose clothes are fetishes (245). On the other end of the spectrum from the dandiacal sect, "poor slaves," mainly Irish with some Scots, also distinguish themselves by outlandish costume. Together, they define the body politic as "Drudgical" and "Dandiacal," existing in mutual, generally hostile, relation. *Sartor* proposes a middle ground of soberly clad, working heroes.

Carlyle's diatribe reflects back on George IV as king and regent. Elaborate in dress and lax in morals, George IV's monarchy defined itself in distinction to the populace from which it separated in almost complete exclusivity yet with which it perforce coexisted in mutual contempt. Sir Morgan O'Doherty, Bart. reported on an encounter with George IV that conveys regency attitudes about clothes: "as to dressing, he had the vilest taste. I remember seeing him one day in a purple velvet waistcoat with a running stripe of a gold tree, surmounted with gold monkeys upon it; and congratulating him on his exquisite taste in the selection of colours, he felt evidently very proud of my approbation, but when I recommended him a yellow coat with purple braiding, I think he smelt a rat."[7] Disagreements about taste between Sir Morgan and the king affirm their preoccupation with it. George IV involved himself in dress with true dandiacal passion, his body fantastically ornamented. Lytton Strachey evoked earlier attitudes toward the sulky reprobate in describing the king's meeting with four-year-old Victoria: "The old rip, bewigged and gouty, ornate and enormous, with his jewelled mistress by his side and his flaunting court about him, received the tiny creature who was one day to hold in those same halls a very different state. 'Give me your little paw,' he said; and two ages touched."[8] Three years later Princess Victoria sat on the king's lap to kiss his swollen face, thick with makeup and patches.[9]

Victoria's resemblance to her Hanoverian uncle in looks underscored her difference from him in morals. The languid scandalous George IV is Victoria's alter ego, the "Anglo-Dandiacal" image against which she dressed. Victoria's unfashionableness reversed George IV's mirror. In dressing the part of a commoner, more impervious to fashion than most, she eventually blotted out the image of her dissolute ancestor. Ellen Moers points out that the dandy's elegance haunts the Victorian imagination:

> the dandy—a creature perfect in externals and careless of anything below the surface, a man dedicated solely to his own perfection through a ritual of taste. The epitome of selfish irresponsibility, he was ideally free of all human commitments that conflict with taste: passions, moralities, ambitions, politics or occupations. . . . Throughout the 19th century the rising majority called for equality, responsibility, energy; the dandy stood for superiority, irresponsibility, inactivity.[10]

Victorian values formed themselves in distinction to those of the Regency. Victoria's gender gave her an advantage to set against the wicked past, while her increasingly unstylish clothes stood for democracy and a religion of earnestness. To counter reports of George IV's outlandish apparel, variations upon a fable of Queen Victoria's simple, unfashionable garments refashioned ideas of the monarchy.

By the time of the Diamond Jubilee, the queen's dowdy dresses had become the stuff of legend. In Sarah Tooley's admiring memoir, for instance, not only can a cat look at a queen, but a shepherd boy can talk to one as his equal. In Tooley's tale Victoria wanders about sketching the picturesque Scottish landscape where she inadvertently arouses the ire of an indignant "herd laddie who found that his flock was timid at the sight of her on the sheep track":

> "Gang out of the road, lady, and let the sheep gang by," he cried. Finding that his appeal produced no effect, he shouted yet louder, "I say, gang back, will you, and let the sheep pass!"
>
> "Do you know, boy, whom you are speaking to?" asked the Queen's Attendant.
>
> "I dinna know, and I dinna care," replied the exasperated lad; "that's the sheep's road, and she has no business to stand there."
>
> "But it is the Queen," was the reply.
>
> "Well," replied the astonished boy, "why don't she put on clothes so that folks would know her?"[11]

The shepherd boy reads rank into clothes, believing in their transparency as class markers. Similar misapprehensions occur in other stories about Victoria, all containing the typical character of an untutored young man confounded by his internal image of a richly clad queen. Simple clothes worn in preference to opulent ones, according to this fable, convey a moral message but sometimes lie about class. In choosing to wear peasantlike clothes, "Queen Victoria" removes herself from the conventions of a symbolic economy where clothes tell the difference between a queen and a servant. In that economy, everyone knows that queens wear crowns. Without a retinue, without opulent clothes, the parable's queen inspires awe by her opacity; the highest woman in the land appears indistinguishable from the lowest. This narrative revises the story about a virtuous monarch disguised in ordinary clothes to learn truths inaccessible to a Highness. In those tales, the monarch dresses down deliberately, but the Victorian version assumes that the queen's wearing a commoner's clothes advertises her character. Instead of gaining her access to the people's secrets, her clothes tell hers. Deciphering the message written on her clothes, the people know the queen as one of them.

⤞   Gender and the Fashion Scene   ⤝

Female apparel now is going to pot, I vow, sirs,
And the ladies will be fined that don't wear coat and trousers
Blucher boots and hats and shirts with handsome stitches
Oh dear, what shall we do, when women wear the breeches.
—*broadside ballad*

Who wears the pants in the family? The question became urgent when Victoria, a married female sovereign, reigned. Cultural anxieties about whether men were losing power showed themselves through the fetishization of dress. During Victoria's reign the first wave of Anglo-American feminism countered femininity, offering a vocabulary of women's rights and desires rather than tributes to feminine frailty. Once women could be imagined as socially constricted, Victorian fashion could indicate imprisonment rather than delicacy. But to change fashion—to loosen women from steel bondage—seemed to threaten the very person constructed from it. Street songs reflected cultural gender anxiety; to wear even the relatively chaste bloomer costume upset the fetishistic value of feminine clothes. If everyone were to wear pants, even loose ones covered with a long bloomer tunic, distinctions between men and women would appear to blur. Since the sexes defined themselves through opposition, the lack of utterly different clothing could be imagined as a dreaded evolution toward a world without real men and women.

In 1869 John Stuart Mill published "On the Subjection of Women," his entry into the debate on the "Woman Question." Mill maintained that women's social oppression prevented anyone from knowing what they might be able to accomplish were cultural arrangements for women to change. His essay, a part of his meditation on liberty, provoked strong reactions in such seemingly unlikely places as magazine articles that denigrated women by ridiculing fashion. An article on "Hair and Head-Dresses" in *Fraser's Magazine* of 1870, written in response to Mill, demonstrates what anxieties the debate on women aroused and how it permeated writings about fashion:

> There are three facts which the advocates of the Rights of Women, so far as these are based upon an alleged equality of the sexes, will find it extremely difficult to get over: 1. The peculiar functions of the fair sex touching the continuation of the species; 2. That no woman has ever manifested the highest order of genius in any walk of literature or art; 3. That women have never been able to emancipate themselves from the tyranny of fashion, however absurd, ridiculous, destructive to beauty, or ruinous to health. Without entering on the main question, or seeking to break a lance with Mr. Mill, we wish to call attention to the third of these social phenomena and point the concomitant or resulting moral.[12]

Congenitally addicted to clothes mania as slaves to fashion, women deserved their inferior cultural position. When they were not performing their biological function of reproducing the species, they were deforming their bodies in other ways.

The article's "moral"—that women's willingness to pay any price for fashion indicated their essential irrationality—posed a problem Victoria had to contend with in presenting herself as a female monarch. If she were fashionable, she risked dismissal as a frivolous woman. If her dresses muted her feminine attributes, she might be accused of mannishness. If too unstylish, her dress could be deemed unpatriotic, but if too stylish, she opened the way to charges of francophilia and disdain for English clothing manufacture.

The popular imagination, reflected in street ballads, used images of

cross-dressing to ridicule the royal couple's topsy-turvy gender authority. In one song, a greedy but passive Albert worries about dominance
in terms of clothes:

> She's all my Lehzen painted her,
> She's lovely, she is rich,
> But they tell me when I marry her
> That she will wear the *britsch*.[13]

Many songs and stories find the idea of a Victoria in trousers a matter
of great hilarity. A long story about the morning after imagines Victoria
leaping out of the honeymoon bed into her husband's pants, deaf to his
ineffectual protests. In a street ballad Victoria ditches her constraining
underwear to wear men's clothes as a sign of marital victory:

> Prince Albert and the Queen had such a jolly row, sirs,
> She threw off the stays and put on waistcoat, coat and trousers.[14]

The ballad reflects early perceptions that there were in fact family rows
about who ruled the roost in Buckingham Palace and that Prince Albert
struggled for a properly manly activity as consort to a sovereign. Albert
himself expressed the matter succinctly when he complained to a
friend that "the difficulty in filling my place with the proper dignity is,
that I am only the husband, and not the master in the house."[15]

Queen Victoria's clothes stirred up anxiety about women in power.
Is she a phallic woman? Or does her feminine attire confirm male masculinity? The phallic woman, a woman in power but hiding the sign of
it, shows her secret by wearing the pants. But she does not have to go so
far as to wear men's clothes. Victoria eventually "threw off the stays" by
refusing the fashionable tight lacing and thus negotiating a thin line
between comfort and mannishness. Cultural concerns about who wears
the britches magnify the drama of royal rule, clothes signifying an anxiety about gender roles from which no Victorian was entirely free. The
royal couple struggled with the representation of rule throughout their
marriage, since the terms of Victorian masculinity were measured in
part by the management of one's wife.[16] Wearing the pants in the family (as Victoria had to by virtue of what she saw as her "anomalous and
trying position"[17]) turned into an all too frightening reality when
applied to the royal family. So the perception that Victoria wore the
pants, or could should she so choose, threatened to turn the gender
hierarchy upside-down. Victoria's marriage proposal to Albert touched
off fantasies about such an eventuality, with all women taking unseemly

initiative. One street ballad imagined that marriage vows could no longer keep women down:

> Since the Queen did herself for a husband "propose,"
> The ladies will all do the same I suppose;
> Their days of subserviency now will be past,
> For all will speak *first*, as they always did *last*!
> Since the Queen has no equal, "obey," none she need,
> So, of course, at the Altar, from such vow she's freed;
> And the women will all follow suit, so they say—
> "Love, honour," they'll promise, but never "obey."[18]

Victoria elected to vow to obey, but by choice. Her option heralds a new regime, opening up possibilities for other women to choose otherwise.

As the song demonstrates, Victoria stimulated fantasies independent of facts. She upheld traditional views about womanly propriety, discouraging feminist hopes that she might support their cause. To the proposal allowing women to attend medical school, the queen wrote Prime Minister Gladstone in horror: "She is *most* anxious that it should be known how she not only disapproves but *abhors* the attempts to destroy all propriety and womanly feeling which will inevitably be the result of what has been proposed."[19] Dressing and speaking the feminine part failed to calm anxiety about her sovereignty's ability to upend convention. Although she eventually opted for comfort in dress, Victoria never wore pants. But even her crinolines could not calm fears of how monarchical attire might destroy the gender system and could change men into "skirts." With Victoria on the throne, so another street song imagined, the power of the petticoat takes over England, signaling female dominance through the transformative power of dress:

> They say that the Queen has a crinoline on
> And so has Prince Albert and buxom Lord John
> We expect to see Palmerston next week afloat
> Strutting around May Fair in a hooped petticoat.[20]

In wearing the skirts rather than the pants, the queen wields such great power *as a woman* that she feminizes every powerful man. The ballad not only ridicules women's absurd styles, it points out how dress influences body movements. The male cannot easily stride manfully but must float. Skinny prime minister John Russell grows breasts to set off his stylish flounces.

The ballad's cross-dressing fantasy balances the queen's authority against the age's use of clothes as a signifying system. The leader mandates whatever fashion exists, using it to augment her authority. The crinoline (which grew to extreme widths in the late 1850s) seemed to more than the balladeer a dangerous fashion excess. Women caught fire and died, imprisoned by their cages of steel. Women lost their balance and were upended. Pornographic photographs show women's crinolines covering their faces but exposing their nether parts.[21] Because the crinoline deprived the wearer of easy mobility, writers on fashion history have also marked its rise as a response to women's moves for increased independence. In *Dressed to Kill*, Colin McDowell considers the crinoline as an outward sign of gender ideology. "Most men were dizzy with joy," he claims, "at the increasingly impractical and varied feminine fashions—especially as developments such as the crinoline and the bustle made any advance in a man's world as difficult literally as it was metaphorically or idealistically."[22] To wear a cumbersome, ballooning garment meant that fewer women could occupy a room—an increasing problem in the crush of palace ceremonials. In addition to these practical problems, the crinoline advertised women as impractical and irrational, not fit for men's intellectual and physical activities. On the other hand, its sheer size exaggerated woman's bulk, arguably reflecting her growing centrality, not in entering a man's world but in occupying more symbolic importance in it.[23] Floating in a crinoline, Victoria hampered the proper workings of the social order. Whatever she wore in the cultural imagination—whether pants or skirts—she could potentially disorganize the body politic.

Victorians imagined fashion power as sowing revolutionary seeds. The ballad envisioning Palmerston's crinoline suggests that as foreign minister he will influence the world population to become like women. Although the song ostensibly ridicules female fashion, it also satirizes what was frequently called "petticoat rule." For the most part, the representation of Victoria's clothes elided what Valerie Steele considers the primary meaning of clothes: sexual attractiveness. If the queen played up her sex—whether tastefully or not—one could imagine a government swayed by erotic enticement. Yet she possessed good features, which she emphasized, and she was vain about her shoulders. The Diamond Jubilee number of the *English Illustrated Magazine* attributed the court fashion for the low bodice to Victoria's vanity: "Like other children, as you will note in all the early portraits of her, the pretty little Princess wore the low-necked, short-sleeved gown of the time, as she always had beautiful shoulders, the reign of the *décolleté*, which has ever obtained at the Court, started with good reason."[24] Albert's favorite portrait, by Winterhalter, shows a languid Victoria, hair flowing down bare plump shoulders. Many paintings of the properly Victorian royal family portray Victoria in a bare-shouldered evening dress, even if the scene is set in broad daylight, whereas most photographs show the queen in more conventionally covered up daydresses.

Until Albert's death, Victoria in fact admired clothes. Far from uninterested in dress, she noticed and judged what other women had on. Her curiosity about what people wore and her specificity about clothes in letters and journals denote pleasure and interest in a woman's world. Her early journals, subject to Mama's examination, rarely break out of a perfunctory listing of sights and activities, but she allotted herself more space to describing women's dresses. During an annual trip through the countryside, the thirteen-year-old Victoria wrote in her journal: "We were received . . . by Lady Bulkeley whose dress I shall describe. It was a white satin trimmed with blonde, short sleeves & a necklace, ear-rings and sévigné of perridos & diamonds with a wreath of orange-flowers in her hair."[25] After describing the dress, the journal resumes its mechanical noting of time passing.

Feeling in her twenties and thirties what was perhaps a national inferiority in matters of dress, Victoria looked to other women for guidance: first to her elegant, French-born aunt Louise, wife of King Leopold of the Belgians, and then to Empress Eugénie, the Spanish-born wife of Napoleon III. What she and Eugénie wore received precise notation in the journal entries during the reciprocal royal visits with France in 1854–55. The thirty-five-year-old Victoria still loved to dress up. When the emperor and empress arrived at Windsor, Victoria and the children excitedly called upon "the Empress's rooms, and saw her dressers." For the "great meeting of the Sovereigns," she notes, "wore a light blue dress with shaded trimmings, and a pearl necklace." Before she mentions Eugénie's personality, she describes her outfit: "a plain plaid silk dress and straw bonnet, with a black velvet mantilla. She is most graceful and pleasing, with a very charming kind expression."[26] Victoria wrote about her eager examination of Eugénie's jewels and dresses, after which the two royal women agree to play dress-up: "looking at her dress and splendid jewels, many of which were Crown jewels, which the Empress has had reset, we agreed to dress our heads, and lunch in that way."[27] Victoria meticulously recorded their other costume changes during the visit.

Three years later, Victoria dressed her oldest daughter for a crucial political role. Her correspondence with Vicky upon Vicky's Prussian marriage elided directly the political questions that made the marriage so desirable to Albert and Victoria and centered on Vicky's wardrobe. Victoria wrote the seventeen-year-old bride to ask about the matter of dress, pointing out that others could fill her in on politics. She wanted to know about what she called "little interior details":

> February 6, 1858: 1st What dress and bonnet did you wear on landing? And what bonnet the 2 next days?. . . What cloak did you wear on the road . . . ? . . . February 7, 1858: Then I see by the papers you wore a green dress at the Cologne concert. Was that the one with black lace?—You must not be impatient about all these details which I am so anxious to know, for I am anxious to know how all my toilettes succeeded? The pink ball dress at Brussels was so much admired. . . . February 10, 1858: Don't worry yourself to write long letters while you are so busy and so worried, only let me have an affectionate little line—but by and by let me hear how every thing is and what your feelings and impressions are. I am particularly vexed at hearing nothing about your dresses. February 18, 1858: I hear from all sides how much your dresses and toilettes are admired, so I take a good deal for myself as I took such great pains with your dresses.[28]

Victoria shows concern for the kinds of statements that dress can make. Victoria and Albert depended upon the marriage of their eldest daughter to create their vision of a Europe led by England and Germany; clothes talk and political talk come together in these letters.

Without access to her journals and with only the evidence of their eyes, her public assumed that the queen was not interested in her own attire, perhaps because of her perceived dowdiness, her unaesthetic shape, and her evident bewilderment about proportion and scale in dress. Mistaking bad taste for disinterest, her subjects could assume that their queen had other things than dress on her mind. The sense that Victoria could wear the pants if she so chose, or that she could mandate the wearing of the crinoline, existed at a different level of consciousness from the perception that, all things being equal, Victoria R. was not a beauty queen.

✦ Fine or Finery? ✦

To assume that Victoria existed on a different plane from ordinary women, free of dress anxieties, beyond fashion consciousness, suited the symbolic economy. A woman too enamored of fashion risked her respectability in loving what the Victorians disapprovingly labeled "finery."[29] The code word indicates not simply a frivolity inappropriate for a Victorian queen but also suggests the underworld of the fallen woman, the prostitute, and the kept woman. Bad morals advertised themselves on such a woman's finery as if an expensive and flamboyant dress were a billboard selling her wares.

A Victorian queen needed to draw attention away from her possible allure, a necessity made less of a problem for Victoria because of her unfashionable proportions. Victoria's body did not conform to western standards of beauty. At four foot ten, she was short, she was plump, and by 1839, the year of her engagement, she was referred to in street ballads as "England's fat queen."[30] Her Hanoverian head and face tended to a coarseness of feature and modeling. Her body shielded her from the worst of finery's lures.

Victoria's reputation for tasteless clothes became international. On her first official visit to France in 1855, her clothes seemed provincial. By this time France had established itself as the sophisticated haute couture capital, with the English expatriate Worth at its apex. But the French eye for style extended to all areas in society—to the army, for example. General Canrobert, commander-in-chief of the French forces in the Crimea, provided a charming dinner companion for Victoria: "He sat next to me, and I was delighted with him," she wrote in her journal, "such an honest good man, so sincere and friendly, and *so* fond of the English, very enthusiastic, talking with much gesticulation."[31] In contrast to Victoria's almost naive appreciation of the French ways, the general's charming manners did not prevent him from Gallic attention to Victoria's attire. Proving himself proficient in the science of sartorial analysis, he described the queen stepping from a newly emblazoned carriage at St. Cloud:

> In spite of the great heat, she had on a massive bonnet of white silk with streamers behind and a tuft of marabou feathers on top. . . . Her dress was white and flounced; but she had a mantle and a sunshade of crude green which did not seem to go with the rest of her costume. When she put her foot on the steps she lifted her skirt, which was very short (in the English fashion, I was told) and I saw she had on small slippers tied with black ribbons which were crossed round her ankles. My attention was chiefly attracted by a voluminous object which she carried on her arm; it was an enormous reticule—like those of our grandmothers—made of white satin or silk, on which was embroidered a fat poodle in gold.[32]

From the English point of view it might be just as well that the French found fault with Victoria's fashion statement.

Victoria's taste, not fine but flamboyant, could be seen as unworldly. Valerie Cumming describes the queen's "taste for the raffish and exotic," showing disregard for her personal bodily enhancement and almost wearing clothes as objects in themselves, independent from the body wearing them. She dressed as if she were tall and stately, "in shawls, wearing over-decorated dresses cluttered with lace, ribbons, bows and flounces, and under the prince's guidance . . . she had taken to swathing her dresses in huge floral trimmings . . . sometimes real, sometimes artificial or embroidered."[33] For an international stage, her clothes created no illusions of hauteur. The poodle purse was reputedly made by one of her daughters.

The problem in representation was not so much the actual taste or fashion of the queen, for she made little overt attempt to set fashionable standards. To set or even to follow Victorian fashion trends might suggest personal instability, even perhaps sexual desire not utterly limited by matrimonial devotion. Like her great-great-granddaughter, Queen Elizabeth II, Victoria's private eroticism manifested itself in the dress of her beautiful and fashionable daughter-in-law, the Princess of Wales. Victoria's dowdiness, like Elizabeth's, added to her moral authority.

While Albert was alive, she solved the problems of her unstylish body and the possible erotics of feminine dress by presenting herself as a docile wife subservient to her husband's taste. Prince Albert's organizing zeal extended to the fashioning of his wife's wardrobe. Popular biographies present Albert as dressmaster:

> After some years of marriage the Queen, when discussing clothes . . . seemed to find happiness in declaring, "I have no Taste—I depend entirely on Him." As a young queen she had given great satisfaction by her attractive and sometimes rather dashing ensembles; but a new factor had entered into this matter. Prince Albert was always present when the traveller from Paris with his hats and bonnets was brought in to the Queen. Propped against the wall, his arms folded, the Prince gazed earnestly at his wife's head as each piece was set upon it. "It won't do!" he muttered, and the article was replaced by another. . . . He tackled the royal gowns as he tackled the hats, and took entire responsibility for the Queen's ensemble from head to foot.[34]

Queen Victoria, photograph by Southwell Brothers, c. 1858. Victoria poses inside but wears an outdoors ensemble: scalloped flat hat, fur muff, and jacket trimmed with matching fur. Her plaid skirt is fashionably wide, probably with a crinoline. *Illustration from the Royal Archives, by permission of The Royal Collection © Her Majesty Queen Elizabeth II.*

Dressing not only *for* Albert but being dressed *by* him promoted the image of Victoria as a good wife rather than a ruling monarch.

A related narrative involving a man's re-dressing of his woman forms a plot in George Eliot's *Felix Holt, The Radical* (1866). In that novel, the superficial but basically virtuous Esther Lyon renounces her concerns about appearance through the exhortations and love of Felix Holt, a man concerned with the conditions of the working classes. Esther's admirable development transpires within a discourse of taste, finally manifested by her turning away from a love of finery inherited from her French mother and consolidated in a French school. Esther first appears in the novel weighted down with biblical allusions: "There will be queens in spite of Salic or other laws of later date than Adam and Eve; and here, in this small dingy house of the minister in Malthouse Yard, there was a light-footed, sweet-voiced Queen Esther."[35] In the beginning Eve ruled Adam to their mutual sorrow, Eliot suggests, but to counter that dangerous precedent, Queen Esther, not a queen in her own right but a consort, saved her people. Eliot informs her reader what everyone in the time of Victoria knows about the laws governing monarchical succession: most countries have Salic laws prohibiting female monarchs. In appealing to a universal category of "queenliness," however, Eliot approximates a leveling discourse, like Ruskin. Queenship, not an unmixed blessing, dwells in a dingy house, and by moral rather than birth right earns the position.

Eliot writes of an ordinary woman's queenliness five years after the black dress became the permanent uniform of her English queen, elevating the character of women such as Victoria who ignore fashion. The values in *Felix Holt* insist that to worship taste enslaves one to its dictates, betraying superficiality in the tasteful cut of one's dress. Felix presents himself as Esther's guide, leading her beyond shallow tastes to discover her own profound character, the queen beneath the clothes. He confronts her on a Sunday while her dissenting minister father preaches.

As a sign of unfortunate difference from devotional habits, Esther sits reading Chateaubriand's *René*, clad in "her well-fitting light-blue dress—she almost always wore some shade of blue—with her delicate sandalled slipper . . ., her little gold watch, which had cost her nearly a quarter's earnings." (208). Esther's reading accords with the diminutive words in Eliot's description of the young woman's appearance. Chateaubriand, the French romantic novelist, celebrated Christianity's poetical appeal in inspiring mankind to intellectual freedom. For him, Christianity exerted an aesthetic force far different from the truths preached by such dissenting ministers as Mr. Lyon. Following the

French writer, Eliot suggests, leads to spending limited resources on delicate slippers and little gold watches.

In contrast to the romantic Chateaubriand, Felix, the Victorian radical, confronts Esther about her taste: "You said you didn't mind about people having right opinions so that they had good taste," he charges. "Now I want you to see what shallow stuff that is" (209). Their debate, what she calls his "sermon," centers on taste, which he defines as a smaller, more petty, kind of opinion. Esther defends herself: "by opinions you mean men's thoughts about great subjects, and by taste you mean their thoughts about small ones; dress, behaviour, amusements, ornaments." Dress, like "ornament" embellishes essence, but Esther does not make clear by her use of *men's* whether she means this essence as gendered or universal. For if "opinion" and "taste" carry gendered attributions, "taste" would be a womanly virtue, whereas men would commonly hold opinions, the result of cogitation. Furthermore, to acquire taste suggests social climbing. Felix Holt's opinions win the upper hand over Esther, and by gaining opinion, she can relinquish her overly feminine taste that also suggests overrefinement.[36] The proper kind of clothes in this novel simply cover the body. To value taste deprives the person of profundity. The plot's action replaces Esther's taste for finery with opinions about fine causes. Taste opposes rationality, probity, responsibility. In giving up taste, Esther also subordinates herself to Felix Holt, a man driven by passionately held, morally defensible opinions.

Queen Esther Lyon Holt, no cipher for Queen Victoria but affirming the queen's disregard for good taste, is saved from the dangers of acceding to the dictates of fashion. As Victoria aged, the moral of Esther's story—that clothes should cover a woman as simply as possible—conveniently fitted her public image. For a queen to seem to clothe herself as one whose more important concerns prevented her from focusing on the irrevelancies of feminine "nature" could set a moral example, recommending unselfish opinions rather than mere good taste.

⇥ The Worst-Dressed Woman in the World ⇤

Widows weeds became her, at least to those who could see her sorrows in her clothes and who used her dress to respond to her image as both unerotic and ordinary. After Albert's death, the queen without a crown crept into Scottish crofts. In 1862, at the apogee of her grief, an effusive loyal subject evoked a miraculous vision of a queen who was indistinguishable from her most humble cottager:

"'A Visit to a Highland Cottage"

And was she really there, Grannie?
And sat she really there?
Upon that very chair, Grannie
Th auld and oaken chair
And sat she doon a very Queen
In purple and in red,
Jist like the picture I hae seen,
With a crown on her head?

I'll tell you how she cam, Mary,
And whar she sot her doon;
But left her robe at hame Mary,
And left at hame her crown.
And though she leuk't a vara Queen,
I see'd nae queenly pride,
But jist a Wifie's loving mien,
With her gudeman at her side.[37]

Such verse interpreted Victoria's refusal to wear her crown as an identification with a "Wifie." Her prodigious memory for details about humble servant's lives and health, her personal concern for their well-being,
and her understanding of their grief were epitomized in her simple
clothes. In the verse, Victoria looks more like a true ("vara") queen
than she does when she looks like a real queen.

   If her ordinary subjects venerated the shabby image, those closer
to her, particularly those loyal to traditional class structures, did not
always understand its market value. Various officials sought a role as
fashion consultants to convince Victoria to wear a crown on ceremonial occasions. Henry Ponsonby recounts one such governmental
effort:

> On the occasion of the official opening of the Exhibition
> connected with the recently erected Imperial Institute in
> 1886, Lord Rosebery urged that the queen should come in
> full state with a crown in order to impress the imagination of
> the Colonial representatives who would all be present. "The
> symbol," he wrote to Ponsonby, "that unites this vast Empire
> is a Crown not a bonnet." . . . The modestly dressed widow
> had really become for the people the symbol of their sover-
> eign whose intimate homeliness endeared her to her sub-

jects more than ever at this date. Crowns and pageantry may
have been necessary conventions for other monarchs. To
her they were of no significance, and in this her point of view
was quite original. So the bonnet triumphed. She wore it at
both her jubilees.[38]

Victoria, not Rosebery, was right. The symbolic bonnet not the conventional crown united her empire. The queen in her bonnet signified
regal folksiness.

Perhaps no tribute to the power of unassuming dress rivals a children's book written ten years later, at the time of Victoria's Diamond
Jubilee in 1897. Its title, The Fairies' Favourite, alluded in part to
Disraeli's lighthearted allusion to Victoria as a new "faery queen."
Written by T. Mullet Ellis in the form of a fanciful biography, it introduced a new generation to a national fable of the queen's old clothes.
Up to the point when Victoria becomes queen, the tale is mostly
prophetic, foreshadowing, like her name, the queen's future greatness. When the story arrives at Victoria's adulthood, a "weighty question is propounded—Why is the Queen the worst-dressed woman in
the world."[39] The text answers its hyperbolic question first by pointing out that her dressing distinguished her from other queens from
"time immemorial" who dressed in royal purple, royal ermine, and
covered themselves with pearls and precious stones. Unlike these
proto–Queen Esthers, Victoria, who (the story reminds us) possesses
not only the Koh-i-noor diamond but bags and buckets of jewels and
gold, eschews this acme of finery. Jewels do not betoken the queen's
feminine vanity, for she neither seeks them nor particularly values
them. Rather, precious stones signify Victoria's imperial power, which,
like that of any Eastern (male) potentate, could command its weight
in gold:

> Kings from the far East, Princes from Colconda, and Rajahs
> from Seringapatam, the Emperor of Morocco, the Grand
> Llama of Thibet and Fee-fi-fo-fum, had all crawled on their
> bare kness [sic] to the foot of the throne with sacks of jewels
> on their backs, and something special in their breast-pocket
> for the queen. She had all these costly presents, cargoes of
> bar-gold from California and scores of ships chock-full of
> gold in its raw state from Australia—which is a very nuggetty
> island—Her cellars were crammed with ingots of gold, and
> cart-loads of precious stones were shovelled in by the ton.

(31)

"The Queen Receiving the Burmese Embassy," illustration by W. B. Wallen, 1872.

Magnifying the size of the tiny England in comparison to the "island" Australia, the story expands upon Victoria's renunciation of finery: "Yet the Queen never wore jewels" (31). The claim is true only relative to the potential. Before Albert's death, Victoria wore jewels galore, frequently specifying them in her journal: "my opal diadem and opals" on one occasion, "a diadem of diamonds and very large Indian rubies," or "my emeralds and diamonds, including my diadem," on others, including her most fabled jewel: "I wore a white and gold brocade, a diamond diadem, the Koh-i-noor, and the Indian pearls."[40] Even after his death, she wore many jewels, particularly on state occasions.

Portraits of the queen, beringed and bepearled, failed to register; the folk queen prevailed. The favorite of the fairies dresses "more than plainly, or less than plainly, if one may plainly say such a thing of Her August Majesty" (32). Victoria metamorphoses into a Cinderella in reverse by virtue of no taste at all. The point of celebrating the taste others mocked becomes clear when Ellis turns to the kind of dressing that by 1897 had become possible for the most ordinary of subjects. Gowns aping the finest designer's modes could be bought for relatively little money, placing fashion in the reach of all but the poorest, for even the

SHE : " Look at Miss Smith's lovely dress, and the beautiful embroidery on it. Sixty years ago, when the Queen came to the throne, such a dress would have cost a small fortune, but Miss Smith says it cost very little, as she made and embroidered it herself on a Singer's Sewing Machine."

HE : " What a marvellous machine that must be !

THE SINGER MANUFACTURING COMPANY.

Management for Great Britain and Ireland :

42 and 43, ST. PAUL'S CHURCHYARD, LONDON, E.C.

Branch Offices Everywhere.

Singer sewing machine advertisement, *The Graphic, Jubilee Number,* 1897.

moderately poor could dress themselves in secondhand clothing of the more well-off. Ellis points out the economics of fine dressing:

> [A]bout this time Messrs. _____ of St. Paul's Churchyard (I will not mention their name unless they pay me for the advertisement . . .) were exhibiting to anybody and everybody a perfect lady's complete outfit for twenty-seven shillings and eleven pence three farthings,—a dress which both for fit and quality was really superior to that worn by the Most Eminent Lady in the realm.
>
> Therefore it was often asked, Why should the queen of England be the worst-dressed woman in the world when she could get a beautiful dress for twenty-seven, eleven three?

(32)

What with the cost of finery going down, the queen could not distinguish herself from a publican's wife by dressing up. The newly invented sewing machine could easily replicate the fine stitching of the seamstresses lovingly depicted at their slavish labors in Victorian paintings. The song of the shirt became the song of the department store and the song of the sewing machine—eventually underselling even Messrs. ___ of St. Paul's Churchyard. Not only could an English publican's wife dress like a queen, but, by 1897, so could an Australian publican's wife.

According to the *Fairies' Favourite*, Queen Victoria dresses down to advertise her womanly qualities, raising herself above all crass material signs of nobility. After the fairies disguise her in rags, the queen vows to wear them always, delighted that "now I am dressed even as the very meanest of my subjects." Further, the queen knows that she can use her rags as a loyalty test:

> But lo! wherever she went the People knew her, even in the disguise which the fairies had put upon her out of the rag-bag.
>
> For she bore herself, though not of great stature, with so much natural majesty, and with such unaffected dignity, withal the simplicity and modesty that became her so well, that the people, having loyal hearts and loving her so dearly, knew her well for their Queen.   (34)

Ellis alludes to Victoria's reputed grace and authority of carriage. Ponsonby reports on Victoria's ability to transcend the limitations of unprepossessing figure in conveying awesome majesty: "In spite of the smallness of her stature and absence of beauty, she managed always by her wonderful carriage and deportment, which had characterized her from her early youth, to present unaccountably a figure of such dignity and distinction as to arrest the attention of the most unobservant spectator who at once decided that no one else in the assembly mattered."[41] From lack of taste and beauty springs spiritual and "natural" monarchy. Queen Victoria stooped to conquer, thereby winning the people's favor. Clothes no fine woman could admire promote Victoria's unique monarchy:

> "She is one of us," she heard the poor people whisper as she went amongst them. "She is one of us. She is one of the People."
>
> So the Queen came to love the dress that the fairies made for her from the rag-bag, and now she often wears it in preference to any other.
>
> There have been Queens of England before, but Victoria was the first Queen of the People.   (34–35)

The queen's dowdy dress thus manifests an idea of a republican queen, itself a contradiction. In a time of growing republicanism and a population whose franchise was no longer entirely based on property, *The Fairies' Favourite* resolves the contradiction between Victoria's immense and growing wealth and her plain appearance. It reads her sartorial syntax as a statement of identification with her poor subjects, the "People" representing the most humble and simple. In keeping with such Victorians as Carlyle and Eliot, Ellis considers clothes a measure of character. Victoria's antifashion broadcasts the queen's affiliation with her people. In a time of the New Woman and the suffragette movement, Ellis represents Victoria as more subjected than her subjects.

The Fairies' Favourite celebrated sixty years of Victoria's reign by restructuring that reign's ideology through the language of clothes. Although not actually resolving contradictions, the tale rationalizes them, imparting a political meaning to clothes. The story for children recasts a familiar tale that pleased adults as well. Victoria's clothes— unstylishly loose—resolved a gender and class problem for the queen. In what Ellis imagines as her fairy rags, Victoria dresses more "rationally" than most women without seeming mannish. While deeply committed to maintaining the prerogatives of royalty, she appears with her bonnet as a queen of the people. During the triumphant year of Victoria's Diamond Jubilee, stories about her clothes celebrated the seeming incompatibility between Victoria's bluest blood and her sympathy with simple people. An anonymous servant recalled an encounter at Windsor between the plainly dressed queen and an inexperienced young man, a tale resembling that about the Scots shepherd lad:

> There is a story told of a young and newly-appointed Equerry who, in going round the stables one day, came across a simple old lady in a mushroom hat and a countrified black gown. Filled with the importance of his new dignity, the zealous official shouted across the intervening stalls: "My good woman, you must get out of this! Strangers are not allowed here, especially when Her Majesty is in residence." He finished up his remarks by threatening to take her to the gate himself if she were not quick in going. His feelings on discovering that the shabbily dressed intruder was his Royal mistress in person may be better imagined than described; but the Queen, with delightful good-humour, forgave him and at the same time complimented him on his zeal and obedience to standing orders.[42]

Despite its resemblance to other stories and in the face of contradictory reports of Victoria's imperiousness, the writer asserts that this particular story is true. Kind to the lowly and fierce to the well-born, not excluding her own children, Queen Victoria's unaesthetic sensibilities in regard to dress became one of her most endearing characteristics, creating a popular figure that not only seemed to advertise her truest qualities but qualified her as queen of her moment, as her peoples' queen.

After Victoria's death, Henry James, transplanted British subject, personally grieved over the loss of his adopted sovereign: "I mourn the safe and motherly old middle-class queen, who held the nation warm under the fold of her big, hideous Scotch-plaid shawl and whose duration had been so extraordinarily convenient and beneficent."[43] James misses Victoria's safety; he has taken her muted sexuality for granted so that he can depend on her maternal protection. James's image presents Victoria as a folk madonna. Like the other madonna, she opened her ethnic shawl to her peoples. Lovable because beyond fashion and therefore beyond time itself, her common cloak seemed to assure stability. Dressed for access, shabby Queen Victoria offered a haven amidst uncertainty.

4

IMPERIAL TEARS

Oh Queen! Till now thy people's vows were paid
In Joy! New ties this common grief hath made!
—*Richard Bennett, "The Queen and Albert the Good," 1862*

Break not, O woman's-heart, but still endure;
Break not, for thou art Royal . . .
—*Alfred Tennyson,*
Dedication to the new edition of Idylls of the King, *1862*

Queen Victoria performed mourning rituals with theatrical panache. While she undeniably suffered when someone died, her customs also served both the monarchy and the culture. Though extreme, her practices serve to authorize cultural meanings the queen could not have consciously foretold. Because of her long and flamboyant mourning practices, Victoria acquired the epithet the Widow of Windsor. For more than a generation, children pronouncing the alphabet in English could identify queens with widowhood. In 1897, the year of Victoria's Diamond Jubilee, a New York publisher issued *Baby's A.B.C.* with its rhyme for "Q":

> Q is the Queen
> and a widow, poor thing.
> Whose Baby will
> one of these days be a king.[1]

However one construes this jingle, the conjunction of baby, mother, and widow does not compute. In 1897 Albert Edward, Prince of Wales, was fifty-five years old. Even considering the likelihood that the pub-

Q is the Queen
and a widow, poor thing.
Whose Baby will
one of these days, be a king.

"Q is the Queen." The baby wears a blue gown, and the queen
wears a crown.

lishers used material from an earlier English alphabet book, the prince
had passed his nineteenth birthday at his father's death while the ninth
and last child, Beatrice, called "Baby," was a four-year-old toddler.

Q's rhyme creates a time warp where the perpetual widow also per-
petually mothers a baby. Merely pointing out this effect, however, fails
to decipher other possible meanings of Q's impossible image of a
queen with superhuman, though properly Victorian, capacities. What
could be the possible cultural uses in representing two of Victoria's
most extreme accomplishments as a family woman—her nine live
babies and her flagrantly long widowhood?

The rhyme appeals to the readers' pity, imputing to the queen a set
of sorrowful emotions: bereavement, emptiness, grief. Except for its
reassuring gesture to the future, Q's conventions do not associate
mourning with pleasure. Yet Victoria's extravagant mourning included
an additional sensation; if not quite pleasure, it was a quickening, a
devotion or dedication to death itself. Victoria showed intense interest
at the death of someone she knew. After the deaths of her mother, her
husband, two children, many devoted servants, countless relatives, and
hordes of officials, the queen seemed to perk up at the grim reaper's
appearance. When, during a vacation in Grasse in 1891, a servant died,
Marie Mallet, one of the queen's ladies-in-waiting, noted how Victoria's
"interest" in death bordered on the unseemly:

> It is very curious to see how the Queen takes the keenest inter-
> est in death and all its horrors, our whole talk has been of
> coffins and winding sheets. We had a sort of funeral service

last night in the Dining Room, the coffin in our midst not even screwed down, everyone in evening dress, the servants sobbing . . . . The Queen was very grieved and placed a wreath on the coffin rather tremblingly; and then the body was removed to the little English church close by and this afternoon we had to visit it again with the Queen. The final funeral is tomorrow and after that we may hope for a little peace.[2]

Victoria seemed almost to prefer mourning someone's death to paying attention to them when they lived, as if her tears repaired wrongs committed or requited inadequate interactions. Henry Ponsonby noted this characteristic in reference to officials she thought she may have worked to death as a way of "making amends in a post-mortem eulogy."[3] By wearing black, the queen atoned as well as grieved.

Given Victoria's regret at her rejection of Mama when she first became queen and before Albert effected a reconciliation, her histrionic behavior when the Duchess of Kent died in March 1861 exemplifies such reparative mourning. Victoria felt remorseful when she discovered evidence in diaries of the duchess's maternal devotion. For months after her mother's death, Victoria could not stand the sound of voices; she took her meals alone, nothing diverted her attention from her orphaned state, and she suddenly felt very old. Albert bore the brunt of her reaction, taking care of her official business and also arranging elaborate ceremonies, such as a memorial birthday party for the duchess. When the duchess died, the prince had less than nine months to live, and Victoria suffered later from believing that she had strained his already weakened health.

Victoria's reaction to her mother's death provoked rumors that she was mad. If madness here signifies the loss of volition and calculation, Victoria was not insane. If her behavior was unbalanced, it was not involuntary. She knew her grief appeared excessive, but she did not care, agreeing with her oldest daughter that she was committed to grief: "You are right, dear child, I do not wish to feel better. . . . The relief of tears is great—and though since last Wednesday night I have had no very violent outburst—they come again and again every day, and are soothing to the bruised heart and soul."[4] Victoria explained "the sort of quiet, serious state of mind which I am in and wish to remain in":

> Don't worry yourself about me. I love to dwell on her, and to be quiet and not to be roused out of my grief! To wish me to shake it off—and to be merry—would be to wish me no good! I could not and would not! Daily do I feel more the

blank—the loss I *shall* experience—and the power of enjoying other things is not possible at present.[5]

She wishes to be left alone to enjoy, not to overcome, her grief.

Victoria's mourning for Albert needs to be placed in the context of
her mother's death. Because her father died when she was only eight
months old, she knew her mother only as a widow. Victoria's mourning
for her husband beyond the limits of Victorian customs can be understood as homage to memories of her widowed mother as well. After
Albert died in 1861 ceremonies for the dead became a habitual way of
life not devoid of their own particular pleasures. Monuments at
Windsor and Balmoral—and throughout the empire—along with
plaques and memorabilia, constituted a virtual company of memories,
made concrete through realistic statues. Victoria laid fresh flowers by
her own hands on memorials to her husband and later to her beloved
servant, John Brown. Dwelling on and with the dead cheered her up.

Queen Victoria immersed herself in the role of widowed queen-
hood without necessarily calculating its many cultural uses and meanings. Above and well beyond her age's elaborate mourning customs,
she engaged in the rituals and trappings of loss, expanding upon them
to the point where she exhausted her subjects' capacity to enjoy or sym-
pathize with the performance. Histories and biographies stress the
increasingly republican sentiments of her subjects, who resented their
enormous financial investment in a monarch who barely showed her
face. In turn, the queen charged them with having an almost prurient
interest in viewing her abject grief. During the 1860s and much of the
1870s, she found few reasons sufficiently compelling to perform the
most common ceremonies of her position, but, apparently motivated by
impending royal requests to the nation for increased funds for her mul-
tiplying family, she opened Parliament in 1866, five years after her
"angel's" death. Writing to Prime Minister Russell, she explained her
feelings in melodramatic terms:

> That the public should wish to see her she fully understands,
> and has no wish to prevent—quite the contrary; but why this
> wish should be of so unreasonable and unfeeling a nature, as
> to long to witness the spectacle of a poor, broken-hearted
> widow, nervous and shrinking, dragged in deep mourning,
> alone in State as a Show, where she used to go supported by
> her husband, to be gazed at without delicacy of feeling, is a
> thing she cannot understand, and she never could wish her
> bitterest foe to be exposed to![6]

Victoria acknowledges the public's right to see her but at the same time allows no way for them to satisfy that right. To be gaped at as a "Show" violated protocols for an ordinary lady, while not appearing violated her duty as queen. Her widowhood threw into relief her anomalous position. She could not rely on precedent for a model, for England had never had a widowed queen regnant.

After Prince Albert's death the queen interred herself. None of her people could view her, although the mere sight of the queen, it was thought and subsequently proved to be so, would revive British monarchical loyalties. Rather than engage in public ceremonies, Victoria worked privately at official business while creating personal and public monuments to death. Virtually everything associated with the prince became an Albert memorial. What he liked, what he had touched, what he had designed, and what he had decided became preserved as sacred relics. The two homes Victoria owned, Balmoral Castle and Osborne House, both designed by Albert, had to be conserved in their entirety. The entrances to many rooms bore a plaque stating that Prince Albert had chosen the decor; when upholstery wore out, it had to be removed silently, reproduced exactly, and the furniture replaced precisely where it had stood. Her contemporaries, even though they were accustomed to mementos of those who had passed on, such as hair rings and mourning portraits, did not necessarily share Victoria's conviction that Albert's memorials should be "numberless."[7]

All Victoria's surroundings continued to bear the immutable seal of her husband's taste and habits. When Edward White Benson, headmaster of Wellington College from the time it was under the active patronage of Prince Albert, paid a call to Windsor Castle a few years after the prince's death to inform the queen of the school's progress, he reported, "On the table in the ante-room to the chamber where the interview took place there were laid out his [Albert's] gloves and his white wide-awake hat as on the day when he had last used them."[8] The prince's things contained a whiff of his spirit. They suggested a community of the living and the dead, the objects themselves making concrete—indeed almost seeming to prove—a sense that those living on earth touched things inhabited by those living in the afterworld. Victoria expressed such a belief to her daughter: "All you say about beloved Grandmama knowing every thing better than she did before—and our being not really separated from her—is what I feel. I feel as if she lived on with us—(though alas! I get sudden shocks when I feel I can't write to her)."[9] Victoria's faith in the continuity between life and death maintained a feeling of literal connection. Active mourning seemed to keep the spirits on the alert, more aware, and more present

with their loved ones on earth. The queen shared with many of her subjects the conviction that the dead were right here, in the room though
just out of perception. One was never alone.

Alfred Tennyson found a temperamental soul mate in Victoria; both
seemed at home with dead presences. The death in 1833 of his closest
friend, Arthur Hallam, focused his melancholy temperament on an
actual loss. His great elegy, *In Memoriam* (1850), rings the changes on
the themes of loss and longing; writing the poem over seventeen years
kept Hallam among the living, much as Victoria's active mourning vivi-
fied Albert in a more concrete sense than a later century might recognize. Spirit rappings, séances, and other antics of the spiritualist extend
the belief in the living dead to a level that Victoria did not subscribe to,
although some thought that John Brown acted as her medium to the
spirit world. For the queen, mourning sites replaced the spiritualist's
table to bring the dead among the living. *In Memoriam* indicates that
Tennyson, too, believed that Hallam had access to everything from
beyond the grave. The poem suggests that acts of mourning in themselves kept the communication open between the dead and the living.

To live with such active consciousness of ghosts could be unsettling,
particularly if the mourner felt unworthy. "Do we indeed desire the
dead / Should still be near us at our side?" Tennyson asks, as if the
desire itself determined spectral proximity. He concludes that the living
need not fear, for once the dead are with God, they receive His wisdom
and show divine mercy:

> Shall he for whose applause I strove,
> I had such reverence for his blame,
> See with clear eye some hidden shame
> And I be lessened in his love? . . .
>
> Be near us when we climb or fall:
> Ye watch, like God, the rolling hours
> With larger other eyes than ours,
> To make allowance for us all.[10]

In the course of their first somewhat lugubrious meeting, the Widow of
Windsor cited the stanza above to her poet laureate as having been of
great comfort to her.[11] Albert would know everything she did and
thought but would judge her with a compassion equal to God's.

Given that Victoria believed that the beloved spirit was sentient and
omnipresent, her mourning habits not only kept the dead in her own
memory, they also showed them how much she cared. She performed

her grief for an audience composed of both the living and the dead. Consciousness of dead relations just "beyond the veil" may be particularly acute for sovereigns. As their assured place in history takes its particular shape, they daily pass a procession of painted ancestors on the walls of what will be their descendants' castles. As much as the birth of successors, ancestral deaths create continuities of history where nursery and sepulchre join. Boundaries between rooms where living monarchs conduct their business and those where they become part of the past have been more permeable than those separating ordinary people's lives from their funereal monuments. An obituary from the *Daily Telegraph* the day after Albert's death meditated upon this melancholy royal condition:

> It is part of the state of princes to be buried almost by the sides of their beds, and to look from their palace windows into the mouths of their sepulchres. The meaner sort can stave off the remembrance of the grim hour until its very imminence of chiming. . . . But those of Royal lineage have, in their decease, no such immunity from parade. . . . Not for him are the quiet country churchyard—the verdant "God's acre," where the lambs browse and the wild flowers bloom— the Prince must pass but a few paces from the Chamber of Death to the House of Silence.[12]

In the end Albert possessed both a chamber of death and a house of silence. Victoria's memorial rooms testify to a Victorian trait of concretizing feelings as if a material object were equivalent to an emotion. One felt grief privately, while one mourned in more visible ways. The two may be incommensurable. Whatever constituted the personal dynamics of her grief, Queen Victoria performed her mourning in carefully staged scenes.

⤳ The Chamber of Death ⤶

Albert's death from typhoid fever was preceded by a restless movement from bed to bed, from the large one he shared with Victoria to a small one at its foot. After wandering in a delirium from room to room, he settled in the Blue Room—"the King's room where both George IV and William IV had died."[13] There Albert passed on. To die on the deathbed of kings seemed to confirm what Victoria had worked for but failed to achieve during her angel's life: except in name, Albert was king. Her initial distrust of Louis Philippe, king of the French, dissipated when he showed elaborate respect for Albert: "What an extraordinary man the

The Blue Room, Windsor Castle, watercolor by William Corden, the Younger, c. 1868.
Illustration from the Royal Archives, by permission of The Royal Collection © Her Majesty Queen Elizabeth II.

King is!" Victoria wrote to Uncle Leopold, "What a wonderful memory, and how lively, *how sagacious!* . . . The King praised my dearest Albert most highly, and fully appreciates his great qualities and talents—and what gratifies me *so much,* treats him completely as his equal, calling him "Mon Frère," and saying to me that *my husband* was the same as me, which it is—and "Le Prince Albert, c'est pour moi le Roi."[14] That sentiment could serve as the motto for the Blue Room. By dying in the bedroom where previous kings had also expired, Albert made possible the considerable slide or blur in representation from husband of a queen to king in his own right. In preserving the room as a living shrine, Victoria reserved this symbolic possibility.

The queen wrote a memorandum officially removing the room from the vicissitudes of change:

> *Memoranda from the Lord Chamberlain:*
> *March 25, 1862*
>
> *It is Her Majesty's command that the Blue Room at Windsor Castle in which His Royal Highness the Prince Consort died (No.*

202) should remain in its present state and shall not be made use of in the future.[15]

The queen dedicated the Blue Room as a shrine to the prince as he might have lived, had he lived there. Rather than keeping the room as it was at the moment of Albert's death, she redecorated it with wreaths laid upon both beds, repainted the ceiling, and ordered new china. William Theed, a sculptor who had made other objects for the royal couple, won a commission to fashion a marble bust, the first posthumous sculpture of the prince; the bust was placed between the two beds. Albert's dressing case, opened and at the ready, sat on a table near a window for good light. Fresh towels and hot water were replenished every day; clothes were laid out, ready to wear. Mundane necessities of daily civilized activities, such as changing sheets and pajamas, washing up and shaving, became sanctified for ritual consumption.

The enshrined Blue Room altered a German custom of the *sterbezimmer*, where time stops and the only change is measured in the accumulation of dust. The queen's intention, in her words, was to "dedicate the room to him not as a Sterbe-Zimmer—but as a living beautiful monument,"[16] in line with her conscious intention to treat the dead Albert as if he were alive. Diurnal rituals of consumption—getting and spending—kept him "alive." Except that no one actually saw Albert performing those rituals, the daily housekeeping witnessed to an apparent person's all too human condition of dirtying things and using things up.[17]

The family gathered for a service of ambiguous meaning in the Blue Room on the first anniversary of Albert's death, December 14, 1862. Victoria described the event:

> Dr. Stanley most kindly held a little service for us, reading Prayers and some portions of the 14th and 16th Chapters of St. John, and spoke a few and most comforting and beautiful words. The room was full of flowers, and the sun shining in so brightly, emblems of his happiness and glory, which comforted me. I said it seemed like a birthday, and Dr. Stanley answered, "It is a birthday in a new world."[18]

The mourning ritual in the Blue Room was a *translated* birthday party, an extreme example of the Victorian habit of concretizing belief and feeling. The ritual both acknowledged mortality and denied it, while it also gave a religious sanction to Victoria's private emotions. Victoria felt that Albert's immortal spirit attended the party.

Victoria's ways of keeping Albert alive, as she herself sensed, verged on sacrilege. She was convinced, however, that God sanctified her worshiping the dead Albert as if he were a god. Without divine permission, she explained to Vicky, she could not love so strongly: "Yes, I ever did and ever shall love adored Papa more than anything on earth or in heaven and God sees and knows and approves that, for He gave me that heart, that feeling of love and gave me that blessed precious object to gaze only upon, and love beyond all and everything—and keeping him safe for me!"[19] Becoming in death Victoria's guardian angel, Albert could be imagined as her heavenly king. The queen met with her ministers with Theed's bust of Albert on a table between them. For at least fifteen years, Albert was both alive *and* dead, a fact (if something so irrational could be called fact) influencing the existence of huge numbers of people.

⤇ The House of Silence ⤆

'Tis the voice of Prince Consort! I heard him complain
She is gone to that damned Mausoleum again!
—Attributed to Robert Browning

In an uncanny way, Victoria and Albert were in the mood for death in the year preceding the terrible events of 1861. They began to prepare their tombs. Their desire for a mausoleum to hold their remains originated with Albert's family, the Saxe-Coburgs, who started a family taste for internment in mausolea in preference to traditional royal burial in churches. In 1860 Albert and Victoria visited the Coburg mausoleum, which had been designed by Albert and his brother Ernest for their father in 1844. Victoria thought it both beautiful and "cheerful" and commissioned a combined small mausoleum and summerhouse for Victoria's mother near Frogmore House on the grounds just outside Windsor Castle; unfortunately the duchess died before she could use it as a summerhouse. Victoria and Albert made plans for their own Royal Mausoleum, also on the Frogmore grounds. Externally the building is Romanesque, on a Greek cross plan with an overcrossing octagonal dome. Albert's effigy rests on a bier, with room for his wife. Victoria had her own effigy made at the same time as Albert's, for, although she genuinely believed that she was not long for this world, she wanted their likenesses to match in age should she manage to endure. It would not do for young Albert to be paired with an aged Victoria, almost forty years older by the time of her death. Taken together, the effect of the two mausolea, among houses rather than among other tombs, is to rep-

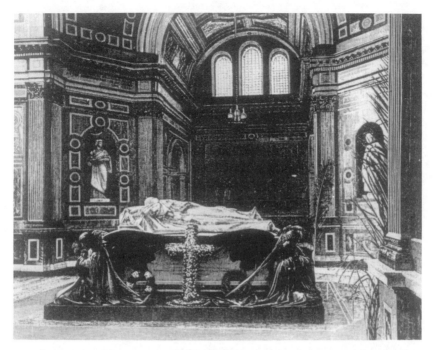

Prince Albert's tomb in the Royal Mausoleum. Queen Victoria's effigy, executed at the same time as Albert's, was stored in an almost forgotten place until it was found and placed next to her consort forty years later.

resent the structures as extensions of family life. The mausolea, in full view of where the duchess lived, seem to be little more than new houses in the neighborhood.

To many British subjects, however, the idea of a mausoleum seemed not domestic but foreign. The architectural design reinforced the notion of alien forms of death. An anonymous pamphlet, *Frogmore Follies*, dwelt upon the strangeness—and the expense—of the plan:

> This Mausoleum place the learned say,
> Is built in crucial form of Maltese cross,
> As worn by th' Knightly Order of St. John,
> With an Italian roof and gilded fane;
> And that eight thousand pounds of British gold
> The Queen did freely give to decorate
> Within, to one who came from Italy, —
> As if no British hand could trace such work,
> Although twelve times that sum is yearly spent
> By Parliament, these same Fine Arts to teach.[20]

The writer evokes hermetic rites of the Knights Templar, a secret society, possibly unorthodox, certainly not British. The private space, closed off to visitors, stimulated fantasies of rituals fortunately unfamiliar to true English sorrow:

> For eight long years now past once more renewed,
> An un English rite of mourning—
> . . . a rite unknown
> To English sons . . .

(6)

Imagined non-Protestant rites, even perhaps non-Christian ones, raised the same questions about Albert's religion as those arising at the marriage, when rumors spread that he was secretly Roman Catholic, not Lutheran. The idea of Victoria, clad in "widow's cheerless weeds," along with her mournfully dressed children gathering together for private ceremonies brought out chauvinistic suspicion mingled with pecuniary outrage. What was the secret within the "mosaic" mausoleum walls?

The answer to the suspicions seems almost banal, certainly anticlimactic. The tomb was turned into an extension of the home, and the home bore signs of the tomb. Victoria commissioned a fire screen painted with a scene of the family mausoleum, so that the home of the living could display a likeness of the home of the dead. The building itself served as a family gathering place, where Victoria went every day when in residence at Windsor, either alone or with family members.[21] She frequently enjoyed a picnic on its lawns. The very ordinariness of the rituals the royal family performed reach across death to conserve family unity. The family met at the mausoleum to feel Albert's presence, to visit with him, even to receive his judgments. For instance, the day before the Prince of Wales's marriage to Princess Alexandra of Denmark, the queen, with her daughter Helena or "Lenchen," took the bridal couple there; Victoria memorialized the event in her journal entry for March 10, 1863: "Drove with Alix, Lenchen and Bertie to the Mausoleum where Vicky and Fritz met us. I opened the shrine and took them in. Alix was much moved and so was I. I said, 'He gives you his blessing', and joined Alix and Bertie's hands, taking them both in my arms and kissing them."[22] Conveying her husband's benediction, Victoria acted as a medium for him.

Theed's bust of Albert served to complete the wedding portraits, playing out what may appear to a later century to be a weird family romance. Instead of blessing the nuptials and its promise of continuity, the queen's pose in those portraits appears to pledge her to the past

After the wedding of the Prince and Princess of Wales, 1863.
The women look one way and the "men" look the other, incor-
porating the missing Albert in the picture. *Illustration from the
Royal Archives, by permission of The Royal Collection © Her Majesty
Queen Elizabeth II.*

and to death. After the wedding, which the queen found a terrible trial
but where she fought to "master her emotions" (not only grief but
envy), she waved Bertie and Alix off to their honeymoon at Osborne,
then returned to the mausoleum with Lenchen and "prayed by that
beloved resting place, feeling soothed and calmed."[23]

☀ "Pillars of Domestic Peace" ☀

Victoria attempted to assimilate the person of her husband into her
own identity. Her wedding benediction underscores, or rather takes to
the familial plane, what she attempted to perform in her sovereign role:
to carry out what she imagined were the prince's mandates. By taking

The Queen at Osborne, engraving by W. Holl after a portrait by
A. Graefle, 1864.

on the person of the prince in her actions and opinions she represented herself for a while as both prince and queen.

Theed's bust sometimes signaled the prince's conscious mental presence to Victoria. The portrait of an attractive young widow by Graefle
(1864), commissioned by Victoria, shows a pensive queen, finger at her
chin in a pose that conventionally signifies not mourning but deep and
profound thought. Albert's bust in the right of the portrait indicates
that the queen feels her consort's influence. Victoria gazes into the middle distance, while Albert's bust seems to look at her, its ghostliness
emphasized by the strange lighting, at once from behind on the fore-
head and from the front in the draperies. Her body clothed in deep
mourning, Victoria is surrounded by white: her widow's cap and veil,
the ermine draped on the left, and Albert on her right. The blank back-

Mourning photograph of Queen Victoria and Princess Alice
by Prince Alfred, 1862. *Illustration from the Royal Archives, by
permission of The Royal Collection © Her Majesty Queen Elizabeth II.*

ground enhances the scene's timelessness. Through meditation
Victoria merges her spirit with her moral guide. The allegorical picture
represents the metaphor "living memory." Like the Blue Room, it seems
to blur boundaries, but in this instance not those between the person's
life and his death but those between a living person and a dead one.

Using the bust and other statues as effigies, the royal family performed the queen's mourning. A mourning photograph, particularly
interesting because it was taken by her second son, Prince Alfred, boldly
places the statue in the center, with two women reacting to its domination in a pose that resembles a tableau vivant personifying "Devotion."
Queen Victoria leans up to the bust while her second daughter, Princess
Alice, looks out at the camera, her small white face a study of grief.

Victoria's pose, typical of allegorical representations of fidelity,
echoes a familiar attitude, such as that in Sir Edwin Landseer's *Old
Shepherd's Chief Mourner* (1837), in which a sheepdog's chin resting on

The Old Shepherd's Chief Mourner, by Sir Edwin Landseer, 1837. *Printed courtesy of the Board of Trustees of the Victoria & Albert Museum.*

his master's coffin resembles Victoria's pose here and in Bertie's wedding picture. Like the Blue Room, Landseer's painting depicts a room as a living monument to the one who lived there, a visual allegory of the shepherd's character. The dog not only mourns, showing a similarity between human and animal emotions, he also reveals the character of the one he mourns; the dog's sorrow indicates the dead man's worth.

Unlike the coffin in the Landseer painting, which foregrounds its sense of death's finality, Victoria's scenes, or tableaux, contain a stone embodiment of their subject who mingles sociably with his family. This scene of ghostly domination will be replayed, with a variety of children. For instance, Emilie Chaese, a primitive painter, reconstructed a "portrait" of the entire royal family, with Windsor Castle in the background, the queen in black in the center with every child, grandchild, son, and daughter-in-law stretching to the bounds of the frames east and west, and a full marble Albert on a pedestal at the center presiding over the multitude.

Preserving the father's memory as if he were alive makes sense in maintaining the stability of a family unit. Tennyson provides a literary analogue to the domestic effect of Albert's statuary ghost, admonitory and, what is probably most to the point, defending the home from

Queen Victoria's Family, by Emilie Chaese.

incursions of a subsequent paterfamilias. Victoria's poet laureate was preoccupied during his entire poetic career with the effect of the return of the husband to a household that had overcome the effects of his loss, either through death or, as in "Ulysses," after long years of war and adventure. What should be the consequences of a wife's remarriage? Most typically, the returning mate comes back as a ghost to upset the reestablished domestic "joy." Stanzas of *In Memoriam,* Victoria's favorite poem for comforting herself, warn that the "domestic pillars" representing the stable married couple would be destroyed by the unbodied interloper, the dead husband returned:

> But if they came who past away
> Behold their brides in other hands
> The hard heir strides about their lands,
> And will not yield them for a day.
>
> Yea, though their sons were none of these,
> Not less the yet-loved sire would make
> Confusion worse than death, and shake
> The pillars of domestic peace.[24]

By keeping Albert in view of as many people as possible, Victoria's mourning rituals preserve domestic peace. Although rumors married off the relatively young widow, such an eventuality was out of the question for Victoria, who generally disapproved of widows remarrying and believed that she would reunite with her husband in the afterlife. Not for her the scene portrayed by Richard Redgrave in his painting of the widow throwing off her weeds. To comfort others in their bereavement, she quoted the first lines from the last stanza of Adelaide Procter's "The Angel of Death":

> O, what were life, if life were all? Thine eyes
> Are blinded by their tears, or thou wouldst see
> Thy treasures wait thee in the far-off skies,
> And Death, thy friend, will give them all to thee.[25]

In addition to its personal meanings, Victoria's refusal to give up the ghost ensured no shaking of the political mansion. Had Victoria revived her early self-presentation as a single, unattached, autonomous queen, she would disrupt Victorian gender conventions. Nine children complicated the image, for Victoria could no longer appear as an appealing virginal maiden queen. What she provided by invoking a ghostly Albert—still there albeit marmoreal—was a husband, a ruler of the queen, someone who kept the woman—and the nation—in line.

Since he had spent his last conscious hours redrafting and softening the language of a harshly worded memorandum to the United States government about their belligerent act against an English ship during the Civil War, Albert was credited with preventing a war between England and its former colony. Thus the ghostly presence was enforced symbolically by conceptualizing Albert as a Christ figure who died for his people. The image of the prince, so ill that he could not dress, reading his draft in his robe and slippers, death at the doorstep, was disseminated. This image gave him a status closer to deity than angel; he enjoyed an apotheosis as the Prince Albert of Peace.

Princess Alice connected Victoria's adoring stance with religious iconography in a sketch of Queen Victoria "garbed as a nun, standing with clasped hands in the presence of a vision of Prince Albert."[26] Married to her bridegroom, Victoria dedicates her life to him, reinforcing her fealty by means of her favored mourning outfit, which resembles a nun's habit. The subtext suggests the erotics of mourning while it removes Victoria from the dangerous amorousness attributed to merry widows. Sister Victoria satisfies her desires within a spiritual marriage.

After Albert's death, Victoria commissioned literary memorial tributes. One, a six-volume life of the prince, became the life work of Theodore Martin. With the help of General Grey, who had served as

Albert's secretary, she also compiled a volume on Albert's young life. Published in 1867 and entitled *The Early Years of His Royal Highness The Prince Consort, 1819–1841*, the work ends with the christening of Albert and Victoria's first child on "the 10th of February, 1841, the first anniversary of the Queen's happy marriage."[27] The volume concludes with numerous appendices: reminiscences about the family by King Leopold, some of Albert's letters in German. More important, the bulk of the appendices contain documents and lengthy descriptions of Victoria and Albert's nuptials and wedding, including a list of members of the privy council present at the betrothal declaration; the service and festivities in Coburg announcing Albert's betrothal; and detailed descriptions of the wedding ceremony, including who was in the wedding carriages, what jewels the queen wore, and the festivities that evening and the next day. Victoria thus concludes her memorial to her husband's childhood with the account of his wedding to her. By emphasizing their marriage, the volume not only suggests that marriage made his life meaningful but also leaves the reader with a final image of Victoria and Albert together beyond the end of the volume—and beyond the borders of time.

The following year Victoria published *Leaves from a Journal of Our Life in the Highlands*. Not publicized as a tribute to their marriage, this book nevertheless memorializes Albert as fully as his official biographies. Like the biographies, it presents the prince as the primary actor in the royal cast, this time in the context of family life. The couple live in the home designed by the prince, and Victoria offers selected glimpses of family activities among close family retainers. Victoria's glosses on her journal convey her nostalgia for the absent main character. The dialogue between text and gloss produces a double sense of time, a past where the prince acts out his noble character and a present where his legacy remains. Victoria offers the servants' simple family histories to magnify the prince's benevolence to them. Grant, the head keeper, she writes, was "most devoted to the Prince and myself. . . . The Prince was very fond of him. . . . His mother . . . 'stops' in a small cottage which the Prince built for her in our village. . . . He himself lives in a pretty lodge called Croft, . . . which the Prince built for him" (107–108). The prince very much likes his retainers and builds cottages for them.

Leaves had an enormous influence; it was far and away the best-seller of the year in many languages. Taken together, the widow's ventures into print maintain a living picture of her marriage beyond the grave. By presenting herself as married, as still married, Queen Victoria kept the prince alive in the face of growing rumors of an illicit connection between her and the gillie John Brown, whose increasing importance to her, coupled with his familiar manner and aggressive manliness, had stimulated scandalous stories. Victoria's gloss on John Brown, on September 16, 1850, takes up almost the entire page. Putting Brown in his social place, yet elevating his character, Victoria tries to dispel the rumors of a liaison. She recounts the history of his service: his appointment as gillie in 1849; his position as the queen's regular attendant out of doors in 1858; and then, his promotion in 1865 "most deservedly" to become "an upper servant, and my permanent personal attendant" (December 1864.) Victoria attributes her need for someone with Brown's qualities to her "state of health . . . sorely tried and weakened." Brown has "all the independence and elevated feelings peculiar to the Highland race, and is singularly straightforward, simple-minded, kind-hearted, and disinterested; always ready to oblige; and of a discretion rarely to be met with" (128). After praising the man, she then describes his simple Scots family. Published first for her family and most intimate friends, most of whom either disapproved of Brown's increasingly authoritative position or were jealous of it, Victoria's journal attempts to remind them of her eternal marriage.

To reinforce the impression that she was connubially, if not actually carnally, plighted, Queen Victoria took Albert to bed with her wherever she went. During the year of the Diamond Jubilee, one of Victoria's servants published an unofficial and forbidden commentary on the

Queen Victoria's bed with posthumous photograph of Albert on his side of the bed, from the unauthorized *Private Life of Queen Victoria, by One of Her Servants*, 1897.

queen's private life. In describing various rooms, she revealed Victoria's practice of sleeping on her half of a double bed, the other half "occupied" by a photograph of Albert taken shortly after his death: "The Queen's bed is large and of wood, as are all of the beds at Windsor, the hangings being of fine crimson damask. It is most pathetic to note that above the right side of the bed there hangs against the rich silken background a portrait of the late Prince Consort, surmounted by a wreath of immortelles. The same sad memorials are in every bedroom that the Queen ever occupies." When the servant repeated the same information later in her reminiscence, she elided possible erotic meanings with reverent respect: "Her Majesty's touching fancy to have a portrait of the Prince Consort taken after death, and a wreath of immortelles always fastened at the right hand side of the head of her bed, is too sacred to be commented on."[28] Bedded with the dead Albert, for some time sleeping with his nightclothes in her arms, Victoria's behavior keeps alive a carnal union and wards off the remarriage that would complicate a global political image of a steadfast, undeviatingly loyal queen. Queen Victoria became a sacred icon, her faithfulness to Albert a paradigm of loyalty, of compassion, and of patriotism.

Victoria created sets on which to perform the inconsolable widow in accommodation to the gender requirements of her century. England had never had a widowed queen regnant, and Victoria had to write the anomalous role while she played it. Although few saw her performances of mourning in the flesh, they were well publicized and were derided by many. Margaret Oliphant, whose widowhood (eventually in Windsor) left her with no choice but to continue writing to support herself and her family, compared her own vigorous survival to Victoria's theatrics:

> I doubt whether *nous autres* poor women who have had to fight with the world all alone without much sympathy from anybody, can quite enter into the "unprecedented" character of the Queen's sufferings. A woman is surely a poor creature if with a large, happy affectionate family of children around her she can't take heart to do her duty whether she likes it or not. *We* have to do it, with very little solace, and I don't see that there is anybody particularly sorry for us.[29]

Yet Victorian gender ideology made the queen's subjects party to the deeds. Despite Albert's general unpopularity among most of the English populace, the keeping of the queen's husband alive cannot be entirely attributed to her personal need. If in deed the queen went over the edge, that precipice was constructed from some of the culture's strictures on womanly propriety that were at odds with the needs of having a queen as representative of a nation state. Victoria's tears exaggerate and thus perform for the culture its construction of properly womanly emotion. At the same time her tears create a space in the cultural imagination that would allow a woman whose husband happened to die to pursue her hereditary right to remain queen. The image of an inconsolable widow (who had nonetheless a husband) served a variety of useful purposes—maintaining the very kind of monarchy that seemed threatened by the queen's absenting herself into a private interior space.

To be chaperoned by a husband (or in Victoria's words, to have him to lean on) seemed requisite for a respectable Victorian monarchy. Without a husband the youngish Victoria could be seen as a destabilizing figure, resembling the "redundant woman" made into a social problem in W. R. Greg's polemics, where there is no cultural place for a surplus of unmarried women.[30] Furthermore, a sexually experienced woman without a mate at the top of the social hierarchy generates a disorderly image for the body politic. Solving the problem—at least imaginatively—a happily married couple as rulers of the realm, one of them inconveniently dead it is true, preserves Victorian propriety. With Albert's effigy hovering over everything, Victoria becomes plural, both man and wife. Victoria's connubial tears signify her pleasure in being two who, once joined, cannot be separated throughout eternity or throughout the globe.

The alphabet rhyme "Q is the Queen" telescopes a married woman's life to create a mythic queen. In the gap between biological clocks and representation the nursery rhyme performs its cultural work. From Q's behavior, new meanings become constructed, new imaginings become possible. The reader's awe at a queen's extraordinary prominence, coupled with pity for her ordinary condition ("a widow, poor thing"), opens up meanings of mourning that have little overtly to do with Victoria and the death of her beloved Albert and have nothing at all to do with producing ordinary babies. Rather, "Q" reproduces the queen as Victorian Britannia, a sign of national power.[31]

"Q" could be queen consort, important herself primarily in her roles as mother and wife, a producer of kings, not as a sovereign female monarch. The image of Victoria accompanying the jingle had become a familiar pose. It shows a substantial woman, clad in the black of mourning, crowned with a lace veil, and wearing the ribbon and garter of her rank. On this particular icon's lap perches an infant dressed in a baby blue robe. The iconography resembles the pose of many royal portraits of the queen, with babe in arms or child on lap, the grandmother queen with grandchild. Both allude to the iconography of Virgin and

Queen Victoria with Princess Victoria of Hesse, daughter of
Alice, 1868. *Illustration from the Royal Archives, by permission of
The Royal Collection © Her Majesty Queen Elizabeth II.*

child. Victoria's black dress and wimple also make her look nunlike.
Adding to the allusions to the Virgin, the time warp created by making
the Prince of Wales a babe in arms removes the queen from the realm
of ordinary temporality and universalizes the female roles of mother
and widow by conflating them and making them seem inevitable.

By virtue of a fantasy of her unending fecundity, Queen Victoria came
to represent an imperial mission of continual conquest made tolerable
by being represented as familial. Like some depictions of the Virgin
Mary with her robe opened to shelter all people, Queen Victoria offered
accommodation to the family of man. Her large biological family proved
her capacity. Such a universal function tied in nicely with the nearly universal spread of the alphabet used in England with which the queen
became identified: "Q *is* the Queen." Wherever it goes, she goes with it.

Not until the aged monarch herself became iconic as an object of
unsexual veneration could Albert's ghost be reverently laid to rest. The
windows of Victoria's mournful rooms eventually opened upon a view of
an empire where the sun never set. The image of the empire as a wid-

owed queen with a large supportive family naturalizes conquest as an imperial community with a devoted widow as its protectress. Slowly emerging in her black uniform, Victoria added "Empress of India" to her titles in 1876. Her revived vigor and energies seemed astonishing. In a tone of amazement, E. F. Benson, who was not yet born when the widowed Victoria visited his parents in 1864 at Wellington College,[32] describes a few of her activities in the year after the 1876 Royal Titles Act:

> Hitherto she had wailed and protested at the cruel way in which she was overworked, at the callousness of those who teazed and tormented her to make exertions of which she was incapable: she had been full of self-pity of the lonely lot of the "poor Queen," but now there was an end of that. . . . Instead of having to be urged by her Ministers to a greater activity it was she who spurred and hustled them. . . . All her energy was pouring back: she reviewed troops, she went on board her ships . . . she went to see a game of La Crosse; she received that queer man Mr. Richard Wagner, who wrote such extraordinary music. . . . She had an impromptu dance at Osborne, "and I danced a Quadrille and a valse (which I had not done for eighteen years) with dear Arthur, who valses extremely well, and I found I could do it, as well as ever!" . . . As each New Year came round, instead of looking backwards with regrets for vanished happiness, she prayed for renewed strength to improve, and do her duty and fulfil her arduous task.[33]

Victoria awakened to an empire, however, that prescribed marriage for women but permitted elderly widows some autonomy. The image of a venerable widow could be transported to the eastern part of the empire. In "Ave Imperatrix," Rudyard Kipling's poem of thanksgiving at a failed assassination attempt in March 1882, fighting for the royal widow provides motivation for empire:

> And all are bred to do your will
> By land and sea—wherever flies
> The Flag, to fight and follow still,
> And work your Empire's destinies.[34]

In other moods, Kipling doubted the imperative of attending "the Widow's parties," his mordant term for colonial wars; but whatever one's attitude toward imperialism, the "Widow at Windsor," as Kipling called her, became its sign, all children "bred" to do her will.

Cover of *Baby's A.B.C.*

A mourning custom denoting personal loss and sexual unavailability thus converts into an emblem of universal sympathy. Embracing her world mission, Queen Victoria emerged from memorial rooms with vigor and zest. Returning from the dead, she became mythical. On the cover of *Baby's A.B.C.*, Victoria's image differs from the one for "Q." She wears no crown, no star, no royal ribbon on her black dress, while the baby on her lap wears baby pink instead of the baby blue of the "Q" illustration, where the baby will one of these days be a king. In the sense that mourning strengthens the queen, the baby in the cover picture represents an emblem of Victoria's own renewal, of her aptitude for rebirth through tears.

5

QUEEN OF A CERTAIN AGE

*She is the symbol of law; she is by law, and setting apart
the metaphysics, and the abnormal incidents of revolution,
the source of power.*
—W. E. Gladstone

As Queen Victoria's monarchy entered its fourth decade, the playwright William Schwenck Gilbert and the musician Arthur Sullivan were writing comic operas featuring an adaptation of a stock character, the dame figure, who possesses unpredictable yet strong emotions. Their Savoy Operas allow a disturbing power to those women of a certain age. Born less than a year before the slender eighteen-year-old Victoria ascended the throne, Gilbert (1836–1911) grew up in a world according to Victoria, while Sullivan (1842–1900) lived and died within the years of her reign. The year after Gilbert and Sullivan's first success, *Trial by Jury* (1875), eclipsed the featured production at the Royalty Theatre, the queen acquired the title, "Empress of India." Twenty years later, in 1896, *The Grand Duke*, last of the Savoy Operas, opened before an audience that would the following year celebrate the queen's Diamond Jubilee. During the decades of the creation of the Savoy Operas, the sovereign began to emerge from seclusion, entertain potentates, and participate in ceremonial events. Although suffering from rheumatism in her legs, she nonetheless occasionally danced in Scotland at the gillies' ball, sometimes with her children, eventually with her grandchildren. The dame, an overbearing woman of a certain age, bears many of the sovereign's personality traits, qualities also of interest to the increasingly specialized medical profession. The queen's spirit inspires more than the dame figures' sprightly measures.

✦ A Curious Malady ✦

When Prince Albert died, Victoria, forty-two years old, had reached an age considered dangerous for women. In an intermittent fertile state, the "dodging time," women in their forties were entering the "change of life," what the medical profession called the "climacteric" and W. Tyler Smith, M.D., thought a "curious malady." Its very labels connote danger, a crisis when virtually anything in a woman's physical or mental constitution could go awry. Whereas medical authorities believed that a male climacteric disorder began with a decline of vital powers in advanced life, around sixty-five, they considered that for a woman it loomed earlier and contained more varied dangers. Edward Tilt, M.D., an early specialist in women's conditions, specifically cites age forty-two as "one of the several milestones that leads from the cradle to the grave."[1] Describing a woman "aged 45" who had been suffering from "Climacteric Mania" for two or three years, Smith writes:

> Each paroxysm is a distinct shock to the brain, leaving behind it peevishness, irritability of temper, and eccentricity. . . . Her disposition towards her husband and family has completely altered. She is morose and passionate on the slightest provocation, yet having a full sense of her improper explosions of temper, which at times she deplores most earnestly. Her nervousness is very great; she cannot listen to the same noises, or occupy herself with the same [pastime] long together, without a frantic feeling of delirium and loss of self-control.[2]

Much of Victoria's mourning behavior—sensitivity to noise, outbursts of temper, inability to concentrate—fits Smith's description of a climacteric woman. Smith's diagnosis did not rely on behavior only; no matter what she did, the forty-year-old woman's age itself marked her body as harboring the malady: "The extinction of reproductive power gives an emphatic interest to that period of the lifetime of women comprised within the 40th and 50th years, were it even unattended by many constitutional changes and morbid phenomena," the doctor claimed (v). Medical wisdom was built on the presumption of womanhood itself as a diseased state, as if no observable evidence simply confirmed potential sickness rather than health. Tilt's expert opinion, too, deemed women's fifth decade as charged with "emphatic interest," another way of conceptualizing a culmination of women's potential dysfunctions.

A time of chaos, the climacteric could extend until old age, to the virtual end of one's days. Tilt cites physicians in three European countries who reported on patients of ages ranging from the late fifties to eighty. One woman with a remarkably late reproductive life seems to have been drawn from the pages of Nathaniel Wanley's *Wonders of the Little World*: "a woman who bore her first child at forty-seven, and the last of seven other children at sixty. Menstruation ceased and reappeared at seventy-five, continuing until ninety-eight, then stopped for five years, again to return at the advanced age of 104" (125). By selecting extraordinary cases, medical writing thus represented the climacteric itself as disorderly and interminable. If one survived that crisis, fraught with paroxysmal attacks, one might enjoy life more fully when the constitution rallied "after having been shaken." Queen Victoria could emerge from the malady, but she might not. The multiple vicissitudes of menopause might burden her realm with a queen forevermore at a pitch of symptoms.

If the dodging time itself, "characterised by intense suffering," was not sufficient cause for disordering Queen Victoria, the simultaneous melancholia at the loss of the person she utterly depended upon, coming a few months after the death of her mother, could intensify the malady. In fact, according to Tilt and Smith, the climacteric could be brought on by an emotional shock. "Whenever widowhood or separation takes place at the change of life," Dr. Smith categorically states, "all the distressing symptoms, and the ovario-uterine excitement, are considerably aggravated" (604). The husband, in ways perhaps too indelicate to mention, mitigated the worst symptoms.

Wracked by double losses, Victoria could be imagined as a woman on the verge of yet another monumental death: the end of her reproductive capacity. Physicians in fact used metaphors of morbidity not simply for the reproductive but for the entire ganglionic system, figuring the change of life as a partial death: "This death of the reproductive faculty is accompanied, as it were, by struggles, which implicate every organ and every function of the body," Smith cautions, "but especially the nervous system in all its divisions" (604). It was as if the rest of the woman's body went into mourning for the demise of its capacity to bear children. From a medical perspective, Victoria's entire being suffered losses that it might try to recuperate in unpredictable but documentable ways.

For Tilt, the removal of regulatory functions of the female system during its fertile years left the menopausal body to its own undisciplined devices. Set loose from both marriage and menstruation, Victoria's person could conceivably know no boundaries. The uneducated eye confirmed such dangers. Tilt describes one physical repercussion following the change, a "symptom" observable in the queen. In some people, he noted, one sees the storing up of fat, for the lack of regular bleeding changes blood to fat: "Fat accumulates on women after change of life, as it accumulates in animals from whom ovaries have been removed. The withdrawal of the sexual stimulus from the ganglionic nervous system enables it to turn into fat and self-aggrandisement that blood which might otherwise have perpetuated the race" (54). Whatever else the doctor meant by "self-aggrandisement," the word conjures up an image of a selfish women who, deprived of sexual stimulation, turned her excess blood to unproductive self-indulgence. It is certainly true that Victoria's figure, never willowy, swelled after Albert died. In the 1870s her forty-eight-inch waist made her ten inches less wide in the middle than she was tall. Wearing the long full dresses of her times, she resembled a monumental pyramid. Her most courageous doctor, James Reid, tried prescribing a food formula to encourage Victoria to lose weight, but since she insisted upon eating it in addition to her meals rather than instead of them, the effort was doomed.[3]

In its rotundity, the queen's body resembled a black stove. Victoria detested heated rooms and would not tolerate fires, presumably because she supplied herself with sufficient heat. She kept her household freezing. Excessive body heat characterizes the climacteric. Tilt appeals to his audience to confirm the symptom: "It must have struck many, that at the change of life most women have the power of generating a more than usual amount of heat; they often want less clothing and even in winter leave their doors and windows wide open" (54). Victoria allowed little artificial heat, even in cold damp Balmoral. Marie Mallet's letters report on the Household's chills: "I think she is at last beginning to realize that we are all mortal and not utterly impervious to cold."[4] The queen, seventy years old, froze everyone out:

> Windsor Castle, March 2, 1890
>
> We have gone back to mid-winter, snow and bitter north-east wind; the Queen goes out in an open carriage just the same and does not seem to mind it. I drove with Her Majesty yesterday morning in a Victoria, it snowed hard the whole time.[5]

Other climacteric symptoms, some of which Victoria manifested, were many, varied, yet contradictory. Among the diseases of the brain

H. M. The Queen, woodcut by William Nicholson. *Printed courtesy of the Board of Trustees of the Victoria & Albert Museum.*

on Tilt's list, "nervous irritability, headache, apoplexy, hystericism, hysterical fits, laughing and crying fits, hysterical flatulence, and insanity" accorded with some of Victoria's occasional complaints. She discussed her physical conditions with her doctors, who recorded mentions of headaches and flatulence, suspected perhaps more. Hysteria and possible insanity were items of gossip, stimulated by Victoria's absence from public occasions and her willful behavior. When Henry Ponsonby accepted the job of Victoria's private secretary, Thomas Biddulph, Master of the Household, instructed him in the difficulties of working for an impetuous and inconsiderate mistress. "The fact is," writes Sir Thomas, "the Queen sitting in the garden at Balmoral issues arbitrary orders with what eagerness she determines to unsettle them again."[6] Biddulph's queen issues orders that will be obeyed. Sitting in her queen's garden, she represented the still center of a tornado.

As a somatic equivalent for nonparticipation in monarchical ceremonies, the queen developed trouble with her legs so that she actually could not walk. Medical men attributed the inability to walk as hystericism associated with the change. It is true that Victoria had injured her knee, but in 1883, following John Brown's death, she could not use her legs at all, a temporary condition that had also occurred in 1861, after

Albert's death. Her cadre of doctors diagnosed a possible psychological symptom.[7]

Victoria's paralysis, attendant as it was upon the loss of men upon whom she depended, suggested an erotic disorder. Amorous emotions increased during the dodging time, a distressing contradiction to Victorian formulations of women as asexual moral paragons. According to the authorities, nymphomania and erotomania could persist. "Many women," cautions Dr. Smith, "even those of the most irreproachable morals and conduct,—are subject to attacks of ovario-uterine excitement approaching to nymphomania" (606). Victoria's involvement in Europe's marital alliances, coupled with rumors of her amorous connection with John Brown and her flirting with Disraeli, could be seen as proving that the effects of the change had not abated but had simply shifted in trajectory from nervous irritability to sexual excitement. Her considerable energies as a woman without a mate might wreak havoc as she entered into an increasingly active public role during the final quarter of the century.

⇥ "Capture the Heart of a Queen" ⇤

She is possess'd of tender cares
To wipe away the orphan's tears
While she is Queen of England.
—*Street Ballad*

By the time Gilbert and Sullivan began their brilliant collaboration, the queen had been mourning her consort's death for more than ten years. Her body was expanding, as was the body politic. Britain's influence and conquests were extending into regions whose exotic names conjured up the distinct un-Englishness of their inhabitants. In those acquisitive times, Britain was involved in the Suez, New Zealand became a colony, and the queen's fleet entered Turkish waters. In the following years Britain annexed the Transvaal, gained Cyprus, invaded Afghanistan, and fought the Boers. The British defeated the Zulus, occupied Egypt and the Sudan, formed a protectorate of the Niger and New Guinea. Odd names, such as Zanzibar, Tel-el-Kebir, Isandlhwana, Jalabad, and Kumasi appeared in the newspapers, the last a legacy of a brutal "little war" on the Gold Coast of Africa with the Ashanti.

Gilbert and Sullivan operas represent conquests of vast and remote regions but place them in a domestic context. In the implicit equation between public and private spheres, love—personal conquest—resem-

Isandhlwana: The Dash with the Colours. A heroic moment in the Zulu War during the defeat of the English by the Zulus under the leadership of Chief Cetewayo, the Zulu King: "a defeat so disgraceful that the history of half a century supplies no parallel to it," according to one report. There were no survivors in the British camp after the battle, but England eventually won the war.

bles conquest in the larger political sphere. Many plots equate laws governing love with those ruling the polity.[8] When Dame Carruthers in *Yeomen of the Guard* sings "Joy and jollity / Then is polity; / Reigns frivolity," she equates her amorous conquest with the joy of the commonweal. The equation occasionally reverses, so that a political absurdity reflects on the foolishness of mating practices. As the democratic principle is ridiculous in the state, for instance, so it is absurd in matters of love. *The Sorcerer* and *The Gondoliers* satirize the kind of amorous leveling that also upsets political hierarchies. When in *H.M.S. Pinafore*, for instance, we hear a seemingly nonsensical declaration as "Josephine, I am a British sailor and I love thee," the conjunction seems absurd but it yokes together love for the domestic realm, or, patriotism, with the eventual establishment of a nuclear, or domestic, family.

Politics intertwines with gender disruptions in *Princess Ida*, where Prince Hilarion with his comrades storm Castle Adamant, a female refuge, apparently in order to rescue their women from the "unnatural" female conditions of learning and celibacy, but also to preserve the political order that depends upon Hilarion's marriage to Ida. In this case the men temporarily dress as women to gain access to the women's preserve. Transvestite roles serve the cause of male supremacy, and the men thereby regain authority over the women; equality for females fails as the women acquiesce to the men. Women's assumption of public power again results in disaster in *Iolanthe* as Mountararat, a member of the House of Lords, explains: "This comes of women interfering in politics." But women do so apparently only before the pacific effects of matrimony. Politics resumes its normal inanity when the women leave the political arena for marriage.

But some force blocks the panacea of marriage. Typically, Savoy society suffers from a moratorium on marriage. The pirates of Penzance sing "Here's the perfect opportunity / To get married with impunity," the rhyme implying that marriages are snatched from the grip of punishment, the arm of the law. As a triumph over a punitive adversary, marriage represents a heroic accomplishment. There are no women or no men to marry; laws prohibit flirting or marrying mortals; women segregate themselves from men. If, however, one loving young couple marry, the society will reestablish "normal" marital patterns. But an older woman with covert power, who may ally herself with an older man having overt political power, impedes the marriage. The action of the plot pacifies the older woman; mass marriage ensues. Both pacification and marriage affirm conventional gender arrangements. But as group marriages bring down the final curtain, a quality of defensiveness implies that there is a threat against which all the operas repeatedly reassert the primacy of this established cultural ordering.

The spectrum of British public offices represented in the casts seems unable to maintain the system. These male public figures—the Lord High Chancellor, Head Jailor, Captain of the Queen's Navy, Major General—display the face of British government. The "authority figures" of the repertory company, dressed in various official uniforms, sing lyrics absurdly juxtaposing political matters with family relationships. The officials acknowledge a power behind their authority, for the songs place them in a childlike relationship to an older woman who is either out of control or in too much control. The Rt. Hon. Sir Joseph Porter, K.C.B., First Lord of the Admiralty in *H.M.S. Pinafore*, "snaps his fingers at a foeman's taunts; / And so do his sisters and his cousins and his aunts!"[9] The apparent irrelevancy places Sir Joseph in familial dependency, as if he were still a child and his bravery supported by a matriarchal domestic structure. Public officials' feats resemble childhood games of mastery. The Duke of Plaza-Toro in *The Gondoliers* (Queen Victoria's favorite) leads "his regiment from behind. . . . But when away his regiment ran, His place was at the fore."

In addition to drawing parallels between the public and the private spheres, the same figuration in all the operas locates that political analogy not in the drawing room or the boudoir but in the nursery. The Savoy cultural order suffers from what Virginia Woolf in *Three Guineas* (1938) described as an "infantile fixation." Those heros Thomas Carlyle elevated in his treatise "On Heros, Hero-Worship and the Heroic in History"—judges, captains, kings, and poets—totter and caper about the Savoy stage. Reduced to their boyhood fears, they mask those fears with youthful bravado. Their plotting is as sophisticated, as sadistic, and as ineffectual as the elaborate games of children—not Rousseau's or Wordsworth's educable children but greedily impersonal and cruel ones. These domesticated heroes constitute a society of tin soldiers, of insomniac Chancellors who fear the dark, of Major-Generals who hear scary noises, of pirates who cry at the sight of orphans, and of a Ruler of the Queen's Navy who starts by doing domestic chores: cleaning windows, sweeping floors, and polishing a door handle.

The Lord High Chancellor in *Iolanthe*, who is afraid to fall asleep, describes a childish, surrealistic nightmare in which he is "crossing the Channel, and tossing about in a steamer from Harwich":

> And bound on that journey you find your attorney
> (who started that morning from Devon);
> He's a bit undersized, and you don't feel surprised
> when he tells you he's only eleven.
> Well, you're driving like mad with this singular lad
> (By the by, the ship's now a four-wheeler,)
> And you're playing round games, and he calls you bad names
> when you tell him that "ties pay the dealer."

Sing-song rhythms and childish phrases convey the singer's mental age. The Lord High Chancellor, "the highest officer of the Crown and an important member of the Royal Cabinet," according to the *OED*, "is the highest judicial functionary in the kingdom and ranks above all peers, spiritual and temporal, except Princes of the Blood and the Archbishop; he is Keeper of the Great Seal, is styled Keeper of his (her) Majesty's conscience, and is president and Prolocutor of the House of Lords; he presides over the Court of Chancery, appoints all justices of the peace, is the general guardian of infants, orphans and lunatics; is visitor of hospitals and colleges of royal foundation, and patron of all church livings under twenty marks in value." Gilbert portrays this eminence as dreaming himself the peer of an eleven-year-old, arguing over the rules of a childish game, a concern, Freud thought, of boys between the ages of six and twelve.

In short, the entire Savoy world floats on Her Majesty's Ship *Pinafore*, the uniform of childhood. This ship of state lacks a fully civilized moral code but maintains order through a strong fear of punishment. Absolute retribution for minor infractions—dismemberment, decapitation, kidnapping, extermination—is evaded at the last moment, usually by means of a technicality on the level of childish logic. In *Iolanthe*, for example, the fairies avoid mass slaughter by inserting one word, "doesn't," in the law "Every fairy must die who marries a mortal." This culture makes little distinction between saying something and doing it: "When Your Majesty says 'Let a thing be done,' it's as good as done—practically, it is done—because your Majesty's will is law" (*The Mikado*). Such is the law of His Majesty, the Baby, as Freud called this kind of tyrannizing.

The Savoyard trope infantalizes all characters except the older woman. The operas portray a culture suffering from the arbitrary and thereby frightening autocracy of a particular kind of woman, a woman on the edge—of domesticity, of middle age, of unfemininity. Not only powerful, she resembles a woman in the dodging time. Although she may appear as a governess instead of a governor—and she usually occupies a subplot—these assertive subordinates to state institutions glow in the light emanating from their real-life muse on her throne. In different ways in various operas she interferes with the course of the action. Because female authority in the operas bases itself on the emotions, both repressed and unrestrained, it seems an absurd yet distressing obstacle to male domination. The action corrects the gender upheaval she causes either by tricking her into submission or by marrying her off—or both.

To reinforce patriarchal authority through marriage, Gilbert adapted the performative device of ceremonial transvestism, a ceremony that "captures" the woman out of bounds. Natalie Zemon Davis points out that in ceremonies such as the English May and Epiphany festivals a man dressed as a woman would both claim female power and show how ridiculous a female in power could be.[10] Gilbert refined the traditionally transvestite dame figure of travesty, burlesque, and pantomime to create the middle-aged women of the Savoy.[11] Davis emphasizes that such ceremonies do not favor female rule; they are "ultimately sources of order and stability in a hierarchical society."[12] In the earlier transvestite performances the unattractive, overbearing woman takes off her clothes to reveal the man she really is, whereas Gilbert and Sullivan's operas pair off the frightful thing with a controlling man or an unwilling dupe.

As a stand-in for the Victorian nanny, the dame figure in each opera completes Gilbert and Sullivan's evocation of the nursery. Little Buttercup, Ruth, Lady Jane, the Fairy Queen, Lady Blanche, Katisha, Mad Margaret, Dame Carruthers, the Duchess of Plaza-Toro, Inez, and Lady Sophy all display some traits of the formidable and forbidding creature.[13] The woman is both excessive and sadistic, usually wielding enough power to enable or to prohibit marriages. She is a woman out of her place in the sense that she is dominant rather than submissive, but also, as in the case of Dame Carruthers in *Yeomen of the Guard*, she is only too horribly and symbolically in her place—the Tower of London, location of torture and punishment. The dame ghoulishly sings, "The screw may twist and the rack may turn," celebrating the power of the fortress that she in her person represents. In her sadism she resembles "an Irish woman, aged 40, and at the beginning of menopause" reported on by Havelock Ellis, who "stabbed five men with a hatpin. The motive was sexual and she told one of the men that she stabbed him because she 'loved' him."[14]

The woman is unruly, usually because at her advanced age she lacks a husband. If married, her time of life prevents most attempts to control her. The Duchess of Plaza-Toro in *The Gondoliers* browbeats her husband and smothers her daughter; Lady Blanche in *Princess Ida* tries to keep all maidens away from all men; Lady Jane in *Patience* chases after a younger man. But all three attempt to control the matrimonial patterns of young people. Unconfined by a family circle, the dame's meddling reaches directly into government—as in *Iolanthe*, where the Fairy Queen creates chaos in Parliament. In addition, the woman of a certain age may exert power and authority over the young. Inez in *The Gondoliers* abandons her own son, keeps the prince, and allows him to become lackey to the Duke of Plaza-Toro, while Ruth, the nursemaid in *The Pirates of Penzance*, apprentices her charge to an outlaw. Others, such as Lady Blanche, the ambitious intellectual in *Princess Ida*, and Lady Sophy, "an English lady of mature years and extreme gravity of demeanor and dress" in *Utopia Limited* (1893), serve to restrain spirited female behavior by denying it expression: Lady Blanche forbids sexuality; "learn your appetites to sub-due," she preaches; while Lady Sophy restrains all spontaneity whatever. In a parody of respectable Victorian behavior, she rehearses her Utopian charges in civilized English manners:

> English girls of highest class
> Shun all unrehearsed emotion.
> English girls of highest class
> Practice them before the glass.

Lady Sophy schools those English girls in sexual repression and patriotism, linking the two qualities.

Victoria's schooling of her children, grandchildren and eventually great-grandchildren in the proper ways to gain a mate resembles the repressive tones of Lady Sophy. In 1880 she wrote to her granddaughter Princess Victoria of Hesse, child of Alice, who had died: "You are right to be civil and friendly to the young girls you may occasionally meet, and to see them sometimes—but never make friendships; girls' friendships and intimacies are very bad and often lead to great mischief. . . . And at the dinners remember not to talk too much and especially not too loud and not across the table."[15] Like a nanny, Victoria acted as surrogate mother for many royal children, in the Savoy rituals represented by all Victoria's subjects. Like no other body of Victorian work, Gilbert and Sullivan's Savoy Operas present a world under Victoria according to a masculine subjectivity's infantalized gaze.[16]

Only once does Gilbert explicitly connect Savoy antics to the queen as an all-purpose mother surrogate. *The Pirates of Penzance* makes a point of motherlessness: pirates are orphans, the Major-General's daughters have no living mother, and Frederick's nursery maid decides his fate, for he has no memory of his mother. The denouement occurs when mass slaughter turns into a mass marriage because all the battling men suddenly kneel to the queen, as if she were their holy mother. Patriarchal marriage can then occur "with impunity" because fealty has been paid.

When not a schoolmarm or a mother, the Savoy dame shows evidence of a raging sexual appetite, akin to the climacteric woman's erotomania. The woman may fawn over uniformed men, not always of a proper rank or station in life. Sometimes she pursues any man whatever. The Queen of the Fairies in *Iolanthe*, for example, irresistibly adores "manly beauty" as embodied in Private Willis, B Company, first Grenadier Guard, a mere sentry: "Now here is a man whose physical attributes are simply godlike. That man has a most extraordinary effect upon me. If I yielded to a natural impulse, I should fall down and worship that man." In addition to her flirtatious behavior with Melbourne and Disraeli, Victoria's regard for handsome men of all ranks and stations was well documented and overt. Her attraction to a man in uniform seemed almost formulaic. That Disraeli referred to Victoria as the Fairy Queen would be known to many of the Savoy audience. Adding to her resemblance to the queen, the Fairy Queen remarks: "I see no objection to stoutness, in moderation." The Fairy Queen affirms Dr. Tilt's contention that the climacteric woman's ganglionic nervous system turned to fat, self-aggrandizement, and sexual desire.

The aging but still unruly Savoy woman's chaotic sexual desires inhibit others' ability to pair more conventionally. Unless governed, her relentlessly sexual urges disturb order. Lady Jane, the oldest of the "rapturous maidens" in *Patience*, sings a eulogy to her dimmed eyes and thinning hair and rhapsodizes upon the benefits of "rouge, lip-salve, and pearly grey / To 'make up' for lost time." Lady Jane's immoderate passion is fiercer than that of her younger rivals. Her body seems to swell, pumped up by the power of her emotion, as she not merely succumbs to but ferociously anticipates her middle-aged climacteric spread:

> Fading is the taper waist
>   Shapeless grows the shapely limb,
> And although severely laced,
>   Spreading is the figure trim!
> Stouter than I used to be,
>   Still more corpulent grow I—
> There will be too much of me
>   In the coming by and by!

Distorting by manic or hysterical exaggeration, Lady Jane voices not simply her own concern but a cultural fear that the menopausal woman will be too much to accommodate.

To control the aging woman's excess, the operas ritually end with a comedic marriage. But that conventional happy ending obscures life-threatening dangers. Dame Carruthers's "bloodthirsty words" need to be silenced with marriage—"Meryll's hand, not his heart." Since love is equated with conquest, the woman does not care what part she gets as she gloats:

> Rapture, rapture!
>   When love's votary,
> Flushed with capture,
>   Seeks a notary . . .

This rapture, based upon capture, resembles rape. Meryll sadly comments about the same captivity: "Doleful, doleful!" Thus, when the principals in *The Yeomen of the Guard* point out that the aim of the games of both love and war is to "capture the heart of a queen," the word in its context means much more than simply "most desirable woman." Capturing the queen in the sense of representing, burlesquing, and thereby defusing anxieties about Victoria herself is the point of these performances.

⇥ "Mine Is the Largest Circulation in the World" ⇤

Gilbert's aging but still forceful women are not direct allegories of the queen. Rather, Victoria's monarchy provides a political and social context for renewed energy and for the relevance of a stock figure, with counterparts in fairy tales, folk drama (Punch and Judy, for example), and the popular theatrical forms of the times. The constant source of her power derives from a needy woman's ability to thwart marriage and to interfere with the smooth running of the state. Each opera presents different aspects of the type, but the composite character, emerging from the oeuvre, presents not so much an equivalent as a symbolic counterpart of Queen Victoria.[17]

Savoy plots present a frustrated rite of passage—usually one symbolic of the passage from private to public world. Typically, a powerful woman interferes with this essential moment by interposing her own needs, by insisting upon her own arbitrary laws, or by coercing the male leader. The action overcomes the impediment by conquering the woman, pacifying her, and fragmenting her power. By means of the ritual, the dames of misrule become ruled, and civilization, symbolized by the marriage ceremony, continues. *The Pirates of Penzance, Ruddigore,* and *The Mikado* exemplify the general Savoy pattern of a ritual of pacification.

The Pirates of Penzance (1880) opens with a rite of passage: the pirates toast Frederick's twenty-first birthday, the end of his pirate indentures. The Pirate King defines the importance of this rite: "Yes, Frederick, from to-day you rank as a full-blown member of our band." But Frederick, idealistic, militaristic, and simple-minded, so strongly disapproves of his mentor's values that he pledges himself to the Pirate King's "extermination." Frederick thus enters a patriarchal world divided by male rivalry. Although apparently opposed, both pirates and sailors espouse the same social values. The pirates supposedly revolt against convention, but at the end confess that they are "all noblemen who have gone wrong." Because of their childlike vulnerability, they subvert their own rebellion. Every commandeered crew dupes them to the point of tears by claiming to be orphans. The pirates relent: "Of course," explains the Pirate-Lieutenant, "we are orphans ourselves, and know what it is."

No more heroic, the policemen describe themselves as "timidly inclined" and confess: "when the foeman bares his steel / . . . We uncomfortable feel." Because of their sympathy for, even identification with, the criminal, they find that "when constabulary duty's to be done . . . a policeman's lot is not an 'appy one." On both sides of the rivalry, the men act like boys who always wanted to be either outlaws or sheriffs but find themselves repelled by the reality of those roles. The father of the female chorus, Major-General Stanley, knows no more about military matters than a "novice in a nunnery." He rescues his daughters from marriage to the pirates by telling the lie that he is an orphan, claiming he would be lonely without them. He then allows himself to be captured by the pirates because he sings a paean to the beauties of nature as the enemy advances. Since the men represent different social classes as well as opposing sides of the law, in spite of posturing in uniforms, no male really wants to be a man.

Mabel and Ruth, the two female principals, compete for the love of Frederick, but the young Mabel encourages the youth to grow up and become heroic, whereas Ruth, the older woman, tries to impede his maturation and thus to maintain his dependence on her. As opposed to the squeamish males, the females do not find male violence particularly distasteful, sending their cowering swains to the fray: "Go to death and go to slaughter / . . . Go to glory and the grave." But while both young and old men alike dote upon the maidens, the old maid Ruth receives no mercy. She accurately describes herself as a "piratical maid of all work," true in more than one sense. In spite of her forty-seven years, she is still a "maid," a virgin looking for a mate. And she is "piratical," not only working for the pirates but, in her former work as a nurserymaid, pirating away her charge and apprenticing him to a pirate instead of to a pilot "through being hard of hearing." As a surrogate mother, Ruth fails to protect Frederick. Even worse, she does so not through neglect and only once in the past because of her infirmity but because of her over-bearing possessiveness.

Ruth's unwillingness to relinquish her charge when he comes of age bears uncomfortable similarities to Queen Victoria's relationship with Bertie, the Prince of Wales, who was kept in political infancy by not being allowed to exercise any authority. Like a boy who thinks his mother beautiful because he knows no other, the imaginatively limited Frederick admires Ruth only because he has no one with whom to compare her. "But I have been constantly at sea since I was eight years old," he explains, "and yours is the only woman's face I have seen during that time. I think it is a sweet face." Ruth's efforts to keep her charge innocent, like the efforts of Bertie's parents to shield him from carnal temptation, backfire when Frederick stumbles upon the entire female chorus. The initiation into adulthood brings with it the knowledge of other women, younger and more beautiful, and inevitably results in his rejecting Ruth. Such expected transfer of affections turns in this opera into a reason for revenge. Refusing to keep her place, the older woman seeks to extend her power beyond the nursery. This desire, frighteningly fierce and explicitly sexual, comes from an older woman, a woman in the dodging time. As Frederick readies himself to renounce Ruth, he sings:

> Your love would be uncomfortably fervid, it is clear
>> If, as you are stating,
>> It's been accumulating
> Forty-seven year—forty-seven year!

Ruth boils with climacteric nymphomania.

The combined revenges—of Ruth for having been renounced and the Pirate King for having been deceived—lead to military maneuvers between the pirates and the policemen. Just when the Major-General is about to be slaughtered, the whole company invokes the name of Queen Victoria, which reconciles their differences. "With all our faults, we love our Queen," warble the pirates. In a script connecting the lack of mothering with lawlessness, the queen represents the congruence of private maturation and public institutions. The nurturant aspect of mothering has been split off from its destructive capacity, represented by Ruth. The queen functions as the reconciling mother, while Ruth is the wicked stepmother. In the opera, Queen Victoria, unlike Ruth, has no body, no desire. Having been reduced to an invocation, she can be loved without ambivalence.

The woman invoked in *Ruddigore* (1887) represents the absolutely unlovable woman. Dead long before the curtain rises, her power outlasts her demise. The title announces a bloody subject, while its subtitle, *The Witch's Curse*, hints at its ominous initiator. The witch, the quintessential unruly woman, interferes with nature by mysterious means. Since cursing was a ritualized form of recourse for an unjustly treated member of the underclass,[18] this witch's curse represents a judgment against the Baronets of Ruddigore. Sir Rupert Murgatroyd, the first-cursed baron, delighted in breaking witches' bones, ducking them in the lake, and burning them. As one woman roasts on the village green, she hurls a curse from the midst of the flames. She requires a ritual daily crime from all descendants of Sir Rupert: henceforth the wages of virtue are death. The assumption behind the action of this opera, then, is that the cause of criminality in a family springs from an uneasy struggle for power between ruling men and unruly women:

> Sir Rupert Murgatroyd
> His leisure and his riches
> He ruthlessly employed
> In persecuting witches.

But worse, he committed these extraordinarily sadistic acts with gusto and with "no sense of shame or pity."

At the point where the action begins, the Baronets compulsively commit one daily crime. Learned by ghostly ancestral conditioning, their crimes curse the countryside with celibacy. No one can marry while the bad Baronet keeps himself alive by diurnal criminality. Linked to "the curse," the barons' actions parody it by releasing a tide of daily gore, or "ruddigore." Though trivialized by silly crimes, identified by the current bad Baronet with the naughtiness of children ("Poor children, how they loathe me—me whose hands are certainly steeped in infamy, but whose heart is as the heart of a little child!"), this child's world manages to stop everyone's reproductive clocks.

The opera opens as an endowed corps of professional bridesmaids languish for lack of employment. The principal women—Dame Hannah, Rose Maybud, and Mad Margaret—are paralyzed in their maidenhood by the Bad Baronets. These women act as "muses" to the Baronets' crimes and in turn represent female reactions to male aggression: Mad Margaret's wild frustration; Rose Maybud's seductiveness; Dame Hannah's meek, nervous victimhood. Mad Margaret, the dame figure, crazed by thwarted desire, traces her lineage not only to theatrical mad ladies but to the maddened fury represented in such paintings as Brueghel's terrifying *Dulle Griet* (meaning: "Mad Meg"), where a huge figure of a sword-and-skillet-wielding housewife seeking mastery breaks through the boundaries of the kitchen. Even in hell she is a menace. With her ravaging army of housewives, Mad Meg may be understood as archetypal of all women who usurp masculine prerogatives or otherwise defy propriety. Walter S. Gibson connects Brueghel's portrayal of this ferocious woman with the ascendancy of female monarchs in Europe at the time:

> When *Dulle Griet* was painted the Netherlands, France, England and Scotland were all governed by women. . . . It would be natural for Breugel and his contemporaries to ascribe ills of their time to the malice and ineptitude of female rule, and it is not impossible that their fears were given con-

crete expression in the figures of Dulle Griet and her horde
pursuing their reckless way past the portals of Hell.[19]

In a similar way and for analogous reasons, nineteenth-century fears
of ruling women were aroused. England, Spain, and Russia had queens
with memorable personalities. In addition, France's Marie-Antoinette's
alleged great sexual appetites (including accusations of incest with her
son) influenced nineteenth-century images of dangerous queens.[20]
Queen Isabella of Spain's hasty marriage to someone she loathed and
who apparently did not find women sexually appealing was performed
for political reasons but also to curb and mock what were seen as her
enormous and precocious sexual appetites. The German ancestry of
Catherine the Great, whose malicious sexuality was legendary, might
have appeared an all too close analogy to Victoria's German blood in
an age that believed in the inheritance of racial propensities.

If Dulle Griet's hellish terrorism reflects a misogyny fired by the fear
of ruling women, Gilbert's comic figure, "Mad Margaret, Daft Madge,
Crazy Meg" (also an object of pity: "Poor Peg"), expresses an affectionate misogyny employing the weapon of humor. Utterly disorderly,
Margaret dresses wildly, speaks extravagantly, and wanders wantonly on
the borders of the civilized village. Both in appearance and in emotion
she is all most un-English and unrehearsed. Killing obsesses her, but
she's killed only a fly and an affidavit. The etiology of her madness?

> No crime—
> 'Tis only
> That I'm
>   Love—lonely!
> That's all!

Mad Margaret suffers from curable erotomania. Having jilted her only
because of the witch's curse, Sir Despard Murgatroyd keeps his marriage promise after he discovers he is not really the eldest brother.
Under the benevolent despotism of marriage, Margaret binds her hair
and her wild impulses, rules a national school, and becomes a district
visitor, that precursor to a social worker. Marriage restores Mad
Margaret to partial sanity only, however, for she continues to lapse into
fits of passionate rhetoric. Sir Despard praises her for being "orderly,
methodical, neat; you have your emotions well under control; she
replies: "I have! (*wildly*) Master, when I think of all you have done for
me, I fall at your feet. I embrace your ankles. I hug your knees! (*Doing*

so.)" To control these fits, Margaret herself suggests that Despard employ a word charm to use "whenever I am about to relapse—some word that teems with hidden meaning—like 'Basingstoke.'" The admonitory charm identifies pacification with a middle-class Victorian town and pokes fun at the sovereign whose values were considered appropriate for those dwelling there. Her erotomania largely absorbed by sacramentally sanctioned sex, Margaret's other climacteric symptoms are disciplined not in the madhouse but in the suburbs.

Although the parallels between Margaret and Queen Victoria—as in most "dame figures" of the Savoy Operas—are broad, the spectacular adoration practiced by Victoria for Albert resembles that of Margaret's for Despard. Victoria's letters and diaries record the voice of a woman of extremes, with underlining running to as much as triple or quadruple; some of Victoria's favorite adverbs: intensely, excessively, "schockingly" (sic) show her verbal attempts to match her affect. The day after her wedding, her words throw themselves at Albert's knees, at his ankles: "I [am] the happiest, happiest Being that ever existed. Really, I do not think it *possible* for anyone in the world to be *happier*, or as happy as I am. He is an Angel."[21] Gradually regulating her immoderate passion, Albert properly Basingstokes her. By the time of *Ruddigore*, Albert lived only in effigy and memory, and the living men who filled Victoria's heart—John Brown, Benjamin Disraeli, Abdul Karim—had neither rank nor privileges to control her. Her heart could be won, but, barring marriage, how could anyone keep it captured?

Not simply controlling women's sexuality, matrimony, when judiciously entered upon, offers social advancement. The Ruddigore bridesmaids attest to this value when they welcome the gentry as appropriate lovers in preference to the honest but awkward "shepherds and plowmen and drovers and cowmen" who populate their unpastoralized countryside. Rose Maybud, the most likely bride, may be bewitching, but she changes amorous allegiances with heartless rapidity. Marriage to someone or other is her goal. She quotes her particular gospel, the etiquette book in the same way as the devil quotes Scripture: to get her way.[22] Her name (like Mabel's in *Pirates*) is appropriate, since May, Flora's month in the Roman calendar, was thought to be a period in which women were powerful, their desires at the most immoderate.[23]

Queen Victoria's obsession with marrying off her children virtually endowed a corps of bridesmaids, although she could be squeamish in the matter of her daughters' marriages. She arranged marriages as supreme matchmaker of Europe, writing to her daughter about suitable mates for her progeny. In 1862 she commented to Vicky about her son Alfred's (Affie) marital interests:

> I think . . . dearest, Dagmar [sister of Alexandra, eventual
> Princess of Wales] should be entirely dropped and the
> mother encouraged to give her to the future Czar if that
> will secure Alix. . . . The young Princess of Altenburg would
> be a very good match for dear Affie—as well as the
> Hanoverian and possibly the eldest Weimar may turn out
> less ugly. There is also the young Princess of Württemberg
> for him; never mind equality of age. How many marry peo-
> ple of the same age?[24]

The queen could also believe she distrusted marriages, despite her own
marital happiness. In reference to Beatrice's impending marriage, she
remarked, "I hate marriages especially of my daughters."[25] She seemed
to justify her feelings by reference to her deceased daughter Alice's
opinions:

> One thing I know she felt most strongly about and that was
> against early marriages for her girls—or getting them mar-
> ried for marrying's sake. Besides a married daughter is
> never, as a rule, the same use to her father or mother as an
> unmarried one—whose only object is their home and its
> interests. The longer I live the more I think marriages only
> rarely are a real happiness.[26]

Atmospheric ambivalence regarding marriage pervades *Ruddigore*,
as if it captured Victoria's double messages. The endowed corps of professional bridesmaids betokens the political stakes in the marriage
industry; "the witch's curse" restrains the same action that maintains
monarchies. Queen Victoria allows, eventually blesses, her daughter's
marriage; likewise, in the opera, the witch's curse is lifted, and Rose,
"queen of maiden-kind," marries.

If Mad Margaret marries up to the relatively low aristocratic title of
a baronet, Katisha in *The Mikado* (1885) aspires to marry royalty. As in
Ruddigore, the ritual aspects of this opera partly explain its bloody pre-
occupations and further suggest some fantasies behind its obsession
with decapitation. Purportedly set in Japan, the behavior issues from an
English nursery. The fake Japanese names resemble baby names,
expressive of primitive desires, functions, and judgments in baby talk:
Yum-Yum, Peep-Bo, Pitti-Sing, Ko-Ko, Nanki Poo, Pooh-Bah, Pish-Tush,
Titipu. Yet, despite the nursery perspective, the town of Titipu concerns
itself with violently repressing courtship rituals.

Ko-ko, a "cheap tailor," is condemned to die for flirting, but his outward demonstration of desire elevates him instead to the position of Lord High Executioner on the logic that "he can't chop off another's head until he's cut his own off." The Mikado, a great totem figure, attempts to "steady" the passions of young men by decreeing "that all who flirted, leered, or winked / (Unless connubially linked) / Should forthwith be beheaded."

Poised in this sexually charged environment, the city of Titipu functions precariously on illogic and hypocrisy until the arrival of Katisha, a woman fiercely out of her place, upsets the balance. As daughter-in-law elect, she avoids direct blood relationship with the Mikado while actually ruling him.[27] Whereas the Mikado himself does not appear until act 2, Katisha arrives at the end of the first act, at the crucial prenuptial moment, to prevent the temporary marriage of Nanki Poo and Yum-Yum. The chorus recognizes her elemental power: "Why who is this whose evil eyes / Rain blight on our festivities?" they ask. The evil eye emanates from the vengeful soul of the older woman abandoned for a younger one. Her unappeased energies loosed upon nature, pervert it, raining blight. "Give me my place," she wails, calling upon the elements to wreak vengeance. But for the comedy, she invokes the primitive world of Lear, of elements out of their place:

> Ye torrents roar!
> Ye tempests howl!
> Your wrath outpour
>   With angry growl!
> Do ye your worst, my vengeance call
> Shall rise triumphant over all!

Such rage cannot go unanswered; it needs a victim to appease it—in this case, a prey/spouse. Formidably ugly, Katisha appeals to an "adult taste" with an "educated palate." She nonetheless claims esoteric attractions. Although her face is a "caricature," her left shoulder blade is a "miracle of loveliness," and her right elbow has a "fascination that few can resist." As the Mikado is a totem figure, so Katisha is a grotesque saint, a "part object" in the Kleinian sense, who can be worshiped only in pieces. In her entirety she is hard to endure, alternately coy and fierce, like the queen whom she resembles in part—or in parts.

Katisha, like Victoria, was "tough as a bone with a will of her own." Katisha is the only figure who is exempt from the Mikado's decrees. All his subjects "cheerfully own his sway, except for his daughter-in-law elect." The object of pilgrimages, she holds court on alternate Tuesdays and Thursdays. People travel miles and miles specifically to view her elbow. "My circulation is the largest in the world," she boasts. Her claims for herself ally her body with the British Empire upon which the sun never sets. She resembles Queen Victoria as *Mater Mundi*.[28]

To intensify her similarity to Victoria, Katisha indulges in ecstasies of mourning. Two of her songs bewail her loneliness in dirges evocative of the queen's excessive grief.[29] By 1885 in *The Mikado*, a huge woman moaning over her solitary state would recall the flamboyant bereavement of the queen, who typically referred to herself as alone, even when surrounded by crowds of relatives:

> The hour of gladness
>   Is dead and gone;
> In silent sadness
>   I live alone!
> The hope I cherished
>   All lifeless lies,
> And all has perished
>   Save love, which never dies!

Katisha's loneliness echoes her sovereign's. The experience of being alone dates from the first day of Victoria's reign when it expressed her wonderful sense of release. At first a declaration of independence, Victoria's claims to be alone became a dirge to her widowed state. In the midst of the Jubilee celebration at Westminster Abbey, for example, she meticulously noted her family with sober but manic accuracy. Surrounded by "sons, sons-in-law, grandsons . . . and grandsons-in-law . . .Daughters, daughters-in-law . . . granddaughters, and granddaughter-in-law," not to mention the clergy, the enormous crowds from the palace, the Chelsea pensioners, people sitting on houses, the queen described herself: "I sat alone."[30]

In another solo, "The Living I," Katisha echoes the "evil eye" of her initial appearance, giving another explanation for the blight that "reigns" over the land. In her unabashed lusts, her large body, her sacred parts, and her need for power, Katisha is Gilbert's most explicit parody of his female sovereign.

⟿   "Beauty in the Bellow of the Blast"   ⟾

Gilbert's depiction of large, aging, ruling women symbolizes the threat to Victorian patriarchal structure that a woman in power poses. While the operas are not conventional political allegories, every plot depends on the apparent contradiction in terms implied by a female sovereign.

Advertisement for "The Mikado" bustle in a booklet commemorating Queen Victoria's Golden Jubilee, New York, 1887.

By figuring the society as an immense nursery, they parody the topsy-turvy gender protocols of Victoria's long reign.

The unruly women in the Savoy Operas together represent a composite portrait of the object of social, political, and psychological concerns. Gilbert's images of the woman out of her place function together as a cracked and crazed mirror, reflecting a figure of ridicule, looming too large, exaggerated in the infantile eyes that view her. She is shameful and outrageous, vigorously but chaotically expressive: "There is eloquence outpouring when the lion is a-roaring" (*The Mikado*). But she is also a figure of instruction, repressive and reproving, prudish and seductive. When Nanki Poo asks Katisha, "Do you fancy you are elderly enough?" she identifies herself with romantic ruins and affirms, "I am sufficiently decayed." The Savoy climacteric woman, paired off with somebody or other, calms down.

Making light of fears of the woman of a certain age, the Savoy's political body fears and loves her, "with all our [and her] faults." Queen Victoria's influence as muse has not been sufficiently recognized, but the Savoy Operas present an oeuvre that performs the body politic, paying its sovereign modified homage.

6

DOMESTICITY; OR, HER LIFE AS A DOG

The good Earl of Shaftesbury once said: "Domestic life, by
the all-merciful Providence of God, is the refuge and stronghold of
morality: the honour, dignity, and mainstay of nations." How well
this great truth has been understood in "England's Royal Home"
we need not say. The Queen's household has been—what every
palace should be—a model home.

—*Charles Bullock, 1897*

Given the English love of dogs, it is not surprising that Queen Victoria should be associated with them. There is more to the association than simple sentiment. Many cultural historians find direct relationships between eighteenth- and nineteenth-century English attitudes toward animals, colonial subjects, women, and the lower classes. Her intimate friendships with dogs, her own womanly service to her realm, and the "ethnic" servants in her Household form a loose pattern of interconnections that compare to representations of Victorian home life.[1] By considering the Victorian monarchy as both constructing and being constructed by these attitudes, and by giving precedence to the animal perspective, one might devise a fable of Queen Victoria's life as a dog.

When would one begin such a fable? Would it be in 1835, when the Princess and her mother, the Duchess of Kent, became patrons of the Society for the Prevention of Cruelty to Animals (SPCA)? (Five years later Queen Victoria permitted the SPCA to affix "Royal" to its name.[2]) Or would it be 1837, when on June 20 Victoria became Queen of England and also owner of Edwin Landseer's painting, *Dash*, a "pet portrait," a genre that would become associated with her? The year

Dash, by Sir Edwin Landseer, 1836. *Illustration from the Royal Archives, by permission of The Royal Collection © Her Majesty Queen Elizabeth II*

1838 is also a good choice; on June 28 that year, the day of her coronation, the nineteen-year-old queen threw off her weighty robes, gathered her skirts, and ran up to her room to bathe Dash, her best friend at that time. Whichever date one chooses, the queen spent the early years of her life in the intimate company of dogs and never forgot her debt to them.

As late as 1880, for instance, Victoria wrote a condolence letter to Vicky, upon the slaying and mutilation of the princess's pet cat. Her daughter had confessed to shame over her inability to stop crying:

> And now let me say how horrified and how distressed I am about your cat! It is monstrous—and the man ought to be hung on the tree [the dead cat was hung on a tree, with her nose cut off]. I could cry with you as I adore my pets. . . . We always put a collar with V. R. on our pet cats and that preserves them. . . . I think it right and only due to the affection of dumb animals, who (the very intelligent and highly developed ones) I believe to have souls, to mourn for them truly and deeply.[3]

Although Victoria preferred dogs to cats, in comforting her daughter she did not exaggerate. Dash's epitaph on his gravestone read:

> Here lies DASH, the Favourite Spaniel of Queen Victoria,
> By whose command this Memorial was Erected.
> He died on the 20 December, 1840 in his 9th year.
> His attachment was without selfishness,
> His playfulness without malice,
> His fidelity without deceit.
> READER, if you would live beloved and die regretted, profit
>   by the example of DASH.[4]

On the grounds of her dwellings, pet gravestones marked sites for mourning their loss and praying for their immortal souls.[5] Dash's epitaph indicates that pets could also set a moral example. Victoria apparently quoted Schopenhauer: "If it were not for the honest faces of dogs, we should forget the very existence of sincerity."[6]

Victorians revised their thinking about animals, first recognizing their ability to suffer pain and, as an extension, to have other feelings in common with humans. Their idea of the human place in the animal world marked a changing relationship to animals, signaled first by the founding in 1824 of the SPCA and written into succeeding acts of Parliament, in 1839 and 1854, against cruelty to dogs. The English had long regarded their dogs as companions who may have possessed souls but who spoke in a different tongue and whose transgressions could be punished as one would punish a human: by hanging, for example.[7] But the idea that the canine world deserved respect independent of its effect upon human character and human needs and the concomitant excusing of animals from legal penalties grew from a late-eighteenth-century sense that all creatures were fellow mortals, though by and large the domesticated ones were more lovable.[8] Victorian pets, in particular, could yearn and grieve and could act with moral rectitude. What's more, they expressed themselves within domestic spaces resembling ideal Victorian homes.[9]

Paradoxically, the romantic notion of a commonality among creatures gave license to human domination of the animal kingdom; appropriation of their creaturehood as humans once or twice removed assumes that humans could speak for animals and, by extension, for human diversity as well.[10] If animals were no longer hanged for human crimes, they were no longer admired for their difference from humans. Rather, loved animals were assimilated into human likeness.

⇝ Victoria's Domestics ⇜

Osborne, 14 Aug. 1886: respecting the dogs:
I. As regards her poor dear friends the dogs, she would repeat that
no dogs should ever be killed by police unless the veterinary surgeon
declared they were mad. That dogs who were close to their masters
or mistresses or their house door, poor quiet dogs, should be left
alone and not molested. A faithful dog will often snap and
snarl and bite if interfered with by strangers.
—Queen Victoria to Henry Ponsonby

Queen Victoria embodied contradictory meanings of the domestic. Hers was an inspired use of the concept not simply that the domestic is political (a more recent perception) but that the political could be domestic. She herself blessed the domestic construction of her power, attributing her popularity to her happy home life. Following publication of her Highland journal, she liked best the responses from the "cheap edition for the poor": "It is very gratifying to see how people appreciate what is simple and right and how especially my truest friends—the people—feel it. They have (as a body) the truest feeling for family life."[11] She knew that her portrayal of family life promoted the dissemination of domesticating values, with herself as their symbol.

One kind of authority identified with Queen Victoria's domesticating virtues could be wielded by any housewife. Rather than grand or queenly, such domestic authority seems trivial. As many studies of Victorian gender relations show, middle-class women came to represent the domestic ideal, the end of the civilizing process. Because it was seen as secondary to public affairs, womanly domesticating ability became a gentle way of representing British imperialism. Victoria's domestic virtues—seen as middle-class—played out a global metaphor of the empire as one happy family. Queen Victoria embodied an imperial feminine figure, a domesticated queen who was imagined as civilizing all creatures in her empire.

Domesticated energies serve men's larger needs. Some heroines in Victorian novels are presented as inadequately civilized and undergo the sort of taming that will suit them to Victorian parlors. Bella Wilfer in Dickens's *Our Mutual Friend* (1864–65), for instance, provides an example of "happy" domestication, while George Eliot's Maggie Tulliver in *The Mill on the Floss* (1860) illustrates the consequences of its failure. Both characters, unhappily blessed with minds and tempers of their own, inflict typical damages upon families unable to govern them. As opposed to Bella's problematic values and willful temperament, however, Maggie suffers from nonconformity to conventional femininity. Her father believes she would have been better off had she been a boy, while her extended family describes her as "half-wild," a frequent description also of colonial subjects. Maggie displays her sense of regal entitlement by running off to "Gypsydom," where she thinks she could be queen. By allying Maggie with a nomadic group who live on the semi-wilds of proper English towns, the novel positions her, like them, as half-domesticated. When she encounters some gypsies, she inquires about their present queen's qualifications: "I'm only thinking that if she isn't a very good queen you might be glad when she died, and you could choose another. If I was a queen, I'd be a very good queen, and kind to everybody."[12] In less than an hour, she abandons the idea: "Maggie felt that it was impossible she should ever be queen of these people, or even communicate to them amusing and useful knowledge."[13] Although modified by experience, her aspiration remains. She does not want to be queen consort; she wants to rule. As a queen in her own mind but frequently in disgrace, feared as unmarriageable, yet passionate in all her attachments, she can find no place in the world. Implicitly linking notions of a queen with freedom to shape others to one's will, Maggie Tulliver exemplifies her author's inability to imagine a world where vigorous independence and incomplete domestication might find rewards. One queen does not make room for others; Queen Victoria did not necessarily ease the way for ordinary women to gain autonomy. Her family persona parodied the most domesticated wife of her most vigorous patriarchal subjects. On their part, Victorian novelists found no happy ending for a woman with longings beyond the garden gate.

For that reason, Dickens's Bella Wilfer offers a more likely model for a Victorian woman as a queen. She becomes an obedient wife, queen of her husband's heart—what Queen Victoria came to desire for herself as well as for her female subjects. Like Victoria, Bella initially enjoyed being the boss, but devotion to a man tames her. John Harmon Sr. watches an unknown savage little girl intimidating her father by throwing a tantrum. Inspired by Bella's disposition, Harmon designates her in his will to be his son's fiancée. Convinced of Bella's ungovernability (an indication of class bias as well), he concocts a plan that will either subject his son to a domineering, selfish wife, or will disinherit him. Though participating in the transaction, Bella accurately characterizes herself as akin to a domesticated animal: "Was it not enough that I should have been willed away, like a horse, or a dog, or a bird?"[14] She allies herself with those animals identified with Victorian women—the first two associated with women in pornography, the third with kept women. Dickens's plot confounds such corruption and malice through further domestication. Bella meets her moral superior in Lizzie Hexam, whose selfless love resembles that of the best pet, the sort whose impulses are more pure than men's but who nonetheless unquestioningly adores its master. Bella then recognizes and is repelled by her own nature, calling herself a "limited little brute."[15] Upon feeling humanizing love, she relinquishes her animal ambitions and marries a man she believes lacks a fortune.

As proof of her domestication through marriage, Bella cooks for the first time in her parents' house. New docility arises through study of "a sage volume entitled The Complete British Family Housewife, which she would sit consulting, with her elbows on the table and her temples on her hands, like some perplexed enchantress poring over the Black Art."[16] Thus civilized, Bella all but trots to her beloved master with the newspaper she has been trying to comprehend in order to make herself worthy of his love. Through figuration Dickens acknowledges domestication's precariousness. Who would like to have a sorceress, a Vivian in the guise of a British Family Housewife out of Mrs. Ellis's *Wives of England*, stirring the kettle and delivering one's newspaper? In a flash, domesticity could break down; the soup reveal itself—too late—as speckled eel's broth.[17]

Queen Victoria stamps her approval on Bella's domestication. Bella writes a conciliatory letter to her mother after she had eloped with a man—John Harmon disguised—whom she knows as John Rokesmith. They mail the letter: "Then John Rokesmith put the Queen's countenance on the letter—when had Her Gracious Majesty looked so benign as on that blessed morning!"[18] A contingent domesticity changes the dour image to a benevolent one. Victoria's graciousness could turn to something else on a morning not so blessed, but that possibility occurs in other domestic arrangements in the novel—the Lammles' marital disaster in particular—that comment on Bella's happy ending.

In the years leading up to the 1864–65 publication of *Our Mutual Friend*, the stamp was the most commonly recognized image of the queen. Meditating on what he calls "the idea of the Queen," W. T. Stead, editor of the *Pall Mall Gazette*, thought back on his earliest images of Victoria and remembered the stamp John Rokesmith affixed to Bella's letter: "the first picture of the Queen that ever attracted my attention. It is the portrait by which she is best known to millions, the only picture of their sovereign indeed which many of them have ever seen. It is the Queen's head on the penny-postage-stamp. The old unperforated red stamp was commonly called in our home a Queen's Head."[19] The stamp in Dickens authorizes the kind of domesticity that resolves problematic family structure by means of sentimentality. By giv-

The Queen's Head: first penny postage stamp.

ing the queen's head the power to bless Bella and John's marriage, Dickens pays homage to Victoria as goddess of the English hearth.

⤳ Her Life as a Dog ⤴

Nothing brutalises people more than cruelty to dumb animals, and to dogs, who are the companions of man, it is especially revolting.
—*Queen Victoria*

Our Queen . . . may defy any sovereign line to show a loftier pedigree.
—*George Russell French*

Victorian animal painters showed animals as family folk, with recognizable family values. Dogs appeared on valentines, while Sir Edwin Landseer, painter of Dash, gained a reputation as the "Shakespeare of the world of dogs." Largely because of the queen's patronage, his pet portraits set the standard for the genre. Queen Victoria so loved the Dash portrait that she commissioned *Queen Victoria's Favorite Pets*, a painting that includes the greyhound Hector, Dash majestically ensconced on a velvet footstool, and Nero, a deerhound. The animals, not merely humanized but entitled, enjoy their regal surroundings.

Landseer added the human royal family to the pet portrait to create a representation of domesticity that became one of the most reproduced paintings of Victoria and Albert. *Windsor Castle in Modern Times* (1841) captures a characteristic Victorian sentiment. The title directs attention to the royal dwelling, emphasizing how the new regime differs from the various monarchies preceding it. *Modern* refers to Victoria and Albert's domestic pastimes: a regulated life producing happy progeny and well-trained pets. Despite its luxurious setting, their domestic life institutes a moral ideal to which those of humbler dwellings could aspire. The painting shows a formally dressed Victoria with a flower in hand, standing as the highest figure, a position proper to the monarch. However, her pliant attitude and her standing erect along with the child and dogs convey authority to her husband. She faces him as a servant

Her Majesty's Favorite Pets, also known as *Hector, Nero and Dash with the Parrot, Lory,* by Sir Edwin Landseer, 1837–1838. *Illustration from the Royal Archives, by permission of The Royal Collection © Her Majesty Queen Elizabeth II.*

Windsor Castle in Modern Times, by Sir Edwin Landseer, 1841–1845. *Illustration from the Royal Archives, by permission of The Royal Collection © Her Majesty Queen Elizabeth II.*

might approach a seated master or mistress, for in royal protocol the monarch requires others to stand unless given permission to sit. Whereas Victoria looks demurely down, Albert's clearly visible gaze reinforces his authority. Two dogs, Albert's Eos gazing into her master's eyes and Dandie, the Skye terrier, sitting up to lick the prince consort's hand, act out Victoria's adoration. Queen Victoria joins the household paraphernalia, on a par with pets and children, a happy subordinate within a domestic setting.

The window tenting underscores the room as an inner sanctuary, with disciplined gardens out-of-doors, where the queen's mother takes her circumscribed exercise, pushed in a perambulator by a liveried servant. Wild tree limbs outside the garden wall contrast to well-regulated interiors. By shooting every undomestic creature encroaching upon the domestic space, Albert has exhibited his fitness as man of the house. Vicky plays among Islay, the Skye terrier, who is begging, and dead wild animals. The painting might be read as allegorical of a new kind of monarchy, a modern one. Its generic allusions to pet portraits enlarge the possibilities of both kennel and castle to represent various denizens

Queen Victoria and Princess Beatrice with Retrievers, etching from a photograph, c. 1875

of the English imperial imagination. Its title could be Her Life as a Dog, with Windsor Castle the best doghouse in the kingdom.

Victoria herself seemed to blur the boundaries between her human family life and her life among the dogs. She had a special cottage built on the border of her kennels. From its bow-windowed parlor she could watch her dogs exercising while at the same time view Landseer's dog paintings hanging on its walls as if they were family portraits. In the many photographs in which Queen Victoria self-consciously poses her pets, she and the animals frequently seem almost to be one species. An elegantly structured photograph of herself with her youngest daughter, Beatrice, portrays both her and her daughter on the lawn with their pet retrievers. Beatrice leans over so that her silhouette nearly imitates the dog at her knees, while Victoria's pose seems to provide a frontal view of the two dogs in profile who flank her. With no other frame of refer-ence—no houses or other humans—the two women blend with the pets, creating an integrated portrait, Pets on a Lawn.[20] In a formal por-trait, the dog seated on a Gothic chair completes the outline of Victoria's dress, so that the two seem to be the same person, an impres-sion reinforced by the matching color of their "coats." Read another way, the pose resembles many photographs of Victoria and Albert,

Queen Victoria and her dog Sharp, 1867. *By permission of The Hulton Picture Company.* The portrait follows the genre in which one of a married couple sits while the other stands. Mayall took a series of such portraits of Victoria and Albert in 1860, which became well-known as cartes de visites.

where one is standing and the other seated. The Gothic chair resembles a throne; the two figures seem, if not as one, at least as one species.

Landseer's genre scenes of dogs imply the influence of human values. *There's No Place Like Home* (1837), for instance, painted the year of Victoria's accession, portrays a similar sentiment to that of *Windsor Castle in Modern Times* but at the opposite end of the social scale. A nondescript dog stands in front of a house constructed from a recycled barrel, whose unpainted wood indicates his class as a common terrier (pedigrees did not become regularized until 1840, the year of Victoria and Albert's marriage).[21] The snail in the foreground signifies that all creatures need homes, this one emblematic of such a "natural" need. Snail and dog bring the viewer into the commonality of all living things.

There's No Place Like Home, etching by C. G. Lewis from a painting by Sir Edwin Landseer, 1837.

When Landseer exhibited the painting at the British Institution Show in 1842, the catalog caption quoted the familiar ballad lines:

> "Mid pleasures and palaces though we may roam
> Be it ever so humble etc."

These typical sentiments encourage all Victorian classes to consider the domestic ideal as a universal one.

Dickens represented that same domestic ideal by democratizing the castle. His comic character Wemmick, the law clerk in *Great Expectations* (1860–1861), dwells in the humble suburb of Walworth in a castle fit for the modern worker. When he is in the city, the clerk accepts "portable property" from convicts about to be hanged, but when home he sweetly shows "the Castle" to his new friend Pip:

> Wemmick's house was a little wooden cottage in the midst of plots of garden, and the top of it was cut out and painted like a battery mounted with guns. . . .
>
> I think it was the smallest house I ever saw; with the queerest gothic windows (by far the greater part of them sham), and a gothic door, almost too small to get in at.
>
> "That's a real flagstaff, you see," said Wemmick, "and on Sundays I run up a real flag. . . . After I have crossed this bridge, I hoist it up—so—and cut off the communica-

tion." . . . It was very pleasant to view the pride with which he hoisted it up and made it fast. . . . "At nine o'clock every night, Greenwich time," said Wemmick, "the gun fires. There he is, you see! And when you hear him go, I think you'll say he's a Stinger."

The piece of ordnance referred to, was mounted in a separate fortress, constructed of lattice-work.

"Then, at the back," said Wemmick, "out of sight, so as not to impede the idea of fortifications . . . there's a pig, and there are fowls and rabbits; then I knock together my own little frame, you see, and grow cucumbers; and you'll judge at supper what sort of a salad I can raise. So, sir," said Wemmick, . . . "if you can suppose the little place besieged, it would hold out a devil of a time in point of provisions."[22]

Wemmick's castle parodies the castle at Windsor, including Albert's model farms at the back. During the year of Victoria's Diamond Jubilee, the Reverend Canon Wilton, M.A., acclaims Victoria's ability to transform an austere castle, a palace, and country houses into a national model, what he called a "sympathising Pattern":

A Good Queen

A nation's myriad homes in thee
Their sympathising Pattern see;
For thou hast dignified Home-life
As daughter, mother, friend, and wife
And round the brow of England's Queen
A fair domestic wreath is seen.

If Windsor's grey historic pile,
Or sea-breeze of soft southern isle,
Call thee; or heathery banks and braes,
Or the loud city's mighty maze:
Where'er thy Royal footsteps roam,
Castle or palace still is Home.

A sanctified domestic space of home, also a fortified space, indicates warlike sentiments protecting domesticity. But Victoria's fair domestic wreath softens the militaristic "grey pile" into a home. To domesticate the world, to turn it into a home, sometimes required severe measures that might nevertheless prove insufficient. On the margins of Canon Wilton's

Comical Dogs, etching by C. G. Lewis from a painting by Sir
Edwin Landseer, 1836.

praise, as in Dickens's celebration of domesticity, lurks some recognition
that the uncivilized may be banished but may return. In *Great Expectations*,
the convict Magwitch is transported to Australia, but his influence never
leaves the country. Part of the price of Wemmick's domestic tranquillity
involves transactions with such untamed Others, who continue to return.
Windsor Castle in modern times provides a fitting emblem not only for
the family within its walls but for the institutions required to maintain it.

Some of Landseer's dog paintings also encode imperial assumptions,
not of banishing the imperfectly socialized but of socializing them.
Making explicit the connection between these animals, human domesticity, and imperial attitudes, *Comical Dogs* (1836) draws on the relations
between Victorian convictions about home, marriage, and the kind of
domestication involved in colonial practices. Landseer's humorous
painting connects Scottish nationality—or better, its "ethnicity"—ani-
mality, and domesticity. The viewer appreciates the comedy not as one of
the Scots who might wear the dogs' tam-o'-shanter or poke bonnet but as
one who would experience an affectionate condescension. The dogs
form a domestic couple, happily conjoined in a ménage à deux. While
the male dog gazes cannily at the viewer, the tuft of hair before one eye
making him appear to wink, the female sits demurely on a rug, smoking
a pipe, disclosing her class and rural background. The husband poses at
the doorway of their simple wooden dwelling, its honest weathered

boards signifying the inhabitant's character. These "comical" dogs reflect a colonizing attitude, where picturesque natives charm the viewers by being somewhat like themselves yet somehow lesser. Domestication controls their potential for danger. Nationalized—domestic as opposed to foreign—their difference from the viewer confirms colonial power to classify and dominate. Much like the "Balmorality" of the royal family's Scottish identity, the Scot and the dog are assimilated to British desires.

Landseer first came to the Highlands in 1824 to see Sir Walter Scott and loved the land.[23] His visit, a pilgrimage to the author who had most contributed to the nineteenth-century idea of Scotland, inspired paintings that can be understood in the context of the racializing project that sought to bring Scotland into the idea of empire.[24] Michael Hechter terms that English assimilation of "the celtic fringe," a kind of "internal colonialism" that predates and postdates the empire. Whereas internal colonialism, experienced as an affectionate recognition of inferior copies of a British ideal, finds comic expression in Landseer's painting, Charles Kingsley's 1860 alienated reaction to viewing the Irish uncovers a brutality in the animal metaphor:

> I am haunted by the human chimpanzees I saw along that hundred miles of horrible country. I don't believe they are our fault. I believe there are not only many more of them than of old, but they are happier, better, more comfortably fed and lodged under our rule than they ever were. But to see white chimpanzees is dreadful; if they were black, one would not feel it so much, but their skins, except where tanned by exposure, are as white as ours.[25]

Victoria sometimes characterized the Irish as "horrid people," but she also could find them beautiful. When in 1850 she visited Ireland, she encountered the same misery that caused Kingsley to recoil: "You see more ragged and wretched people here than I ever saw anywhere else," she noted to Uncle Leopold. "*En revanche*, the women are really handsome—quite in the lowest class—as well at Cork as here; such beautiful black eyes and hair and such fine colours and teeth."[26] Victoria regards the Irish with the objectivity of a connoisseur of animal husbandry. As the Irish Question becomes more and more intractable, however, she regards them as undomesticatable. To Earl Cowper, viceroy in Ireland, she wrote in December 1880: "She is sorry but not surprised to see how gloomily and anxiously he speaks of the state of Ireland, and how little hope he has of improvement. It is very dreadful and very disheartening, and the more one does for the Irish the more

Dignity and Impudence, by Sir Edwin Landseer, 1839. *Printed courtesy of the Trustees of the Tate Gallery.*

unruly and ungrateful they seem to be."[27] The unruly Irish, without humanizing emotions such as gratitude, cannot be tamed.

Landseer's paintings similarly extend Victoria's realm from the colonial to the animal world, personifying the human variousness of her empire. Landseer's *Dignity and Impudence* (1839) draws on an allegorical tradition of portraying humans in animal forms. In endowing dogs with human qualities, the Victorian painter suggests an imperial family. The painting depicts domestic tranquillity, with the dogs ensconced in their home. At first the dogs—though actually male—might appear as yet another celebration of heterosexual marriage, the sage husband towering over his perky wife. It might be seen as an animalizing precursor to Victoria and Albert's enshrinement of happy home life in a modernized Windsor Castle, shorn of its premodern excess. Related to that generic theme yet more globally, the two different breeds and temperaments confirm that all different types and hues, sizes and shapes, can live under one roof, a British one. *Dignity and Impudence* appeals to a similar

The Scrapegrace of the Family, by Tom Merry, *St. Stephen's Review,* 1886. In 1883 there was a series of dynamite sawdust explosions in Glasgow and London. Queen Victoria believed that a great source for evil in Ireland emanated from what she called "secret societies" and "this monstrous language of the Irish Rebel Fenians."

sentiment as *Comical Dogs* but enlarges domesticity to comprehend differing species. In its multicultural perspective, its subtext gestures to a harmonious imperial sentiment, where persons can all find a home in the British global castle in modern times, with Victoria at the center.

A Tom Merry cartoon, *The Scrapegrace of the Family,* illustrates one version of Queen Victoria's familial image employed in that domestic imperial figuration. Races and ethnicities, representing parts of the empire, cluster about the queen, who sits in front of the Albert Hall, while a Fenian with a dynamite can stands outside the family circle.[28] He has become the dangerous undomesticated Other.

Queen Victoria as global civilizer receives an additional dimension when the domestic is embodied in domestic servants who are dark-skinned colonials. These people are both domestic and foreign.

⤳ The Secret of Her Greatness ⤶

I hate making war even upon black beetles. . . . They have as much right to live as black Zulus. But what can one do in either case?
—An animal lover, 1879

Much like the different breeds of dogs who confirm imperial aspirations

The Secret of Her Greatness, also known as *Queen Victoria Presenting a Bible to an African Chief*, by T. Jones Barker, 1861?, possibly completed in 1865. *Courtesy of the National Portrait Gallery, London.*

by their ability to cohabit, the domestic servant who is also a foreigner enters the royal household as an emblem of imperial England's greatness. (At the beginning of her reign, a Pekinese dog named Looty was taken from the Chinese imperial palace and given to Victoria as a similar symbol.) Domestication lies at the core of many tropes for the complex nineteenth-century British version of imperialism. It makes the violent conquest of far reaches of the globe acceptable to a culture beginning to acknowledge certain admirable qualities in the darker-complexioned peoples. To bring the "savage" into the compass of a large family seemed a more desirable figuration for empire than rawer economic and military motives. Not only could one establish properly Victorian family life in India, including English teatime and English sports, but Victoria herself brought the other lands within the compass of her own domestic setting. By entering the Royal Household, the empire's representatives become domesticated as part of a symbolic nuclear family.

An influential painting of its day, *The Secret of Her Greatness* (1861?) by T. Jones Barker, traveled to the provinces showing English power to subdue even to those English who had never seen an African or an

Indian. This painting, also known as *Queen Victoria Presenting a Bible to an African Chief,* does not include the normal trappings of domesticity but includes a likeness of the prince consort (who had just died) in the background. The prince, with other officials, stands under a canopy. In the foreground, Victoria, elegantly overdressed in evening finery, conveys a Bible to a kneeling, gorgeously attired, bejeweled African. The African prince's outstretched arms show off his fine muscles, used to receive the Book from his superior. The barbarian undergoes domestication under biblical and monarchical authority. Painted at the start of the American Civil War, *The Secret* conveys the superiority of the English manner of domestication over American violence.

W. T. Stead evoked the powerful impact of the Barker painting in his Golden Jubilee memoir. As a young boy he remembered viewing the painting as it traveled to the far reaches of the British Isles, including an 1864 showing in Belfast.[29] He vividly recalled what the painting meant to a strictly reared Protestant of a Methodist cast whose family leaned to republicanism. Stead saw the painting in a gallery in Newcastle upon Tyne:

> The swarthy African, highly idealised, I fear, flashing with gems and picturesque in his native garb, bows low before a youthful queen—resplendent in white satin, if I remember right—who advancing to meet the inquiring savage, presents him with a copy of the Bible as the answer to his question. "What is the secret of England's Greatness?" . . . All that I remember distinctly is the dusky envoy, with the flashing eye and upturned face, and the white Queen with the sacred Book. The picture stood all by itself in a gallery in which it was not elbowed or profaned by meaner pictures. It was as if Art had solemnly revealed The Monarchy in loyal obeisance before the Book. . . . It struck the imagination of the common people, this tribute of earthly Majesty to God's word. Rude coalheavers . . . used to tell over and over again how the Queen had given the Book of Books, the Book of our Salvation, to the heathen from afar who sought to know what it was that made England Great. . . . I began to gain a glimmering of the uses of the Sovereign as Grand Certificator for the truth and excellence of that which is best worth holding by in church and state.[30]

Only in retrospect did Stead appreciate the appropriative politics encoded in Barker's painting. To Nonconformists, the nation cannot own the word of God as it had been institutionalized in the Church of England.

Unsophisticated viewers believed the queen felt herself subject to the Bible much as they did. Her attitude as shown in the painting blends personal humility with chauvinistic imperialism. In retrospect, Stead appreciated the painting's political uses in its condescension:

> In the delight of the uncultured artizans and labourers of my native village over the queen's act in giving the Bible to the savage lay the germ of the sentiment which in its full development proclaims the queen *Fidei Defensor*, and regards even the Christian Church itself as somewhat wanting in the necessary credentials until it is surmounted by the royal arms, and certified to be the Church of England as by law established under the sign manual of the queen. But all that was mercifully hidden from our eyes in those days.[31]

Although the actual scene has not been documented, it probably occurred in some form.[32] Marie Mallet described a much later ceremony similar to the one in the Jones Barker painting:

> Windsor Castle, November 20th 1896

> We had a most interesting ceremony this afternoon, i.e. the reception of the African Chiefs. . . . We had a State Lunch, I had . . . Chief Bathoeu on my left; he seemed the least attractive of the blacks but enjoyed his food thoroughly and ate in a very civilised manner. Indeed their manners were excellent, quite a lesson to many Britons! They are all tee-totallers and drink nothing but lemonade but Khama is the finest of them. . . . Lord Selborne says he is a better Christian than anyone he knows and a very intelligent man to boot, a great hero. . . . The Queen received the Chiefs in the White Drawing Room seated on a Throne like a chair, and the Chiefs advanced through a long line of Life Guards with drawn swords. . . . The Queen welcomed them and they presented their gifts, three Karosses or rugs of leopard skins of doubtful smell but intrinsic worth. Then the Queen spoke saying she was glad to have them under her rule and protection and felt very strongly the necessity of preventing strong drink from entering their lands. This was duly interpreted and they replied each in turn. Then the Queen gave them a

New Testament in their tongue with her own hands and
huge framed photos, and an Indian Shawl was handed to
each of them by Lord Clarendon, and with grateful grunts
they retired backwards leaving us much impressed by their
quiet dignity and wonderful self-possession. I could see they
were immensely impressed but they tried not to show their
feelings and succeeded admirably.[33]

Mallet's sense of racial superiority does not prevent her from appreci-
ating some civilized traits of the domesticated chiefs. In a nice touch,
the queen personally conveys the spiritual secret of her greatness while
lesser dignitaries bestow gifts representative of a crasser secret involving
trade and global competition.

Attesting to the power of this image in our present moment, the contemporary Irish poet Richard Murphy encapsulates British imperialist
attitudes in an image of the annual Orangemen's parade with its reproduction of the scene Mallet described:

> On Belfast silk, Victoria gives
> Bibles to kneeling Zulu chiefs.
> Read the moral, note the date:
> "The secret that made Britain great."[34]

As a banner bringing reassurance to the queen's embattled Protestant
peoples in Ireland, the motto reveals its political domesticating function. Its unsubtle analogy to the "blacks" of Ireland, the Catholics, resonates with Charles Kingsley's shock at seeing the white Irish as akin to
blacks.[35]

Victoria liked to give India shawls to foreign visitors. For if she had
not personally visited the jewel in her crown, she imported India to
England, not simply through such relatively light things as shawls but
through animals and people as well. India captured Victoria's imagination, but one can only infer what Victoria's India might have meant to
her or what she imagined it was like. For her, as for many subjects, India
gave Britain a symbol of empire.[36] The East India Company transferred
India to the Crown in 1858; in 1876 the Royal Titles Bill officially con-
ferred the title Empress of India on the queen. Eventually Victoria
brought her new realm home by employing Indian servants as visible
evidence of her title. She set about to learn Hindustani and decreed
that the natives should not be expected to convert to Christianity. In
this she opposed evangelical missionary zeal but, like the evangel-

ical and the utilitarian, she disparaged the Hindus in favor of the Mohammedans.

She respected the Indians' right to maintain their indigenous religions and respected subjected peoples' autonomy, but in safeguarding their religion and customs, Victoria also appropriated their exotic bodies for aesthetic as well as territorial pleasure. This almost contradictory thinking—respecting creatures' right to difference while assimilating their persons into one's national identity—resembles the logic ceding rights to animals, forming societies to protect them while never doubting humans' right to rule them. Victoria expressed this dual attitude to the Others of her empire when she discussed with Lady Harris, the governor of Bombay's wife, plans to educate "Indian ladies and women" to become nurses. The queen both shares with Lady Harris her firsthand knowledge of India (gleaned in part from discussions with one servant) and reinforces her maternalistic charge:

> Midwifery and the care of young children, of whom so many alas! die, is the chief object. . . . But to speak plainly . . . : I think the attempt to educate them *highly* . . . or to encourage their going out and about as Europeans, I am quite sure would be most dangerous; and, if that is to come, it must be the work of generations and very gradual. This of course applies very strongly to the Mohammedan widow, who never could go out; and though there may be, and should be even, modifications in the extreme strictness of their seclusion, I think no attempt should be made to induce them to alter their mode of living, or to interfere with their religion, which, when well known and understood, contains so much that is fine and to be respected and admired.
>
> With the Hindus and Parsees, this is of course very different, as their religion is idolatrous. But for them also over-education might be most dangerous if it led to reading objectionable European literature, or to the imitation of freedom of manners.[37]

Victoria had learned about the superiority of the Mohammedans from her Mohammedan servant, Abdul Karim, who had attracted her particular attention from the time of his employment.

Bringing over living examples of the Indian population demonstrated the mother country's ability to summon the Other; those who had never left London could take in England's power with their own eyes. Victoria approved of ceremonials manifesting imperial sway. "The

Queen was delighted to hear of the ideas of a small Representation of the Empresses of India's troops being brought over to be presented to their Empress," she wrote to Sir William Harcourt, in 1882, when the controversy over the Royal Titles Bill had died down. In 1886 India and the other colonies came to South Kensington in the form of the Indian and Colonial Exhibition. In that show, actual people were part of the exhibit, displayed like the products of Industry at the earlier Great Exhibition. The next year, an Indian honor guard, largely composed of Sikh officers, arrived for the Golden Jubilee. In 1893 the government of India sent to London some non-commissioned officers specially selected from Indian cavalry regiments to form a guard of honor for Victoria for the opening of the Imperial Institute and the Duke of York's marriage to Mary (May) Teck. One of them, Jemadar Abdur Razzak, of the 1st Madras Lancers, wrote a diary of his visit, first in Hindustani, then translated by himself into English. His commanding officer, Major E. E. M. Lawford, commends the Jemadar, "a Mahomedan of Vellore," as coming of "good old fighting stock . . . and he has many relations now in the service, some holding high positions."[38]

Razzak's journal describes what he thought notable. The diary conveys the perspective of a person whisked to a world for which he has little frame of reference yet one that he accepts. He mentions his comfortable quarters on the journey and gives the names of the other officers and the precise amounts of their provisions; he notes that all their servants are Europeans, a remarkable fact for him. The honor guard arrived in London on May 2, 1893, having lost six soldiers and an officer to "some sickness which prevailed on the ship" (4). Razzak finds his English accommodations comfortable, even beautiful. He walks in a lovely garden, he notes with approval that their cooks were "Mahommedans." They live a life fit for a king: "Three coaches and 6 horses were employed for our use. Besides these we were provided with several other things as long as we remained there, from King & Co" (5). Razzak views royalty as his family might have—King & Co replace the East India Co. as the company in charge; he ratifies King Leopold's perception that modern monarchy resembles a trade, here a corporation bringing great profits to its members.

The Indian honor guard waited four days to meet the Queen:

> Soon after the Empress's arrival we saluted Her Majesty. . . .
> after the saluting the Empress approached to us with the
> Princesses and Moonshi Abdul Karim, who, with whom, had
> come and enquired to every one of us of his name, the name
> of the Commandant and the No. of our Regiment to which

we belonged, and said to us in Hindustani that she was much
anxious to see us, and she is very much pleased by seeing us;
a few minutes after we were dismissed.   (5)

The honor guard posed for many photographs and paintings. They
viewed the spoils of empire: "There we saw the thrones of the Indian
kings, studded with gold and precious stones, likewise their arms and
also the valuable presents made to Her Majesty by Kings and Nawabs"
(6). Razzak passes over without comment his country's subjugation; his
presence substantiates it. In "Mugalai dress" the Indians tour Lord
Rothschild's estate. Some London entertainments defy adequate
description, for instance, a ventriloquist: "two idols shaped like a boy
and a girl and singing with the curiosity of three different voices, one
like a man, the other like a body [sic] and the third like a girl, in all
these he didn't shake his lips, but the lips of the mentioned idols were
shaked in their turns of voices afterwards" (14). Some sights he finds
bizarre, some things pleasant.

    That the Duke of Connaught and the Queen-Empress spoke to them
in Hindustani and seemed to care about them impress him. Midway in
their visit they all receive an image of the queen to take home with them:
"We received the Photos of Her Majesty the Khaiser-i-Hind [Hindustani
for "Empress"] at one each, and return sent a supplication that we were
all much pleased with it, &c" (22). They do tourist activities: shop, go to
a tea factory, see animal and magic shows, go to Madame Tussaud's Wax
Museum where they see "the images of almost all the rulers and Begams
of Hindustan in their own dress in suitable places" (30). They visit
national monuments: the Crystal Palace, and the Tower of London,
where they see the crown jewels. At the obligatory tour of the royal mausoleum they see "a statue shaped like Her Majesty's husband" (44).
After their two official duties at the wedding and the opening of the
Imperial Institute, Victoria bids them safe voyage in Hindustani: "At the
last moment were so fortunate that once more visited by Her Majesty
who with great affection like a paternal one spoke to us and by that we
were so glad that no one would have in the world and with an eternal
mind thanked God for Her Majesty's longevity, prosperity and good
health and returned home" (45). Notwithstanding the voyage's few
casualties, Victoria's empire sailed to her.

    The Indian honor guard, their duty colorfully rendered, returned
to India, but India had long established a dogged stronghold within
Victoria's castle walls. At her Golden Jubilee, she received a gift of two
servants. One particular young man captured her imagination.
Razzak's diary indicates that the Munshi Abdul Karim, one of the first

to be hired, had become a fixture in the Household. In fact, like John Brown before him, he had become a domestic above domestics, much to the distress of the Household and to the dismay of the royal children. When Victoria hired him in 1887 as a waiter, she found him attractive. Comparing the two servants Abdul Karim and Mohamed Buxsh, she described Karim as "much younger . . . much lighter, tall, and with a fine serious countenance. His father is a native doctor at Agra."[39] The queen enhanced Karim's background to suit her own desires, for his father worked at the more modest occupation of prison apothecary. Karim's sense of entitlement provoked the enmity of other Indian servants, the resentment of the Household, and the embarrassment of the royal children. It seemed as if John Brown, still handsome but slighter, darker, and younger, had been reincarnated as an Indian; after his promotion from waiter to scribe and tutor to the queen, Karim occupied John Brown's bedroom.

Respecting their religion and more accepting of their differences than most of the British aristocracy, Victoria also attended to "her" Indians' well-being, but to none as generously as to Karim. From the beginning, she indicated that Indian costume pleased her. She made certain adaptations in the native dress for the harsher British climate:

> Mahomet Buksh and Abdul Karim should wear in the *morning out of doors* at breakfast when they wait, the *new* dark blue dress and always at lunch with any 'Pageri' (Turban) and sash *they like*, only not the *Gold Ones*. The Red dress and gold and white turban (or Pageri) and sash to be always worn *at dinner in the evening*. . . . Gradually a warm Tweed dress and trousers can be got for them at Balmoral to go about in, when off duty. . . . But it must be made in Indian fashion and the Pageri always be worn.[40]

Victoria domesticated Karim, her favorite household Indian. He appears in many photographs, gradually thickening in figure over the years. At times it seemed to Victoria's family and staff, however, that the servant had domesticated his mistress to his wishes. He influenced her opinions, but, besides a few ill-written notes and a few letters kept (with permission) by his widow, all written traces of the interchanges between him and Victoria were destroyed by command of her son King Edward VII.

The story of the relationship between the Khaiser-i-Hind and her Indian servant extends the fable of the queen's life as a dog, where people metamorphose into animals or are transformed from peasants to nobles. With an earnestness by now synonymous with Victorianism, the queen thought herself obliged to learn a major language of her Indian empire. Who better to teach her daily Hindustani lessons than a native speaker?

> 11 August 1888: I particularly wish to retain his services, as he helps me in studying Hindustani, which interests me very much, and he is very intelligent and useful. 2 November 1888: Had my last Hindustani lesson, as good Abdul goes home to India to-morrow on leave, which I regret.[41] 8 September 1896: After luncheon did a lesson in Hindustani with Abdul, who has just returned from India. It did not go very well, as I had forgotten a good deal, and not practised at all during his six months' absence.[42]

By royal decree, Abdul Karim was elevated to be an honored member of the Royal household. Victoria's attraction to a man fifty years her junior, barely educated, and innocent of protocol blinded her to his faults. She favored him as a pet, to the point that rumors of the queen's insanity began to circulate as they had during her years of seclusion. Karim gained the title of Munshi Hafiz, teacher and official Indian secretary, entrusted with judging policy and reading confidential papers from the official boxes, although he was barely literate.

If told that the Munshi caused resentment through his pretensions, she accused her informant of listening to gossip:

> 10 April 1894: The Queen . . . would wish to observe that to make out . . . the poor good Munshi . . . is so low is really outrageous and in a country like England quite out of place. . . . She has known two Archbishops who were the sons respectively of a Butcher and a Grocer, a Chancellor whose father was a poor sort of Scotch Minister, Sir D. Stewart and Lord Mount Stephen both who ran about barefoot as children and whose parents were very humble and the tradesmen M. and J. P. were made baronets.[43]

The queen's notable color blindness leads her to impute to her household class prejudice but not racial bias. When one of the queen's brooches was missed and found, sold by an Indian servant, a relative of Karim's, the queen would not heed the proofs of her servant's duplicity. She permitted him to send for his relatives, perhaps more than one wife, euphemistically called "aunts."

Victoria continued to promote Abdul; she decorated him with the Companion of the Order of the Indian Empire. She forced his company upon the Royal Household, although he was snubbed by them. She gave him a furnished residence at Osborne House, and, when his feelings were hurt by what seemed the household's race and class bias, she salved his pride with an additional residence at Balmoral Castle. At all his residences the royal doctors treated various Mrs. Karims. Dr. James Reid reported on an "interesting talk" with the queen about a recurrence of Karim's venereal disease.[44] On another occasion, when Abdul suffered from a carbuncle on his neck, the queen visited him in his room twice daily, "stroked his hand," and, when he began to recover, commenced her lessons in his room. In 1896 Victoria sent Marie Mallet to call upon Abdul's wife at Balmoral; Mallet reported the visit's effect upon her:

> I have just been to see the Munshi's wife (by Royal command). She is fat and not uncomely, a delicate shade of chocolate and gorgeously attired, rings on her fingers, rings on her nose, a pocket mirror set in turquoises on her thumb and every feasible part of her person hung with chains and bracelets and ear-rings, a rose-pink veil on her head bordered with heavy gold and splendid silk and satin swathings round her person. She speaks English in a limited manner and declares she likes the cold. The house surrounded by a twenty foot palisade, the door opening of itself, the white figure emerging silently from a near chamber, all seemed so un-English, so essentially Oriental that we could hardly believe we were within a hundred yards of this Castle.[45]

In the condescending tone of an English lady, and with her wonder that such essential orientalism should invade the precincts of "this Castle," Mallet encounters the domestication of empire, what she appreciated as a "curious bit of history."

Abdul, with his various wives and aunts, geographically superimposed upon Balmoral, seems to create a microcosm of Victoria's empire within the imperial outpost that also serves as a country house. Victorian India not only moves close to home, but becomes homely. A photograph of the aged Queen Victoria with the still slender Abdul Karim could be entitled "The Domestication of Her Greatness." Victoria sits at a table in front of a screen, under a tent canopy. Although out of doors, the space has been re-created as a room, with rich and exotic trappings. On the table rest official governmental boxes. Karim, dressed in "native" garb, stands at attention, holding one of Victoria's canes, which in part stands

Queen Victoria and Her Servant Abdul Karim, photograph by Hills and Saunders, 1893. During the week of her Golden Jubilee celebrations in June 1887, Victoria received Indian princes and deputations. "Their head-dresses and uniforms were very fine and the jewels of the Princes magnificent. All the Indian officers held their swords out for me to touch. Just before I went out, saw Dr. Tyler with the two Indian servants he has brought over for me, two fine-looking men handsomely dressed in scarlet with white turbans." These first of Victoria's Indian servants were Abdul Karim and Mohamed Buxsh. *Courtesy of the National Portrait Gallery, London.*

in for her scepter. The cane resting in the domestic's hand suggests that he, too, wields authority. Victoria's other cane, resting on a chair, links the two figures. One's ascendancy over the other—as human ascendancy over the rest of nature—seems problematic, blurred, indicated perhaps by the trace of Karim's heel extending beyond the carpet. India, represented by Karim, resembles a pet at home, but so too does Victoria. Ensconced within the tent and wearing a bonnet, Victoria tamely works for a domesticated empire, enclosed in the compass of black boxes confined in a small, portable habitation. Britannia rules the waves from an out-building. The photograph translates Landseer's dog pictures back into the human figures they allegorize. It captures an imperial ideal as a somewhat fragile domestication of the body politic in the collective person of Queen Victoria and the Munshi Hafiz Abdul Karim. Close up, it is humble and ordinary, a mode of life made intimate, personal, and domestic.

At the end of her reign, Victoria's desires to maintain her empire warred with her pain over the human cost. The Boer War was going badly, with great numbers of deaths, and the queen was dying. Some wanted to believe that her dying utterance conveyed a wish for peace in South Africa. William Scawen Blunt disapproved of Victoria's imperialist fierceness and recorded what he believed to be her final wish: "That her little dog should be allowed to jump up on her bed. . . . It was with her when she died."[46]

7

PETTICOAT RULE; OR, VICTORIA IN FURS

IN MEMORY OF CASEY FINCH

It is she, Venus, but without her furs;
the widow again, and yet it is Venus.
—Sacher-Masoch, Venus in Furs

From childhood Queen Victoria possessed a willful, strong, and tempestuous temperament. When thwarted she raged; always hungry, she devoured her food; very possessive, she presided over her adored playthings. Lytton Strachey interpreted the princess's passionate nature as foreshadowing the queen's sexual liveliness. "The careful searcher might detect, in the virgin soil," Strachey remarked of the princess's conventual upbringing at the time of her confirmation, "the first faint traces of an unexpected vein."[1] Whereas after her death Victoria became a symbol of sexual repression, her contemporaries could imagine her as an erotic powerhouse. The specter of a dominating woman with strong erotic desires inflects aspects of Victorian culture and, offering its subversive message to a culture that placed women as a refuge from an aggressive world, Queen Victoria presides as its reigning, though sometimes disguised, goddess.

Throughout her reign, Victoria made no attempt to hide her amorous disposition.[2] From the time of her accession, she esteemed men who made her heart beat faster. Serving her apprenticeship as queen with Lord Melbourne, a handsome older man with a past, she acquired a reputation for judging men according to their masculine appeal. Melbourne's intimate relationship as elderly political mentor to an eighteen-year-old maiden tingled with eroticism. The knowledge of their frequent, long, and private meetings led to the queen being hissed as "Mrs. Melbourne" when the two appeared together at Ascot. During the long hours they spent together every day, they gave each other emotional and political support. A goddess of romance nourished the body politic.

The queen's Victorian subjects did not deny her sexuality, making the obvious jokes about her honeymoon at Windsor, on the way to which is a town called Maidenhead.[3] Victoria's return from Windsor three short days later, before the stars could fade from her eyes, was regarded as immodest.[4] She made no secret about the sensuous pleasures marriage permitted her to enjoy. "No pudding and no *fun*," she complained in a published Highland entry on an October evening during the last year of her marriage, when the royal entourage was touring incognito and found itself in an inn of meager accommodation.[5] Less than a year later the widowed queen confessed to Vicky her envy of Bertie's "prospect of opening happiness of married life. . . . It wrings my poor heart, which seems transfixed with agonies of longing! I am alas! not old—and my feelings are strong and warm; my love is ardent."[6] Private revelations accorded with public knowledge of Victoria's disposition.

Building on the model of her early flirtation with the Whig Melbourne, Victoria's later involvement with the Tory Disraeli played with the conventions of erotic friendship, accentuating generative political possibilities under the sign of Venus. Disraeli's "Faery Queen" accepted posies and elaborate courtly addresses from her prime minister, while England attained the Suez Canal and the Fairy Queen became Empress of India.[7]

Although no less devoted to his monarch, the Liberal William Gladstone, a prime minister she disliked, experienced another side of the queen's character, a murderous one. When Gladstone remarked to Lord Rosebery that "the Queen alone is enough to kill any man," he was referring to her insistence that ministers consult her at her distant country houses far from the seat of government. Nonetheless, the perception that this woman could kill a man, or at the very least wear him down, applies to many representations of the queen as a dominating, passionate woman who could overpower a man drawn into her orbit. The Tory Duke of Wellington, the most popular figure in England, reluctantly invited to Victoria's Whiggish wedding, suffered a stroke shortly thereafter, apparently upset by the queen's judging him a rebel. As year followed year in her reign, the number of men to whom she was attached dropped off, if not like flies, then with an ominous inexorability: Melbourne, Albert, Brown, Disraeli, Grey, Ponsonby, Napoleon III, Palmerston, General Gordon, Gladstone—some of them a good deal younger than their queen. Not only did Victoria survive them all, including most of her doctors and reverends, but she seemed to thrive. Her temperament ignited fantasies about the fatal woman's destructive power. If she could fell the mighty Wellington, victor at Waterloo, of what else might she not be capable?

While discomfort at the idea of the queen's sexuality expressed itself in jokes, other responses included considering her erotic energies as requiring forcible control or—should they be allowed to dominate— imagining Victoria's sexual requirements as overwhelming a man's sense of his masculinity. While a male subject might fantasize that he were under her care, he might also feel a risk in becoming a victim of her desire. One extreme reaction to the conflict between fear and desire would be to kill the queen.

Seven men tried to assassinate Queen Victoria. Since some attempts were merely symbolic—the gun was not loaded (one was filled with tobacco) or was only a starter's pistol—those would-be assassins played out a ritual ridding the culture of a disturbing element. The attempts occurred from 1840 to 1882, and all the assailants were caught. Some were pathetic, some deranged, some, it is true, expressed a political motive. A psychiatrist, Trevor Turner, proposes that all the men were suffering from "erotomania." Their frustration at being kept from the object of desire, he argues, led them to a sex crime. As a model for the seven "assassins," Turner cites the case of "Captain Jonathan C," who wrote a series of obscene letters to Victoria from 1840 to 1854, the last ones from an asylum. Turner suggests that under the delusion that the queen was erotically interested in him, Captain C., whose erotomania was "secondary to a chronic paranoid psychosis," considered himself betrayed by a government plot to prevent their union. Such fantasies as the captain's transfer Victoria's professed devotion to her subjects to corporeal intimacies. Using the obscene letter writer as a paradigm, Turner extrapolates to the would-be assassins: "One wonders then to what extent these seven men really were lovers, turned to jealousy by continued disappointment."[8] Victoria, it seems, could inspire murderous devotion.

The deluded men who acted out their killer instincts represent an activist fringe of those more private people who also entertained various sorts of erotic fantasies involving sexual connections with their sovereign. The queen's extreme affection for some relatively lowly employees might encourage other humble but anonymous suitors. She openly,

Queen Victoria on a horse with John Brown. Photograph by Wilson, Whitlock, and Downey, 1868. *Courtesy of the National Portrait Gallery, London.*

even extravagantly, favored two servants, John Brown, the gillie, and Abdul Karim, the munshi, and depended on their close daily attendance. Widely circulating rumors about a sexual relationship with John Brown offered hope for those suffering from unrequited love for the queen of their secret hearts.

✦ On the Throne, On Brown ✦

So capacious were Victoria's feelings that she could maintain ardent longing for her departed husband while holding strong affections for others who were still alive. Her amorous relationship with John Brown after Prince Albert's death created a scandal. He shadowed her, and she liked it. The brusque, rude, unceremonious, yet vigorously manly Brown appeared everywhere; fact became elaborated in fantasy.

Depending upon which female stereotype predominated, rumor married Victoria to Brown, gave them a child, or simply gave him to her as her stallion.[9] Victoria heeded no advice about moderating her attentions to Brown while he was alive; after his death, however, she reluctantly allowed herself to be counseled by Randall Davidson, the new dean of Windsor, who risked his position to persuade her not to publish more leaves from her Highland journals, a publication planned by the queen as a memorial tribute to Brown. She consoled herself by constructing memorial tablets and statues to Brown, many of which were, like the munshi's letters, destroyed after her death by Edward VII.

Whether Victoria did or did not enjoy actual carnal relations with John Brown, sexual currents galvanized her appreciation of him. Whatever their points of actual physical contact—and Brown was observed ordering the queen to change her dress and attaching Her Majesty's shawl pin, scolding her as "wummun" to hold still—no one disagrees that Victoria's relationship with John Brown was intimate, intense, and sentimental. A youngish widow of amorous disposition found her rough servant from the Highlands more comforting and supportive than anyone else, a fact insulting to her Household and children alike.[10] She elevated Brown to gentleman status, listened to no one about her behavior, and grieved at his death as if he had been a husband.

When Victoria died and before the coffin lid was permanently sealed, Dr. Reid, following the queen's instructions, placed John Brown's picture and a lock of his hair in one hand, wrapped the hand, then covered it with flowers.[11] Despite that evidence of profound attachment, their further secret intimacies remain surmise. In any case, whatever happened personally pales before contemporary cultural constructions of the anomalous couple. Since for long years after Albert's death, Victoria refused to participate in ceremonials and therefore was rarely seen, the public relied upon news and gossip, one absorbing topic of which was John Brown and the person dubbed "the Empress Brown." The epithet neatly conflates Victoria's two heartthrobs of the late sixties and seventies in that title: Brown and Disraeli. Whatever their import, the stories conveyed the message that Victoria's loving heart was not buried with her husband, much as she represented herself as eternally mourning for him. Indeed, her extravagant mourning lent a necrophilic aura to her grief, one that was augmented by her clutching Albert's marble hands, modeled from casts taken after his death and always placed near her bed.[12] The mausoleum could not contain Victoria's erotic desire. The question was never the dead Albert or someone else: it was both.

JOHN BROWN EXERCISING THE QUEEN.

"John Brown Exercising the Queen" from *Palace and Hovel* by
Daniel Joseph Kirwan, 1870.

In 1870, at the height of the Brown scandal, Joseph Kirwan, an
American traveler in England, took great pleasure in expressing his
republican sentiments and chauvinism, recording his opinions and sights
of England in an illustrated book, *Palace and Hovel*. He attributed the
queen's "irascible" temper to "her fondness for liquor" to the extent of
"half a pint of raw liquor a day," the effects of which could be discerned
in her swollen face and "ungovernable" disposition.[13] Kirwan thought
that Victoria at the very least found a drinking partner in John Brown
who was frequently too drunk to leave his room. Kirwan picked up scraps
of scandal and, in a section entitled "Lucky John Brown," suggested their
import with the double entendre, "Brown Exercising the Queen":

> When the Queen takes her seat in her perambulator it might
> often occur that a servant would spring forward with a lowly
> reverence to assist the royal lady, the unfortunate flunkey . . .
> might have to undergo the mortification of a sneering laugh
> from Brown, who at this crisis would make his appearance—
> strolling in a leisurely fashion toward the perambulator, and
> stretching his long Celtic legs, his arms full of warm wraps in
> which he proceeds to enfold the person of the Queen, with as
> much seeming fondness as if he were the husband, instead of
> the low lackey of royalty, without polish and breeding.[14]

To suggest connections between an image of an infantilized (or inebriated) queen and sexual practice, Kirwan reported on a cartoon parody of the perambulator illustration, published in the *Tomahawk*: "The queen was pictured in her perambulator, and the tall form of Brown behind, pushing the vehicle, while leaning over the back and looking with an affectionate leer into the face of the sovereign of England."[15] Equally leering, Kirwan plays upon the lewd implications of Brown taking his mistress for a ride.[16]

Humor magazines, such as the *Tomahawk* and the more reticent *Punch*, openly suggested how important Brown had become. *Punch* reported on John Brown's activities in a parody of the court calendar. Anonymous pamphlets also provided an outlet for opinions about the strange liaison between Victoria and her liquorous servant. One pamphlet suggests that the Duke of Athole enjoyed political favors because his family is "in the knowledge of some great secret, which can be used with such magical effect." Victoria's and Brown's secret child, a "thumping Scottish Laddie," spirited away to Switzerland, gives the Athole family power to bring down the government, even to abrogate the Magna Carta. The writer characterizes Victoria as "a sort of weak-minded or semi-imbecile creature," and Brown as "exercis[ing] more power over the party than a shepherd or drover can with his collie dog. . . . It would appear that he can order the P____of W____ or D____of E____ about their business."[17] By reporting on Brown's observable role as an occasionally abusive gatekeeper, the writer gains credibility for his lurid, undocumentable stories.

Another pamphlet, *Brown on the Throne* (1871), depends at first on the title's double meaning. Cartoons appeared depicting John Brown leaning on a deserted throne; one, "A Brown Study," was printed in the *Tomahawk* in August 1867. The pamphlet's title allows the reader to imagine Mr. Brown not leaning but sitting on the throne, but the article presents Brown's reflections on (the state of) the throne in England. Brown portrays his wife, "Mrs. Brown," as more independent than the typical Victorian housewife. He justifies himself for giving his missis more leeway than normal: "I do not call a man an indulgent husband because he lets a woman have her own way ben't his way. . . . So it aint because Mrs. Brown has been allowed to gad about by herself that 'Poor dear Brown' is to be put down as an indulgent husband, as a hen-pecked husband, or a fellow that is under what is called petticoat government."[18]

"Petticoat government" labels one threat posed by a female ruler. If husbands suggest that their wives enjoy a certain autonomy, they may be accused of enjoying subservience. Not only misogynistic, condemning women's frivolity, the term evokes a pungently erotic realm, where underwear presides, not skirts. In the pamphlet, Brown's claim of voluntary submission extends both to the realm of the kingdom and that of the bedroom: "Mrs. Brown does what she likes because 'Poor dear Brown' likes it."

Brown's discomfort with the thought of a woman ruler becomes clear when he defines a throne as "the seat of a King." So defined, the position of a queen can be nothing but anomalous, an incongruity underlying the state of the nation:

> Now, you must bear in mind that the Queen of this country of "England and caetera" is a Lady. When that is understood the difficulty of the situation will be fully appreciated by the meanest capacity. . . . What is the use of having a throne if the Queen don't sit upon it? and that I've proved beyond all controversy, that, as Queen is neither a King nor a Pilot, she can't be expected to sit down upon a seat that was never intended to be so occupied. And small blame to her, say I, for I wouldn't do it myself. It aint to be expected. (16–17)

After comparing monarchy to a grocery, in which the departed husband is represented as a once-prosperous greengrocer, and the vegetables used for puns about sex—the grocer gazes into the eyes of his potatoes, studies the stalk of his celery, and so forth—"Mr. Brown" gets to the point: "a fine business being ruined, as you may say,—for I do look upon the 'Throne of England' as a fine little business if properly managed—all going to smash, because there aint no right head, no 'Governor King.' A woman cannot attend to it, like a man" (21). Like Uncle Leopold, Mr. Brown ("husband of Mrs. Brown") considers the monarchical trade; he recommends that the son get serious, throw out his betting book, and take over.

If Mr. Brown seems defensive about his willing acceptance of Mrs. Brown's power over him, a bawdy marching rhyme (sung to the tune of the "Grenadier Guards") portrays a childish Brown proudly yielding his dirty private parts to the queen's authority. She enjoys free access to the promise beneath the Scotsman's male petticoat:

> There was a bonny Scotsman who lived in Waterloo
> He lifted up his petticoat and shewed his toodle-oo
> His toodle-oo was dirty when he shewed it to the Queen
> The Queen took soap and water and washed the bugger clean.[19]

Suggesting that the queen's power reduces the man to a petticoat-wearing boy, the lyrics also play upon English fantasies about the well-endowed Scotsman. The baby talk, however, suggests a wee organ, diminished in relationship to "the queen." The song portrays the queen as a nanny figure who uses her knowledge of the intimate bodily secrets of her male charge to shame him for their functions. This version of Victoria's relationship to her gillie imagines a boyish Brown lifting his kilt to submit his member to the lustrations of a nannylike mistress. The song's Victoria begins to metamorphose into a dominatrix.

Cartoons similarly portrayed the person who most visibly hated Brown—the Prince of Wales—as being infantilized and dominated. Victoria's treatment of her son played into fantasies about her power to humiliate men. She treated him as a case of arrested development, scolding him for misbehavior. An exchange of letters between the heir presumptive and his mother supports public perceptions. At the apex of her seclusion and the Brown rumors, Victoria asked her son to moderate his appearances at the racetrack:

> Balmoral, 1st June 1870
>
> DEAREST BERTIE, — . . . Now that Ascot Races are approaching, I wish to *repeat earnestly and seriously*, and with reference to my letters this spring, that I trust you will, . . . *confine* your *visits* to the Races, to the *two* days *Tuesday* and *Thursday* and *not* go on *Wednesday* and *Friday*, to which William IV never went, nor did we. . . .
>
> If you are anxious to go on those two great days (though I should prefer your not going every year to both) there is no real objection to that, but to the other days there is. Your example can do much for good and may do an immense deal for evil.[20]

Bertie resists his "dear Mama," in her effort to dampen his celebrating "the great national sport of this country":

> MARLBOROUGH HOUSE, 5th June 1870 I fear, dear Mama, that no year goes round without your giving me a jobation on the subject of racing. You know how utterly and entirely I disapprove of what is bad about them; . . . I am always most anxious to meet your wishes, dear Mama, in every respect, and always regret if we are not quite *d'ac-*

cord–but as I am past twenty-eight and have some considerable knowledge of the world and society, you will, I am sure,
at least I trust, allow me to use my own discretion in matters
of this kind.   (*19–20*)

Bertie reminds his mother of his maturity, but she will have none of it.
Not only her children but her Household reacted to the queen as if she
were a martinet. Henry Ponsonby wrote to his wife about the queen's
taking over the Prince of Wales's household during his life-threatening
bout of typhoid fever:

> The Queen controlled the situation . . . to the point of decid-
> ing who should stay and who should go. . . . Yesterday Haig
> and I went out towards the garden by a side door when we
> were suddenly nearly carried away by a stampede of royalties,
> headed by the Duke of Cambridge and brought up by
> Leopold, going as fast as they could. We thought it was a mad
> bull. But they cried out: "The Queen, the Queen," and we all
> dashed into the house again and waited behind the door till
> the road was clear.[21]

Such stories reinforced the idea that the queen's iron fist reduced men
to naughty children.

In 1890 the American humor newspaper *Life* portrayed an infantilized Albert Edward, seated on his mama's lap smoking a cigar. At
the queen's side sits a bottle of whiskey and a bottle of seltzer, but only
one half-empty glass. As if she were a shopkeeper, she guards her
shelves of India shawls (which she bestowed on visitors) and advises
her son on garnering sinecures. By the time of this spoof, Victoria had
the reputation of controlling her grandchildren as well as her children, particularly Kaiser Wilhelm, whom she called "Willie." *Punch*
depicted a monumental Victoria, black from hat to parasol, at the
beach minding Willie who, with a toy shovel, builds sand forts and
plays with his toy fleet.

The most literal cartoon about petticoat government appeared in
Life in January 1889. In it, Bertie's head, top-hatted and full-bearded,
sits on a miniature body. His infant hand clutches not a scepter but a riding crop, and his chubby legs prevent him from clambering on the
throne behind him.[22] Not only ruled by a petticoat, he wears one. The
queen's will to rule turns him into the symbolic equivalent of a little girl.

"A Hint to Wales," by T. S. Sullivan Jr. *Life*, vol. 16, July 10, 1890. Queen Victoria advises her son on how to apply for multiple army pensions.

⤚ Governor/King ⤙

If I were a Queen,
What would I do?
I'd make you a King,
And I'd wait on you.
—*Christina Rossetti*

Masochistic plots often feature a woman whose exercise of power controls men's degree of authority. In the epigraph, the charm of Christina Rossetti's singsong children's rhyme mutes the power dynamic. The queen "makes" a king, choosing her subservient role but only according to her will. Being queen, she could, after all, change her mind. Whereas humorous cartoons and jokes about the dominating woman either ignore pain or consider the dominatrix as a comic figure, other kinds of stories emphasize pain as an essential element in "love." Victoria's increasingly imperial image lends itself to erotic scenes where a woman enforces the rules of love by means of inflicting pain on an eventually willing subject.

If Victoria could be imagined as a type of Venus, it would be as a "Venus in Furs," the title of a novel by Leopold von Sacher-Masoch, from whom the term *masochism* derives. The love goddess, once edu-

In *Life*'s cartoon, January 24, 1889, the Prince of Wales
has suffered infantalization from his long apprenticeship,
shrinking instead of growing into his future.

cated to her role by her lover, learns to hurt him. Strictly regulated
according to a contract, infliction of pain involves carefully orches-
trated scenes of instruction, as in the Rossetti poem, involving conscious manipulation of domination and submission. Severin, the lover,
likes his mistress Wanda to hurt him, while for his part he likes to
choose her clothes.

The narrative of Victoria's relationship with Albert contains fragments of this kind of masochistic plot. From one perspective, Albert's
choosing of his mistress's clothes could be regarded as part of his man-
agerial aesthetic. Yet from an erotic point of view, his insistence on
dressing her while she was his titular superior though connubial infe-

rior begins to intimate faint outlines of a masochistic scenario. If most versions of the royal story portrayed Albert as eventually gaining the upper hand over an increasingly subservient Victoria, many believed that the queen finally overpowered her prince, wearing him out and draining from him his relatively weak will to live. Defending Victoria against this charge, Longford gives evidence of its cultural currency: "A limited interpretation of the word "passionate" has led to another error: the legend that like the female spider she devoured her mate, Prince Albert, and a few years afterwards, insatiable as ever, took another more vigorous partner, John Brown, from the Highlands glen."[23] This particular legend of the devouring spider, like another popular fantasy about the devouring female praying mantis, expresses cultural fears concerning women who satisfy their sexual energies at men's ultimate expense.

Victoria's love goddess is unpredictable yet judgmental, lascivious yet punitive, always insatiable, doting on men but dominating them, forcing all others to submit to her will. This venerean aspect of the queen's image extends the governess image of the John Brown marching song to domination fantasies and acts as a muse to cultural works of the time that have no overt reference to Queen Victoria.

✣ "Fleshly Tablets" ✣

Some narratives connecting love with pain justify the torment by positing its sufferer as one in need of change. Victoria's image as a potentially deadly Venus fits in with a variation on the typical conversion narrative. "I once was lost but now I'm found" sums up a basic kind of conversion story from Augustine and Dante to Rousseau. The pattern commonly occurs in religious conversion declarations, a foundation of the Evangelicalism that was so powerful in the nineteenth century. Many Victorian spiritual and fictional autobiographies include elements of the conversion narrative: Carlyle's *Sartor Resartus,* John Stuart Mill's *Autobiography,* and Florence Nightingale's short autobiographical fragment, *Cassandra,* are a few notable examples.

The narrative relevant to some kinds of "love" stories shifts the focus of the religious conversion narrative by adding erotic pain, accompanied sometimes by abasement.[24] This love conversion experience would read: "I once was independent, but now love's force has trained me to abject servitude." Love accompanies coercion, sweet and half-willing or violent and absolute. The plot takes literally the conventional tropes of cruelty in Western love literature, where the lover suffers love pangs but where the boundary between mental and physical anguish sometimes disappears, to end in death. Another boundary is crossed when figurations connecting body pain with love ask to be taken literally. The fiction actualizes metaphoric potential; pangs become lashings. We then read the figurations as literal descriptions. Pornographic versions act out on the body the pain of love, often depending on a suppressed masochistic conversion narrative to justify torture.

As if to emphasize the cross-over between figurations of pain and bodily abuse, some pornography describes whipping as if it were writing. Skin becomes the blank parchment of the masochistic text. For instance, *The Whippingham Papers* (to which the poet Algernon Charles Swinburne supposedly contributed) contains a poem literalizing the love-pain trope:

> And harder still the birch fell on his bottom
> And left some fresh red letters there to read:
> Weeks passed before the part inscribed forgot 'em
> The fleshly tablets, where the master's creed
> Is written on boy's skin with birchen pen,
> At each reissue copied fair again.
>
> This was the third edition, not the first
> Printed on Arthur's red bottom in red text.[25]

Here wit shares importance with eroticism, spelling out the links between writing, whipping, and pleasure. Formally, the reiteration of words seem infantile in their ability to evoke sexual feelings; words such as *bottom*, occurring in proper names, evoke pleasure in readers, a pleasure not simply of saying a naughty word but of giving a sexual charge as well. For instance, "A letter from Alan Bummingham," another of the *Whippingham Papers*, emerges from the sensibility epitomized by *Life's* illustration of an adult head on a child's body. The volume's title puns on whipping, but its overt sense suggests that the papers issue from Whippingham on the Isle of Wight, a place associated with Queen Victoria. Whippingham church was near Osborne House and was, in the words of Lord Esher, "so closely connected with her [Victoria] and her children."[26] Among many notable royal events, Princess Beatrice was married in the church at Whippingham in the summer of 1885.

In the writings about love and lashing, body pain extends well beyond mental pangs; the person who suffers physical pain does so under the active ministrations of the erotic partner. Havelock Ellis, the late Victorian sexologist, discusses the conjunction of what he calls "love and pain" in his *Studies in the Psychology of Sex* (1897). Ellis views love and pain as constitutive of heterosexual power relations. Using the animal kingdom as his model, he portrays the male nature as pain-giving while female nature enjoys suffering:

> The infliction of pain must inevitably be a frequent indirect result of the exertion of power. It is even more than this; the infliction of pain by the male on the female may itself be a gratification of the impulse to exert force. . . . The tendency of the male to inflict pain must be restrained so far as the female is concerned, by the consideration of what is pleasing to her. Yet, the more carefully we study the essential elements of courtship, the clearer it becomes that, playful as these manifestations may seem on the surface, in every direction they are verging on pain. It is so among animals generally; it is so in man among savages.[27]

By implicitly connecting animals and savages in the conjunction of love and pain, Ellis suggests that the civilized man has moved beyond primitive courtship rituals. Ellis at once recognizes the pain-love element in "civilized" sex yet wants to think of it as perverse.

Women might want to inflict pain in minor ways, such as leading men on. Most commonly, however, women's desire is "to be swept out of herself and beyond the control of her own will to drift idly in delicious submission to another and stronger will."[28] The sexologist describes a paradigm found in sadomasochistic plots, with a significant difference. Whereas Ellis's men and women naturally assume their gendered roles, in the pornographic novel such pleasures are acquired. The woman does not initially know that she desires submission rather than the control of her own will. It is the action of the plot that shows her the way.

Typically, the woman is independent and innocent; through love she becomes a devotee of pain. A vicious example of the genre, *The Way of a Man with a Maid*, features a riding master who sexually subjugates women, one of whom is named Victoria and who, like the queen, has a remarkably pleasant voice. The author of that domination fantasy seems to echo Ellis when he implies that it is man's duty in regard to women "to master, to break in, to conquer and to teach."[29] The riding master trains Victoria by means of various metallic devices, first securing her to a mechanical horse:

> Oh! the horse!" Victoria declared in her softly modulated voice when she perceived what stood before her.[30]

> "It would not do for you to be thrown by a live one," I
> observed solemnly while she gazed with some wonder,
> though not unpleased, at the grey-dappled rocking horse
> which stood in waiting. . . . It was the largest I had been able
> to secure and stood glossy in its new paint on its rockers, with
> a fine saddle and steel and leather stirrups.[31]

After being locked into the horse, her bottom exposed, flogged, sodom-
ized, Victoria, beaten into submission, politely asks for more. Through
love, the woman comes to see the truth of her lot and submits joyfully
to a higher authority. After doing so, she views her past life from the
vantage of her privileged position.

A subtext of Queen Victoria's biography frequently assumes this
shape, its similarity to many coercive narratives—pornographic or
not—unrecognized. The masochistic story closest to pornography,
close to the pornographic Victoria, involves great resistance and a
power struggle. In this version of the queen's life—and no biography is
completely free of some of these elements—an independent, fun-loving young woman, whose outlet from stressful duties is to laugh heartily,
dance until morning, and ride horses daily, loves her sovereignty to
excess. With a nature inclined to gaiety, she is also stubborn. She enjoys
being queen and takes her job to heart as a sacred trust. She drags her
heels about an inevitable marriage, trying to fend off Uncle Leopold's
candidate, her cousin Albert. The moment she sees a newly mature
Albert, passion overwhelms her: "It was with some emotion that I
beheld Albert—who is *beautiful.*"[32]

Prince Albert, serious, ambitious, and eager to rule—although
willing to do so secretly—takes "Victoria" in hand. Although he has
shown no particular interest in women, preferring the company of
men, he marries her, to his great advantage. After the honeymoon the
press congratulates Albert for winning "the grey mare,"[33] an indication of the correspondence between pornographic fantasy and a common metaphor for a highly spirited woman. Determined to have the
upper hand, Albert, a somewhat retiring and earnest intellectual,
reads up on the subject and makes a plan. Used to getting her way,
Victoria resists and fights back. Monica Charlot describes the bride:
"The Queen was in fact jealous of her prerogatives. She was strong-
willed and autocratic. There was, as Lady Lyttelton notes, a 'vein of
iron' running through her character and she was determined to
remain Queen of England in her own right. She did not want to share
her power with anyone."[34] She shuts Albert out of politics; she fights

him. He wants to be master. Albert writes scolding, very long letters; he becomes cold and logical. He clears the path of earlier influences—such as Victoria's beloved governess, Baroness Lehzen—and diminishes the influence of Melbourne, of whom he disapproves; then Melbourne dies.

Finally, the queen's frequent pregnancies bring home to her that biological imperatives govern even a queen's proper Victorian role: to bear children, to allow a husband mastery. David Duff, who does not admire Albert or his Coburg stock, remarks of the prince's desire for dominance: "Albert was of the type who only become sexually dominant at times of power and success. . . . [He] stole one vital gift from Victoria—her blitheness and her buoyancy. Harriet Martineau said that she never saw the queen before her marriage but that she was laughing. Between them, Albert and Stockmar took the zip and the tinkle from a fun-loving girl."[35]

Like Victoria in *The Way of a Man with a Maid* the queen has a conversion experience and sees her past in a new light. No longer idealizing her mentor, Lord Melbourne, she rereads her journal entry for 22 March 1839 in which she says "as for 'the confidence of the crown,' God knows! *no Minister, no friend* ever possessed it so entirely as this truly excellent Lord Melbourne possesses mine!" She glosses her effusion with a postconversion commentary:

> NOTE BY QUEEN VICTORIA, 1st October, 1842.— Rereading this again, I cannot forbear remarking what an artificial sort of happiness *mine* was *then*, and what a blessing it is I have now in my beloved Husband *real* and *solid* happiness. . . . I had amusement, and I was only living on that superficial resource, which I *then fancied* was happiness! Thank God! for *me* and others, this is changed, and I *know what* real happiness is.—V. R.[36]

Victoria speaks in the convert's tongue, troping the religious with the amorous to construct a conversion narrative that blends romance, gender hierarchy, and the body politic. No longer celebrating her power as sovereign, she discovers that good women are not fitted to reign. In helping General Grey compile a memoir of her husband, she wrote a memorandum explaining away her hesitation about getting married as the giddiness of an inexperienced girl let out of confinement, putting "all ideas of marriage out of her mind, which she now most bitterly repents." After repentance and conversion, she conceptualized monarchy in ways congruent with prevailing notions of women's proper position, one, as "Mr. Brown" agrees, off the throne: "A worse school for a young girl, or one more detrimental to all natural feelings and affections, can not well be imagined than the position of a queen at eighteen, without experience and without a husband to guide and support her. This the Queen can state from painful experience."[37] The convert conventionally bears oral testimony to her visionary, though painful, experience.

Victoria's conversion revises history; she once was blind (believed in Melbourne, liked ruling) but now, past the pain and looking through the eyes of love, she sees. In using the metaphor of the school to describe her education in subordination, Victoria echoes many settings for flagellation narratives that take place in educational institutions—the riding master, the governess, the head boy being some stock disciplinary figures.

Whereas Victoria and Albert's story, written as a masochistic conversion narrative, depends upon marriage and childbirth for its enforcement of proper gender rules, the pornographic text resorts to scenes of torture. But in plots similar to Victoria's conversion narrative, widely read, "proper" novels convert their heroines to the dogma of domesticity, including their erotic submission, through a series of adventures involving bodily pain if not torture, often including humiliation. The woman resists taming, scorns her suitor, and asserts her will in many plots of many Victorian novels, the "romance" being a charting of the course of an independent-minded woman brought to domesticated submission through "love." In Charlotte Brontë's *Shirley* (1849), Elizabeth Gaskell's *North and South* (1855), George Eliot's *Middlemarch* (1871–72), and Mary Augusta (Mrs. Humphry) Ward's *Marcella* (1894), for instance, the woman with high-minded aspirations, unconstrained by male rule, is humbled by difficulties in her encounters with the world; then, softened by passion, she serves her happy days by submitting to a man and curbing her independent disposition. She likes her life and, like the tamed pornographic Victoria, glories in her submission as if to a higher calling.

Hardly read today, though popular in its time, *Marcella* captured a wide audience, due in part to its conservative attitude toward a woman's role. A contemporary reviewer in the *Times* praised the novel for treating issues of the day, "the hot fire of living interests," economic ones such as "property, capital, landowners, and employers, and all our economical institutions." At its heart, however, these general issues seem to speak to the situation of what the newspaper imagines as a woman reader. It is finally her willingness to take instruction from the novel's pages that heartens the reviewer: "It is not a faultless piece of art. . . .

But many a generous-minded woman laying down *Marcella* will say, 'This is for me. Here is written what I have experienced or desired.' "[38] The generous-minded woman reader, like the tamed Victoria, thanks her teacher for showing her that erotic submission leads to pleasure. The narrative itself coerces her to that wisdom.

Marcella combines its consideration of contemporary social issues with a romance plot. The heroine, an intelligent young woman who has read Karl Marx and William Morris, lives among a group of socialist friends in South Kensington and studies art. Returning to her father's estate, Marcella brings her socialist passion to the test when she confronts rigid class structures, far different from her quasi-bohemian London milieu. In her quest to ameliorate the condition of the workers, she becomes a district nurse.

Ward describes her temperament as containing something of the demon, unable to adjust to schooling: "The whole of her first year was one continual series of sulks, quarrels, and revolts" (6). In her unhappiness, she imagines herself best friends with the Princess of Wales: "she went here and there with the princess, laughing and talking, quite calmly with the greatest people in the land, her romantic friendship with the adored of England making her all the time the observed of all observers, bringing her a thousand delicate flatteries and attentions" (7). Marcella's daydream betrays her ameliorist social goals as part of her longing for aristocratic, even royal, power. Yet, scorning the charms of the high life of country squires, Marcella places her passionate energies in the service of doing good.

Her conversion from disdain for great wealth to admiration for its healing power derives from her love for Aldous Raeburn, a landowner of immense holdings. She explains her passion for him in terms familiar to many conversion narratives:

> The enormous importance that her feverish youth attached
> to wealth and birth might have been seen in her very attacks
> upon them. Now all her standards were spiritualised. She
> had come to know what happiness and affection are possible
> in three rooms, or two, on twenty-eight shillings a week; and,
> on the other hand, her knowledge of Aldous—a man of sto-
> ical and simple habit, thrust, with a student's tastes, into the
> position of a great landowner—had shown her, in the case at
> least of one member of the rich class, how wealth may be a
> true moral burden and test, the source of half the difficulties
> and pains—of half the nobleness also—of a man's life.

(554)

After Marcella converts to the role of a lady of the manor, she kneels at her beloved's feet and confesses at length to many sins, one of which involves "calm forecasts of a married state in which she was always to take the lead and always to be in the right" (558). By submerging her will in that of her rich husband she achieves a social position whereby she can devote herself to changing the world, but with a worthy help-meet to help underwrite her beneficence.

"Mr. Brown" and others in the 1870s and 1880s believed abdication would repair the gender anomaly of a lady on the throne. Few fictions, whether pornographic or respectably coercive, allow, much less reward, the independent woman for her strength and ability. She must fall to the power of sexual desire, as in Charlotte Brontë's *Shirley*, or she must remain lonely and as ideologically pure as Rhoda Nunn in George Gissing's *The Odd Women*. Victorian gender arrangements do not allow women both power and femininity.

⇥ Governess/Queen ⇤

I must maim and mar.
Your comfort is as sharp as swords;
And I cry out for wounded love.
And you are gone so heavenly far
You hear nor care of love and pain.
—*Gerard Manley Hopkins to Christina Rossetti*

Ellis allows women the minor erotic pleasure of causing pain through teasing, yet maintains that the male victim unwillingly suffers the pain his mistress inflicts.[39] The greater the pain, the more his humiliation. Unlike subjugated women, the male sufferer neither thanks powerful female figures for tormenting him nor asks for more. A spectacular exception to this rule, Swinburne published such sentiments in volumes sold on the open market and caused a scandal. The poet celebrates ruling females who derive and bestow pleasures from giving pain; the speakers in "Dolores" and "Anactoria" (*Poems and Ballads,* 1866) not only thank the dominating woman but ask for more. (Thirty years later, Victoria refused to make him poet laureate because of these naughty ballads.) "Dolores" praises the pleasure of erotic pain personified as a saint; its religious imagery transfers the mystic rose of Christian passion to a debased one, a "mystical rose of the mire." Our Lady of Pain's pagan parents, the Greek Priapus and the Roman Libitina, progenitors of constant arousal, of "unquenchable flame," rule an underworld of exhausted but insatiate acolytes:

Fruits fail and love dies and time ranges;
  Thou art fed with perpetual breath,
And alive after infinite changes,
    And fresh from the kisses of death;
Of languors rekindled and rallied,
    Of barren delights and unclean,
Things monstrous and fruitless, a pallid
    And poisonous queen.

(ll. 57–65)

Swinburne did not model Dolores directly on Queen Victoria, although the queen might have seemed to Swinburne, born the year of Victoria's accession, to have been "fed with perpetual breath," her mourning rituals by 1866 renewing her with "kisses of death." His own propensities for erotic pain are well known and do not depend upon the queen on her throne, no matter how punitive legends and reportage may have pictured her. But Swinburne's verses about a voracious dominatrix, classicized in "Anactoria" or Christianized in "Dolores," take on an added frisson of recognition or relevance in the context of Victoria's rule, a context beyond one poet's sexual proclivities, extending beyond the thrilled undergraduates who chanted his poem.

The queen, though not the overt subject of his poems, rings in his ears. "Faustine," from the same volume, alludes to mother and daughter Faustinas, both licentious, the mother married to the Roman emperor Antonious and the daughter to Marcus Aurelius. Neither woman was queen in her own right, but Swinburne's alteration of "Faustina" to "Faustine" rhymes her name with "queen," implying connections between the Roman and Victorian empires: "Where are the imperial years? and how / Are you, Faustine?" Rotting and reeking in fine Swinburnean fashion, the timeless "queen whose kingdom ebbs and shifts" (l. 10) presides over "shameless nameless love" that returns to haunt the poet's times:

As if your fed sarcophagus
  Spared flesh and skin,
You come back face to face with us,
  The same Faustine.[40]

If Swinburne's queens are not literally Victorias, it is true Swinburne had something of a queen complex. The earthy scent of the queen's favorite patchouli emanates from their bedsheets, as it did from hers. His first published volume was *The Queen Mother; Rosamond: Two Plays,* and he wrote three dramas on the subject of Mary, Queen of Scots. Regarding his own Queen of the Highlands, he delighted in imagining her in various compromising positions, as if a comic yet lethal queen haunted him. His Queen Victoria possesses lascivious appetites linked with murderous ambition. If not an enforcer and torturer, she becomes in his parodies a creature of easy virtue, a sexual harasser of her all-too-willing "ministers."

In one spoof, two immense cultural icons—Wordsworth and Victoria—enjoy carnal relations. The queen confesses her loss of virginity to her mother:

> Ce n'était pas un prince; ce n'était pas un milord, ni même *Sir R. Peel*. C'était un misérable du peuple, en nomme [sic] *Wordsworth*, qui m'a récité des vers de son *Excursion* d'une sensualité si chaleureuse qu'ils m'ont ébranlée—et je suis tombée. [It wasn't a prince; it wasn't a nobleman; neither was it *Sir R. Peel*. It was an ordinary man of the people named *Wordsworth*, who recited to me the lines of his *Excursion*, so warmly sensuous, that they overcame me, and I fell.] [41]

The ponderousness of Wordsworth's long epic, coupled with an idea of an aging impossibly remote widow, gives the scene its humor, in the course of which, however, the speech reconstructs Victoria's emotional susceptibility. Victoria, not merely deflowered but nymphomaniacal, preys on smitten officials in Swinburne's burlesque, *La Soeur de la Reine* (1861?), an operatic parody. Prime Minister Robert Peel, in an ante-room of Queen Victoria's boudoir, madly raves with jealous desire for "cette adorable femme," who at that very moment lies entwined with her lover, Sir John Russell, also one of Victoria's "ministers." When Peel vows to shoot Russell, the Duchess of Kent tells him that if he kills those who have enjoyed the queen's favor, he will have to murder the entire government leadership. After naming them: Palmerston, Bright, Derby, and so forth, Peel concludes: "Cette femme mettrait dans son lit l'univers entier!" [That woman has brought the entire universe into her bed!]. [42] Imperial in her aspirations Victoria turns her bed into a symbolic counterpart of her government.

Not only does Swinburne's Reine wallow in voluptuousness, she also steeps herself in blood, eliminating in one way or another every challenge to her rule. In the burlesque's existing fourth act, she instructs Peel in her ruling ways. More harsh than her predecessors who merely transport enemies, she has them shot or poisoned. She survives all attempts on her life, bragging that she has survived five assassin's pistols so far. By merging the erotic with the murderous, Swinburne lends credence to the psychiatrist Turner's formulation of the assassins' erotic motives. Finally, Victoria gives her body to Peel so that he will eliminate a rival to the throne. She reveals her basic hunger as one for power. "La Reine Victoria" is a humorous but prescient precursor to Rider Haggard's Ayesha, *She-who-must-be-obeyed.*

Victorian gender codes stigmatize transgressive women as the problem, as in their label, "the Woman Question." Victoria often refers to herself as a quirk, a mutant, an exemplar of the Question, despite herself. The pornographic version of a "Woman Question novel" features a dominatrix who trains the male into embracing the transgressed order, with woman on top. It pictures a world where powerful women inflict their authority against helpless or passive males. Victorian femininity seems antithetic to a desire to torture men. A woman who wanted to hurt rather than heal a man would be a monstrous creature. Yet the dominatrix is the nurse's shadowy double, ministering to darker desires for wounding.

Flagellation fantasies dominate Victorian pornography's repertory. Havelock Ellis observes that "those who possess a special knowledge of such matters declare that sexual flagellation is the most frequent of all sexual perversions in England."[43] Henry Spencer Ashbee, born three years before Victoria's accession to the throne and dead one year before his sovereign, amassed an extensive pornographic collection, and his expertise supports Ellis's observation: "The propensity which the English most cherish is undoubtedly flagellation. . . . Only here, I opine, can be found men who experience a pleasure rather in receiving than in administering the birch. . . . Did not discretion forbid, it would be easy to name men of the highest positions in diplomacy, literature, the army, &c. who, at the present day, indulge in this idiosyncrasy."[44]

Ashbee classified erotic novels as domestic fiction. Although to do so may itself seem perverse, that category illuminates a darker aspect of domesticity in both the familial and the national sense. How many of the "men of the highest positions" placed themselves at the mercy of a punitive "queen"? Ashbee explains that "women delight in administering the birch," his collection providing him with evidence from such titles as *The Merry Order of St. Bridget: Personal Recollections of the Use of the Rod, The Birchen Bouquet, A Visit to Mrs Birch, The Birch Discipline, The Quintessence of Birch Discipline*—works that feature Sir Frederick Flaybum, the Hon. Mr. Freecock, and so on. Though Ashbee's authority on the Victorian fictional dominatrix remains unrivaled, his conclusion about the proclivities of actual women may well be questioned, based as it is on the male-authored works he himself collected.

Although Ashbee does not consider this particular passion unique
to the Victorians, he notes a quickened interest in writings on flagellation: "the rapidity with which the first edition of Hotten's *History of
the Rod* was sold," he points out, stimulated publication of four subsequent volumes. *History of the Rod* devotes itself to the whipping of girls,
a topic not restricted to pornography but, according to Ashbee, occupying the pages of such domestic periodicals as *The Family Herald* and
The Englishwoman's Magazine. Interest in the corporal punishment of
girls has invaded the most genteel of girl's schools, he claims, producing devotees of the rod. He cites one book relevant to fantasies of
a dominating queen, *The Romance of Chastisement; or, Revelations of the
School and Bedroom by an Expert* (1870), in which "Martinet, the head-
governess" in a girl's academy, whips the girls into submission.
Heterosexual fantasies deny the homosexual text: "Fear and shame
were both gone," one girl confesses, "it was as though I was surren-
dering my person to the embraces of a man whom I so loved I would
anticipate his wildest desires." Yet, the image of a strong woman pen-
etrates her fantasy: "But no man was in my thought; Martinet was
the object of my adoration, and I felt *through the rod* that I shared her
passions."[45]

"Miss de Vere" adores the Martinet, whom she calls "Her Majesty":

> Her Majesty gave her two flicks more in the same place, and
> then bade them cut her loose. . . . Miss de Vere flung herself
> at Her Majesty's feet, kissed her hand, pressed it to her
> breast, and I declare to you she implored her pardon with
> tears, calling her Mistress—like a child, and promising
> henceforth to do only Martinet's will and pleasure.[46]

The novel is not a schoolgirl's fantasy about being erotically dominated
by a queen. According to Ashbee, the author was St. George H. Stock,
appropriately enough a former lieutenant in the 2d or Queen's Royal
Regiments. The novel turns the abject into a woman, projecting onto a
female character certain male experiences of submitting to a majestic
woman. The girl characterizes his symbolic gender position, the
debasement he desires.

Taking that desire to another level, *Gynecocracy: A Narrative of the
Adventures and Psychological Experiences of Julian Robinson (afterwards
Viscount Ladywood) Under Petticoat-Rule Written by Himself* (1893) superimposes fantasies of being turned into a girl on scenes of domestic life
and, ultimately, on the management of government. Often attributed
to Havelock Ellis, the novel, a masochistic conversion narrative, ex-

plores connections between the pornographic domestic novel and the body politic.[47] It transforms the common metaphor, "petticoat rule," as in the pamphlet *Brown on the Throne*, into a literal situation. Set in the domestic interiors—the schoolroom and bedroom—of a country home in Sussex, the pornographic bildungsroman follows the sexual growth through pain of a young man.

Because Julian is too frail for the rigors of male education but not too feeble to attempt an examination of what might be under a nurserymaid's skirts, "a friend of the family who had some German anthropological experiences [recommended] that the lad should be taken in hand by a lady."[48] The lady, Mademoiselle de Chambonnard, begins his "education," flogging him in front of his three female cousins, a "bevy of laughing girls." Before detailing his birchen education, the "editor" presents a synopsis:

> Ultimately, as the cutting strokes administered by the white round arm of a woman continued to fall with cruel regularity . . . he could no longer withstand the sense of abject humiliation, the necessity for yielding unreservedly to his fair mistress. He spoke of the subjugation and the galling nature of the conviction that they had, despite himself, thoroughly mastered him. But, he added, he could have held out against a man: what sapped his strength was not so much the torture of the punishment as the sorcery of the gender. It was the triumph of the Petticoat.
>
> *(4)*

The petticoat, "emblem of the female sex," explains the governess, subjects males to its power, turning boys into girls. Innocent of women's anatomy but powerfully drawn to it, Julian's feeble attempts at self-assertion meet with strong measures, administered by his governess, first as instructional lectures: "Master Julian you have to realise that I am your governess and that you are my absolute slave. . . . From you I shall expect and shall exact the most implicit obedience and the most abject submission. You will tremble hereafter at the mere rustle of a petticoat; by it you are to be governed" (18). The lesson follows the lecture.

The conversion scene, in a schoolroom, replicates torture scenes of other flagellation novels. The novels follow conventions known to those seeking pleasures on the side streets of Victorian London. As the preface to *Venus School-Mistress; or, Birchen Sports* explains, "Those women who give most satisfaction to the amateurs of discipline are called governesses, because they have by experience acquired a tact and a *modus operandi*, which the generality do not possess."[49] The governess uses a "horse," but unlike the "horse" of *The Way of a Man with a Maid*, theirs, called the Berkley horse after its inventor, resembles an artist's rather than a trainer's equipment. Ashbee calls Mrs. Teresa Berkley of 28 Charlotte Street, Portland Place, inventor of the Berkley horse, the "Queen of her Profession."[50]

Julian's "governess" also employs mechanical devices, but they are more homely than the Berkley horse. Authorizing Julian's treatment, "German anthropology" alludes to a developing science of human behavior and suggests the study of tribal rituals. His education is figured as "initiation" into a feminine universe, his punishment for being "Too unruly! . . . Too indecent! . . . Too inquisitive! . . . Too anxious to know what young ladies have under their petticoats" (18). Julian suffers from "masculine" curiosity. The work thus places the [male] reader for whom it was written in Julian's vulnerable position, being no worse than most boys and being humiliated for a common prank in households full of young servant girls.

The entire novel devotes itself to converting the young man to petticoat rule, a conversion the protagonist fears as a loss of manhood. "I felt I should be shorn of my manhood and made effeminate and good for nothing, that my strength and virility should be suppressed" he confesses (14). His fear is fulfilled, for the terms of petticoat rule involve psychological emasculation. Emasculation, not impotence, signifies a power position; Julian's great sexual feats only serve women's demands.

More than simply a metaphor, petticoats serve as conversion tools. The turning point in this masochistic conversion narrative, Julian's first ordeal occurs when the governess orders him placed under a petticoat, making literal and concrete the symbolic condition of men under petticoat government. After Julian kneels at Mademoiselle's feet—the same posture as Marcella adopts in front of Aldous at the moment of her feminization—the torture commences:

> At last two straps were buckled tightly round my arms, just above the elbows. In each strap was a small metal ring. Elise [a cousin] passed a white cord three or four times through these rings, and then proceeded to pull them as closely together as possible. Oh, how she hurt! I thought she would have broken my arms.
>
> "Tighter," said Mademoiselle.

(19)

She slaps his face with "soft, lovely, dimpled hands," at the same time administering the lesson: " 'You object to a governess, to feminine domination, to petticoat-rule,'—giving me two smacks at each enumeration. 'I think I shall convert you'" (20).

Julian tries to resist, but he is enchanted with the girls who flush with their exertions and exude enervating odors. His head swims from torture and other sensations, at which point Mademoiselle forces him to kiss the back of her hand and thank her.[51] They tear off his trousers and drawers as instruments of false patriarchal doctrine; the clothes, says the governess, "teach you all sorts of resistance and naughtiness, and make you assume airs of ridiculous superiority, which you do not possess. We must make a girl of you" (21).

Julian's feminization involves associating petticoats with an initially unnameable pleasure: "in the midst of my abasement" he notices an "incipient sensation, of what I felt when I lifted the nursery-maid's garments"(22). Sexual desire becomes forever associated with the petticoat and with whippings. The governess places Julian under one of her used, red flannel petticoats: "To enforce your subjection to the petticoat, the emblem of the female sex, and to show your domination by it, you shall stand in the corner with one over your head . . . until . . . in my boudoir I shall birch your bottom for you" (22). With some lapses, requiring lesson reviews, Julian is quelled and conquered until "at last I became a wretched petticoat slave" (26).

Eventually, he marries one of his cousins, gets sent to Parliament by their machinations, and votes according to his wife's instructions. In this plot sequence, *Gynecocracy* resembles Gilbert and Sullivan's *Iolanthe,* where Strephon, the guileless hero, enters Parliament by means of female fairypower. At the end of the novel, Julian meditates on his position, seeing nothing in the political world that contradicts his education by his governess: "Still there is something in me which assures me that man was made for more than the petticoat. This world is woman's earth, and it is petticoated all over. Their's is the dominion, turn and twist the matter as you will. Therefore, I conclude there must be some other world where men will have a ruling part to play" (167).

Gynecocracy supplies an erotic plot to the same threat that *Brown on the Throne* addresses by innuendo. Petticoat government will not do, not only because women can't mind the business but because it threatens to turn the entire nation into girls. Petticoat government obliterates manliness, as in the broadside ballad discussed earlier where Queen Victoria's crinoline monarchy sends Prince Albert, Lord Russell, and Lord Palmerston floating down Mayfair in hooped petticoats.

In its ending, *Gynecocracy* draws an analogy between the domestic

sphere of the Sussex country house where Julian is educated to petticoat rule and the domestic sphere of the nation where the petticoat
also rules, largely from Queen Victoria's country houses, Windsor,
Balmoral, and Osborne. Writing from the perspective of the British
Empire, the author looks out at an earth covered by a petticoat. His
assessment of women's absolute political power when women did not
have the vote envisions a governess who can make abject puppets of all
men. In that "world" the queen stands for the nation. Julian describes
Mademoiselle as one who "dressed and comported herself like a young
Queen" (8) and who, like the queen, requires that her hand be kissed
on rare and special occasions. Lord Esher, drawing on contemporary
reports on the awe Victoria inspired, reports on the ritual of hand kissing: "How rarely the Queen extended her hand! It was a great privilege,
and only on special occasions vouchsafed to her Ministers. Men and
women bent very low to kiss that hand."[52] To Julian Robinson, Viscount
Ladywood's flogging imparts a different meaning to that last phrase.
Bending very low to kiss the hand of his governess, he observes a world
ruled by the petticoat. The observation resonates through the land
ruled for sixty years by a woman with a strong temper, who could scat-
ter terrified royalty by simply walking down a hall, and whose empire
was envisioned as the "world."

✣ Whip-Up Alive ✣

Queen Victoria was associated with the red-flannel petticoat and its
erotic potential at least forty years before the anonymous author of
Gynecocracy wrote his flagellation fantasy. She was credited with import-
ing that humble but effective garment to the attention of the higher
orders. In an article appearing on February 13, 1858, in the *Home
Journal,* a Boston gossip sheet, Queen Victoria is portrayed as espousing
the red-flannel petticoat as a "Piquant stimulus . . . to awaken the flag-
ging take notice-ism and dormant conjugal susceptibilities of Prince
Albert." Recounting an anecdote that gives an uncharacteristic jaunti-
ness to the flamboyantly moralistic Albert, the paper explains Victoria's
unprecedented setting of a fashion trend. The writer describes a scene
where attractive young servants gather at the entrance of Balmoral
Castle to welcome the royal couple,

> arrayed of course, in their picturesque holiday attire. We
> have spoken of the art-sympathies of the gentle Albert. *The
> effect of the looped petticoat, last year, on his sensitive soul was extra-
> ordinary.* He recognized here a new principle of art before

unknown to him, and gave himself up to its study until his
watchful spouse, thinking that perhaps not art alone, but a
little touch of nature might also combine thus to absorb
him,—resolved to afford him the opportunity of indulging
his tastes in the domestic circle. In short, she adopted the
scarlet herself.

The reporter traces the style of dress to the peasant maidens of
Scotland and Ireland, "of coarse texture, to be sure, but worn with
grace and neatly looped up at one side just sufficiently to reveal bright
glimpses of snowy stocking." With its headline, "THE RED-PETTICOAT
CONNUBIALLY WHIP-UP ALIVE," the story evokes a flagellation scenario,
announcing the whipping up of passion, a subtext of domination and
submission. The story further claims that when Victoria took her red-
flannel whip-up to London, the Empress Eugénie "fell in love with it
and all the ladies of rank were seized with the violent scarlet fever epi-
demic, *scarletina.*"

It is difficult to know whether the report is accurate. Flannel petticoats were thought to be healthy, red ones in particular, possibly
because of the warm color. By 1859 women's magazines were reporting
on the fashion for colored day petticoats, particularly for scarlet and
violet. With the introduction of chemical dyes in 1860, magenta was
described as the "queen of colours."[53] The *Young Ladies' Journal* of 1866
instructed its readers that "White Petticoats are worn in full dress
only."[54] By mid-century a woman's underclothes had become, according to a fashion historian, an "integral part of her personality."[55] They
suggested, yet covered what could not be spoken, but their increasing
bulk masked the growing importance of women. When the wearing of
underwear is taken as a sign of the Victorian new morality, coloring it
red signals a moral transgression, the return of the repressed. Whether
Queen Victoria actually introduced red flannel petticoats into high
society hardly matters, for the story enlivens her culture's imaginative
life by linking a jealous possessive queen with the peasantry's erotic
underwear.

A fetish, the red petticoat signals repressed sexual danger for men,
defending them against fears of powerful women. One of masochism's
prime attributes, according to Deleuze,[56] the fetish arouses men,
thereby enslaving them to a condition Julian Robinson called "abasement." The psychoanalyst Robert Stoller's description of fetishization
clarifies the red petticoat's symbolic meaning: "Excitement [generated
by the fetish] . . . is a defense against anxiety," he explains:

a transformation of anxiety into something more bearable, a melodrama. The ultimate danger . . . at the heart of sexual excitement is that one's sense of existence, especially in the form of one's sense of maleness or femaleness, can be threatened. . . . To dissolve that threat . . . one calls forth the mechanisms of hostility . . . , such as dehumanizing others, and then decks the scripts out with mystery, illusion, and safety factors."[57]

Both Julian's ordeal and the scene on the Balmoral staircase (Albert leering at the servants while Victoria scowls at him) outline a melodramatic script. In a similar way that Masoch's fur-clad Venus allows Severin to reclaim mastery, red underwear transforms fear of woman into desire for her.

By the time of its circulation in England, *Gynecocracy* could excite thrills by imagining an antifeminist nightmare of petticoat rule without end. Queen Victoria's image itself becomes fetishized both in her underwear, which servants apparently sold out of the palace, and in pornographic photographs of women with crowns on their heads. To some, adjusting to petticoat rule required a total reversal of normal male authority, with no possible middle ground.

Queen Victoria was obviously no Marie-Antoinette, whose body and sexuality were used in pornographic propaganda for revolution. As Chantal Thomas and Lynn Hunt have argued, the erotic body of the French queen served political purposes; the forces of the Revolution enlisted a pornography that drew on hatreds and fears engendered by the dark continent of the feminine.[58] To imagine the dumpy Victoria in ecstasy with her most unprepossessing prime minister, Lord Russell, seems comical, but it also opens an imaginative door to reveal a power of queens' erotic desires. Like Marie-Antoinette, Queen Victoria's obvious sexuality could generate pornographic fantasies that intersected with fantasies about the body politic. No matter that Victoria found feminism repellent, a shadowy Venus-Victoria could stand for a different revolution, a sexual one, not bloodless by any means, but one that acknowledges its fear of female sexual desire through pornographic expression.

Stoller considers secrets and secretiveness as essential components of sexual excitement. Victoria ruled the erotic imagination of her subjects in secret ways. Her sexuality enhanced, or, charged, the obvious secret of one's mother's sexual experience. As mother of her people, the visible secret of Victoria's erotic propensities kept the game of sex warm, funny, and dangerous. A pornographic imagination could transform the queen to a sexual slave or a sexual dominatrix. Swinburne, for example, drew his inspiration not merely from unlikely couplings but also from Victoria's amorous behavior. His queen could stimulate libidinal fantasies, her perceived power acting as an aphrodisiac. The poet's lurid imagination in "Laus Veneris" presents a Venus from the Tannhaüser legend in a context generated by his *reine*. This love goddess presides over a kingdom "where strong souls of men are bound":

> Their blood runs round the roots of time like rain
> She casts them forth and gathers them again;
>> With nerve and bone she weaves and multiplies
> Exceeding pleasure out of extreme pain.

Queen Victoria's sexuality lived in her subjects' secret hearts.

8

MOTHERHOOD, EXCESS, AND EMPIRE

*Will the Queen never find out that she will have ten times more
influence on her children by treating them with kindness and not
trying to rule them like a despot?*

—Henry Ponsonby

*When the Royal family is so large, and our children have (alas)
such swarms of children, to connect some few of them with the great
families of the land—is an immense strength to the Monarchy and
a great link between the Royal Family and the country. . . . Besides
which, a new infusion of blood is an absolute necessity—as the
race will else degenerate bodily and physically.*

—*Queen Victoria*, Your Dear Letter

Victorians liked to observe that the queen ruled her nation as a mother
and her household as a monarch. Victoria had the ruling business backward, they suggested. Supposedly the queen should rule her kingdom
as a monarch and her household as a mother. Putting the saying right
by reversing the reversal exposes a puzzle that the witticism disguises—
the problem of a model, a figure, an adequate symbol of this queen's
rule. The saying reveals the culture's difficulty in imagining a queen
who is also a mother. Linking the queen's maternal role to her monarchical role transgressed boundaries in the cultural imagination, as if the
two kinds of authority inherently contradicted each other. Motherhood
as a model for a nation appears manifestly humorous. Since nation-
states derive their authority from a military model, a mother's role is
patriotic.[1] Serving the nation, the good mother sends her sons to war,
knits for them, binds their wounds, and buries them. Victoria performed all these functions. During the Boer War, in addition to staying
in close contact with her ministers, she "crocheted shawls for her soldiers [for the Christmas of 1898] and she sent out a box of chocolate
to every man at the front with a coloured print of herself on it."[2]

Moreover, Victoria apparently conducted state business as if it were a marriage bureau. In October 1889 the American humor magazine *Life* elected Queen Victoria "No. 26" in its "Gallery of Beauties" for her matchmaking gifts. "Her principal function for the past few years," they explained, "has been the securing of husbands and wives for her numerous offspring and their progeny to the third and fourth generation." Inevitably, Victoria's marital skills take a martial turn: "She has successfully ravaged every royal family in Europe," but her need for breeders remains unsated. Finally, the columnist concludes, no one in Britain will escape Victoria's matrimonial snares. With the marriage of Princess Louise to the Marquis of Lorne, a commoner, "she has begun to gather in the members of the nobility and gentry. If the fertility of her family keeps up, there is no reason why every inhabitant of the British Isles should not soon be connected by marriage with the reigning family."[3] The accompanying picture imagines Victoria's ascension. As she is borne aloft, she studies a holy book—the peerage? Genealogical tables? The *Almanach de Gotha?* Her crown hangs down her back, a widow's cap replacing it. Buckled over her robes she wears armor and the coronation sword. The monarchical, matrimonial, and imperial businesses venerate their patron saint, Mother Victoria.[4]

Until her letters were published after her death, most people did not recognize the queen's extensive knowledge of and participation in state affairs, particularly in the realm of foreign policy. After reading Victoria's letters, which were published from 1907 to 1932, Harold Laski, a founder of the Labour Party, concluded that no prime minister could afford to ignore the Crown's opinion.[5] Few statesmen could claim seniority over the queen. In addition, her knowledge of world politics, her superb memory, and her attention to details blended with an unmatched common sense and decisive temperament. An image prevailed of the "retired widow," in Bagehot's phrase, who tended to her grandchildren in a matriarchal way, while she exhibited a tender heart to dogs and the poor.[6] Such activities could be figured as a kind of fierce upper-class mother, but to combine maternal sentiments with actual rule produces a seeming incommensurability. If domestic images of queens offer potential for disorder, the maternal idea also produces its own disturbances.

⟶ Thy Nation's Mother ⟵

No English sovereign before Victoria had been imagined as a national mother figure; it is at once a reassuring and a frightening concept. How would the cultural imagination encompass a mother ruling "as a monarch"? The seeming incompatibility between nurture and knowl-

"*Life*'s Gallery of Beauties, No. 26," vol. 14, October 17, 1889. Queen Victoria ascends to heaven, an apotheosis for the matchmaker and universal mother. The label under the hat with little children's heads on a plate says "Bundestag," translated as "Federal Diet" for her proliferating German-speaking descendants.

edge, combined with an uneasy sense that mothers' intimate knowledge would best stay in the nursery, lies at the core of Queen Victoria's maternal imago. The cultural paradox of Queen Victoria's specific kind of monarchy generates its own complex figurations. National fecundity deriving its power from a maternal idea produces figuration whose trope is hyperbole, yielding much of everything from objects, children, slums—in a word: excess. The mother-monarch apparently rules the waves by ruling the nursery and the altar. "Swarms of children" in Victoria's happy phrase, trace themselves to her. They extend to European courts, ultimately to Eastern colonies; they diffuse into everyone's identity. Sometimes the queen's very ubiquity as a national mother translates into invisibility: she is everywhere and nowhere.

By the 1870s Victoria was the only monarch most people had known. Yet if measured according to prevailing standards of a virile nation, Victoria should not have been its ruler. Health as a nation, according to Charles Kingsley, for example, was embodied in the regimens of manly Christianity, [male] "bodies untainted," in his phrase, "by hereditary effeminacy."[7] The queen herself spoke of a dilemma of self-representability that years of rule, numbers of children, domestic and foreign intrigue, did not resolve but seemed only to exacerbate. With the marriages of her children, Victoria's family multiplied geometrically, threatening to fulfill a Malthusian vision of a micronation of royal progeny. Photographs of the queen's family, its sweetest babe cradled in the arms of Her Majesty, or, a standing child leaning on the queen's lap inundated the nation. Victoria frequently sat at the center of a multitude, her descendants surrounding the origin of their generation.

Victoria articulated in her writing as well as in her posed family pictures some of the contradictions of representing her reign, reflecting as well as constituting what she considered its inherent confusion. She presented her rule paradoxically, drawing on the language of femininity, while at the same time exerting a "masculine" power in government, a secret her maternal presentation disguised. In 1852, after she had been a monarch for fifteen years, she stated, "I am every day more convinced that *we women*, if we are to be good women, *feminine* and *amiable* and *domestic*, are not *fitted to reign*."[8] Victoria's statement expresses the paradox in representation I have been describing. The speaker speaks from her own considerable experience as queen, an authoritative position that has been accumulating for every day of the considerable days of her reign. At the same time, that very authority displaces the maker of the statement as being fit to make a statement about reigning.

Was Queen Victoria not fit to reign, or was she not a good woman? Her significant qualification, "if we are to be good women," opens the possibility of a reigning woman as neither feminine, amiable, nor domestic. The concept of a masculine, unamiable, and political female ruler was exploited in some late Victorian literature. But the qualification of the queen's own statement, which derives its authority from her experience as monarch, provided no ground where Victoria, the domestic woman, could stand.[9] While Victoria Regina opens the possibility, at least on the linguistic level, of not being a good woman, were she to advocate that in life, she would violate vows to her people and to her spouse. The contradictions implicit in a feminine monarch are complicated by the contradiction posed by a monarch who is also a wife and mother.

Sixteen years after Victoria's marriage the paradox of matronly authority had not been solved. Recognized in England only as Prince Albert of Saxe-Coburg and Gotha, the queen's husband had no official title. The reluctance to give him one seemed a way to avoid parliamentary recognition of Victoria's anomalous position as sovereign. What to call a foreign male person who was the conjugal superior but national inferior of the ruler? The queen considered something approaching an oligarchy by suggesting "king consort" but above all wished for Albert to receive an official English title. Before she eventually settled for "prince consort" at the time of her oldest daughter's marriage, she wrote a memorandum, dated May 1856:

> It is a strange omission in our Constitution that while the wife of a King has the highest rank and dignity in the realm after her husband assigned to her by law, the husband of a queen regnant is entirely ignored by the law. This is the more extraordinary, as a husband has in this country such particular rights and such great power over his wife, and as the queen is married just as any other woman is, and swears to obey her lord and master, as such, while by law he has no rank or defined position. This is a strange anomaly.[10]

The anomaly of Victoria's reign derives from conventions of authority. The electric current that kept her tiny body in the spotlight—often at odds with the social structures to which she herself subscribed—had to be harnessed into the gender position history had decreed. Victoria liked wielding authority. She preached subservience, even believed in it, but her dominance, figured eventually as maternal, overruled her best efforts to wrestle it down. After her eldest daughter's early marriage—and for as long as she could after Albert's death—she preached the doctrine of anomalous queenship:

> One great advantage however you all (our daughters, I mean) have over me, and that is that you are not in the anomalous position in which I am,—as Queen Regnant. Though dear Papa, God knows, does everything—it is a reversal of the right order of things which distresses me much and which no one, but such a perfection, such an angel as he is—could bear and carry through.[11]

As Victoria and her age saw it, a woman's authority derived from her ability to influence, to set an example to be emulated. As such delineators of the Victorian gender system as John Ruskin and Sarah Stickney Ellis explain, womanly influence disavows mothers' sexuality, imagining the category of motherhood as disembodied, idealized, and revered but also inextricably imbedded in fleshly concerns, an impossible contradiction that ideology but not real lives can ignore. To imagine unproblematic motherhood, one needs never to have borne children. In actuality, Queen Victoria found childbearing an imposition upon her body (our "animal nature," she called it), while referring to Albert as her angel elevated their own sexual relationship to the spiritual plane. She presented herself as physically devoted to her husband. Yet at the same time, she seemed squeamish about sex.

In 1885, before her baby Beatrice's wedding, she confessed her feelings about sex for women to her eldest child. She did not like the thought of her virginal daughters as sexual beings:

> I count the months, weeks and days that she is still my own sweet, unspoilt, innocent lily and child. That thought—that agonising thought which I always felt, and which I often wonder any mother can bear of giving up your own child, from whom all has been so carefully kept and guarded—to a stranger to do unto her as he likes is to me the most torturing thought in the world. While I feel no girl could go to the altar (and would probably refuse) if she knew all, there is something very dreadful in the thought of the sort of trap she is being led into.
>
> I can't help saying to you what has cost me always so much and what in poor, darling, gentle (and not very strong) Beatrice's case almost tortures me![12]

Coexisting with whatever contradictory feelings she had about her children's sexuality and adulthood, her representations of herself as a mother depended in part in having at least one child at her beck and call. In the sentiment quoted above, Victoria has separated her maternal function as the protector of her virginal daughters from the sexuality that produced them. The older Victoria, beyond childbearing years, becomes more of a national maternal figure than she did when she was bearing children.

Whatever her personal objections to babies (she didn't like them) or her own children, after Albert's death she exploited her authority as mother to represent herself as queen. Two years after Beatrice's wedding, at the time of her Golden Jubilee, Victoria capitalized on her image as a mother in ways that suggest she knew its power as a monarchical image. Vetting her children's speeches on her behalf during the Jubilee celebrations, she wrote to her secretary, Sir Henry Ponsonby:

> The Queen approves of these answers, but always wishes the words 'my dear Mother' to be inserted. Not only on this occasion, but always. If Sir Henry thinks that it could come in any other place better, he can alter it. But the Queen wishes it should never be omitted when her children represent her.[13]

To insist upon obeisance to monarchy as homage to a mother and to employ the powerful medium of photography to emphasize its appropriateness invites the ridicule implied in the witticism about motherhood and monarchy.

Despite maternal monarchy's seeming paradox, the image of the widowed mother solves some of the representational difficulties in conceptualizing a Victorian queen. Victoria no longer had to face her problem of anomalous authority in regard to a husband. The Mother Victoria image as a holy mother eventually subsumes, even mutes, that of the wife.

To cast Victoria as a protestant virgin mother, however, inspires bathetic effusions—an excess of reverence. Salutes to Victoria at the Golden Jubilee in 1887 instate the Mother-Queen as a Holy Mother. Diana Mulock Craik, author of the popular novel *John Halifax, Gentleman* and celebrator of woman in her proper place, employed the repertory of virgin mother images in her Jubilee tribute to Victoria:

> Womanliest Woman! queenliest Queen
>   Thy country's Mother, as it sees

> Three generations round Thy knees.
> And all that was and might have been.
>
> O generous Heart, that, bleeding, fed
>   Her people 'neath her sheltering wings,
>   Taught pity for all suffering things
> Out of the very breast that bled.[14]

Craik distinguishes Victoria from Virgin by specifying her temporal reign as three generations, impressively long for a mortal. Then she draws upon the myth of the mother pelican (used also in medieval Christian imagery) who pierces her breast to feed her children, perhaps an allusion as well to both Princess Alice, who had died with her infant child, and Prince Leopold, who had died from hemophilia. Beyond her personal family, Victoria was known for suffering with her subjects, particularly the soldiers maimed in distant battlefields.

Victoria's image as mother generated such contradictions that by the time of the Golden Jubilee, representations of the queen had fragmented and multiplied, as if to comprehend uniqueness, multiplicity, and contradiction. The figurations resulting from the paradox of maternal monarchy included nonsense, exaggeration, and giganticism. An implication of the fantasy expressed in the *Life* satire—that a drop of Victoria's blood might eventually show up in every Briton—also indicates that Victoria's presence could diffuse, sublime, or disappear. That figuration takes excess to extremes. By being everywhere, Victoria was sometimes seen as being nowhere, as being historical nothingness.[15]

⇥ Three Queens ⇤

Lewis Carroll's Alice books present an antic view of Victorian England. In *Alice in Wonderland* (1865) the young Victorian girl discovers a world ruled by an arbitrary Queen of Hearts, whose husband seems completely swamped by her imperiousness and whose realm upsets all logic. The most familiar and powerful of Carroll's queens, the Queen of Hearts rules by terror, her echoing refrain, "Off with his head!" Alice falls into a wonderland where a queen's logic governing the realm consists of doing and undoing and where all the adventures lead to stasis: nothing ever gets done, although everyone frantically does something. The Red Queen's realm takes arbitrary rules for granted. The ambiance of *Alice in Wonderland* verges on delirium, where awakening from a dream mechanically avoids inevitable violent disintegration.

If the first Alice book avoids the Red Queen's ultimate destructiveness, *Through the Looking-Glass* (1872) distributes a queen's illogic among an oligarchy of three. Carroll presents a conversation between three "queens"—the Red Queen, the White Queen, and the newly crowned Queen Alice. Their conversation reveals that not one of them possesses authority. They are certifiable queens, though, for rationality eludes them. Alice makes herself a queen by placing a golden crown on her head. The more experienced queens examine her for her qualifications: "What do you mean by 'If you really are a Queen'? What right have you to call yourself so? You can't be a Queen, you know, till you've passed the proper examination."[16] No queen, even triplicated, can pass the examination; queens do not have the right physical or mental equipment. Or, in the terms of Carroll's world, Queen Alice passes the queen exam by entering into nonsensical discourse, although she loses points for recognizing nonsense when she hears it.

The hyperbolic three queens clearly refer to Victoria's excessiveness, and allusions to other qualities of Caroll's actual monarch appear in the dialogue. "The Queen gasped and shut her eyes, 'I can do Addition,' she said, 'if you give me time . . . but I can't do Substraction [sic], under *any* circumstances!'" (191). Like the White Queen, but transferred to the physical realm, Victoria made astonishing additions to the population and, even more astonishingly, all of her children survived childhood. Queen Victoria added to her brood through marriage, extending British influence by eventually becoming related to the crowned heads of most of Europe. She also advocated enriching royal blood through marrying an extra royal here or there to an indigenous person. At the same time as her children and grandchildren enter royal alliances through marriage, the "little" Victorian wars in Asia and Africa extended the royal family's influence, even if they were not always victorious. The conjunction of the two actions seems to naturalize the idea of empire: multiplicities of queens, multiplicities of nations, all recognizing some form of Victoria's compelling image.

Carroll jokes about royal pronouncements: "When you've once said a thing, that fixes it, and you must take the consequences"; about verbosity, "I'll tell you a secret," whispers the White Queen, "I can read words of one letter! Isn't *that* grand?" (192). Hyperbolically reducing the thousands of letters Victoria wrote, Carroll also comments on the rarity of the public queenly use of "I."[17] There are those who claim that Victoria used the royal "we" to convey that her desires and pronouncements expressed those of her [dead] husband. The practice did not in fact originate with Victoria, but her use of it kept her husband alive and verbally testified that she was still governed by his wishes. Such a vow places dispute out of reach, for who can argue with a dead man? Carroll comments on queenly diplomacy ("Queens never make bargains") and on queenly intrusiveness: " 'I wish Queens never asked questions,' Alice thought to herself" (92).

In *Through the Looking-Glass* Carroll refers to the queen's mathematical logic, her thickening body, and her imperviousness to the discomforts suffered by those entering her freezing domiciles:

> "We had *such* a thunderstorm last Tuesday—I mean one of the last set of Tuesdays, you know."
>
> Alice was puzzled. "In *our* country," she remarked, "there's only one day at a time."
>
> The Red Queen said "That's a poor thin way of doing things. Now *here*, we mostly have days and nights two or three at a time, and sometimes in the winter we take as many as five nights together—for warmth, you know."
>
> "Are five nights warmer than one night, then?" Alice ventured to ask.
>
> "Five times as warm, of course."
>
> "But they should be five times as *cold*, by the same rule—"
>
> "Just so!" cried the Red Queen. "Five times as warm, *and* five times as cold—just as I'm five times as rich as you are, *and* five times as clever!"   (*194*)

Neither thin nor poor, Queen Victoria could afford to impose her mathematics and body temperature on her company. Discussing his queen's particular brand of reasoning, Ponsonby described a method for discussing matters with the queen that could have appeared in Carroll's masterpiece:

> When she insists that two and two make five I say that I cannot help thinking that they make four. She replies that there may be some truth in what I say but she knows they make five. Thereupon I drop the discussion. It is of no consequence and I leave it there, knowing the fact. But X goes on with it, brings proofs, arguments and former sayings of her own. No one likes this. No one can stand admitting they are wrong, women especially; and the Queen can't abide it. Consequently she won't give in, says X is unkind and there is trouble.[18]

Carroll translates the typical mathematical metaphor for obvious illogic to literal absurdity, while conveying a similar impossibility to Ponsonby's dilemma of negotiating a border just beyond rational interchange, where will, not logic, is at stake.

In addition, the three queens' conversation about climate draws upon a consciousness that Victoria experienced a different atmosphere from the rest of humankind. If her body temperature could be attributed to an endless climacteric, it also could signify a unique body. That Victoria imposed her superhuman tolerance for cold on everyone seemed part of her bodily mystery. Not only did her own household have to conform to the cold fireplace rule in Victoria's dwellings, private homes also needed to bank the home fires when she appeared. Ponsonby reports on an unexpected visit from his sovereign: "Warned one day at Osborne that the Queen was coming to pay a visit, the Ponsonby family set to work to remove the drawing-room fire in a bucket of water, quickly opening all the windows to get rid of the stench."[19]

Ponsonby also reports on an intense conversation on the relative values of heat and cold:

> We had a fierce discussion headed on each side by the Queen and Princess Beatrice as to whether if you were contemned to one or the other you would rather live at the Equator or the North Pole. Princess Beatrice was for the Equator but the Queen fierce for the North Pole. "All doctors say that heat is unwholesome but cold wholesome." So in rooms and corridors in the castle her preference for the North Pole was noticeable.[20]

Accompanied by a freezing lady-in-waiting on regular three-hour drives through her beloved Highlands, the queen took the air. Her body, mysteriously able to tolerate temperatures five times colder than most people, apparently burned five times warmer. The well-published secret of her body, which never subscribed to Alice's thin way of doing things, revealed itself in contradictions, imparting an added resonance to late-Victorian representations of ruling women who encompass extravagant contradictions in their rule.

⟶ Some Gigantic Allegory ⟵

Was it a human being at all? . . . How much of the worship was
paid to a woman and how much to a fetish?
—Edmund Gosse, 1900

The queen's epic mourning could be transformed into an excess not consciously comic. Sir Henry Rider Haggard published *She: A History of Adventure* in 1887, the Golden Jubilee year. The work could fittingly be considered an ominous literary monument to Victoria after fifty years of her reign. That strange adventure novel presents a fantasy about a queen with immense power who presides over a cannibalistic people. Ayesha's title, *She*, the feminine pronoun alone evoking the eternally feminine—conjures up a secret empire where women dominate and exercise their immense sexual desires.[21] The sovereign ruler transcends time. Her reign has extended for two thousand years, a telling fantasy of the thirty-one-year-old author who had never known another monarch and was six years old when Prince Albert died.

In its descriptions of people regarded as savage and therefore inferior, Haggard's novel draws from ethnological researches of Victorian anthropology. The savages in *She* reflect some experiences and consequent fears of a "civilized" tribe who had been ruled for time out of mind by a woman whose own ancestry was more important than that of the minor German prince who had sired her children, provided an heir to the throne and numerous understudies, and then died exhausted. The words of Haggard's hero, the English Holly, in describing the genealogy of the tribe he seeks, the Armahagger, resemble those of Victoria's genealogist, French, whose interest in the prince consort seemed merely polite:

> Descent is traced only through the line of the mother, and while individuals are as proud of a long and superior female ancestry as we are of our families in Europe, they never pay attention to, or even acknowledge, any man as their father, even when their male parentage is perfectly well known. There is but one titular male parent of each tribe, or, as they call it, "Household," and he is its elected and immediate ruler, with the title of "Father."[22]

Haggard's novel draws racial lines similar to those separating Victoria from the subject races: Ayesha rules the Armahaggers but is racially different from them—she is white and they are black. Above the elected prime minister, removed from but at the same time part of government, the queen herself reigns, not only over her biological children and her subjects but also over her large staff, her Household.

Haggard lived through the queen's survival of rumors about her imminent abdication and through the twenty-five years of her extravagant mourning. Albert's preeminent importance as a quasi-live person informs Ayesha's reincarnated lovers. Like the beautiful Leo Vincey,

Ayesha's reincarnated lover, Albert remained eternally young. Victoria's memorials to him kept alive an image of a relatively young man; the clothes laid out year after year remained the size of a person before middle-aged spread or wizened old age. Explaining that *She* has overcome the "change, that ye call death" in order to await the rebirth of her dead lover, Ayesha mourns in a primitive rendition of the Italianate mausoleum at Frogniore.

Ayesha takes Holly and Vincey, who is the reincarnation of her lover, Kallikrates, to the tomb that, like the Royal Mausoleum, serves an alternate home for the queen:

> "Here," went on Ayesha, laying her hand upon the rock—
> "here have I slept night by night for all these generations,
> with but a cloak to cover me. It did not become me that I
> should lie soft when my spouse yonder," and she pointed to
> the rigid form, "lay stiff in death. Here night by night have I
> slept in his cold company—till, thou seest, this thick slab . . .
> has worn thin with the tossing of my form—so faithful have
> I been to thee even in thy space of sleep, Kallikrates."
>
> *(157)*

Emulating Victoria, Ayesha brings people to the mausoleum to commune with her dead spouse. Unlike Victoria, she momentarily achieves her desire: her lover, younger and still vigorous, returns in the body of an Englishman:

> stretched upon the stone bier before us, robed in white and
> perfectly preserved, was what appeared to be the body of Leo
> Vincey. I stared from Leo, standing *there* alive to Leo lying
> *there* dead, and could see no difference; except, perhaps, that
> the body on the bier looked older.
>
> *(158)*

Proliferating Albert statues might inspire in those with mystical leanings a fantasy of returns from the dead. Ayesha's bed in the tomb evokes the space next to Albert in the Royal Mausoleum where Victoria planned to place her already sculpted effigy. Marble's sensual feel and look also could evoke fleshly desires, resembling Victoria in her royal bed, Albert's picture on his side of the bed, the queen clutching his marble hands.

Haggard virtually explains to his readers that the story exceeds the bounds of mere fantasy and hints at some uncanny reality, closer to

The Jubilee Monument by Alfred Gilbert (1887). Jubilee celebrations extended to all of the empire. Every part of India put on a Jubilee show; the most dazzling feature of Calcutta's fireworks wrote the Earl of Dufferin, viceroy of India, to Victoria, "was the outline of your Majesty's head, traced in lines of fire, which unexpectedly burst on the vision of the astonished crowd." Victoria commented to the Earl of Rosebery, "It is impossible for me to say *how deeply, immensely* touched and gratified I have been and am by the wonderful and so universal enthusiasm displayed by my people, and by high and low, rich and poor, on this remarkable occasion, as well as by the respect shown by Foreign Rulers and their peoples."

home. He puts this clue to *She*'s secret model in the mouth of the "editor" who assumes the duty of publishing the incredible tale:

> At first I was inclined to believe that this history of a woman on whom, clothed in the majesty of her almost endless years, the shadow of Eternity itself lay like the dark wing of Night, was some gigantic allegory of which I could not catch the meaning. Then I thought that it might be a bold attempt to portray the possible results of practical immortality, informing the substance of a mortal who yet drew her strength from Earth, and in whose human bosom passions yet rose and fell and beat as in the undying world around her the winds and the tides rise and fall and beat unceasingly. But as I went on I abandoned that idea also. To me the story seems to bear the stamp of truth upon its face. Its explanation I must leave to others.
>
> *(6)*

She bears a stamp of truth visible on the monarch's face. Ayesha, both allegory and real queen, possesses the same larger-than-life quality also inhering in Victoria's reign. "My empire is of the imagination" (118), explains Ayesha, speaking for herself and for Haggard's queen. Her full title, *She-who-must-be-obeyed*, always in italics, pays (possibly unconscious) homage to Victoria's favorite emphatic writing style. The title evokes both an authoritarian mother who lays down the (domestic) law and the passionately willful nature of the monarch. "As my word is, so be it!," asserts Ayesha (118).

✛ Massive Mother—Queen of the Masses ✛

Many of my people don't understand that a person can live so many years as Queen, and many even go so far as to say that she must long ago have gone to her rest, and that it is her fame and glory which remain. . . . For us, it is a curious thing that a woman should be a Queen.

—Letsie, Basoutos chief, July 1887

A little discussed and rarely visited but glorious Golden Jubilee statue provides a visual example of hyperbole during the late years of Victoria's reign. It stands in the Winchester Great Hall near King Arthur's authentic Round Table, which hangs on a wall. The sculptor, Sir Alfred Gilbert (who was also the sculptor of *Eros* in Piccadilly Circus), has represented the queen as a maternal body through the use of proliferating images.

Victory on Victoria's lap; the Jubilee Monument by Alfred Gilbert. *Courtesy of the Conway Library, Courtauld Institute of Art.*

Gilbert's conception of it could not be more explicitly maternal; he used his own mother as a model, in addition to photographs of Victoria, explaining, "One was the Queen of my country—the other Queen of my heart."[23] In fact, Gilbert's mother ruled his emotional life; after years with a wife, he left her to return to his mother, living out her days and his in primal domesticity. Her image, stamped on his heart, also reveals itself in the configuration of the Jubilee Victoria. Representationally Gilbert transferred his attachment to his biological mother to his regard for his monarch. In doing so, he conflated what occurred in many Victorians' internalization of the queen's authority. Gilbert's symbolic equation between the ruler of his heart and the ruler of his nation demonstrates that Victoria ruled her nation *and* her household as a mother. Her subjects responded with appropriate figural complexity.

Gilbert's original design seated the queen on a plain throne. He solved the aesthetic problem of her pudgy body not by making it conform to a more stylish, slender ideal but by enlarging it, swathing it with yards and yards of bronze draperies. Her invisible feet rest upon a huge plump cushion with a long, elaborate fringe. She wears a small crown and holds the scepter and orb. Enhanced by her draperies, the queen's figure dominates the throne. But Gilbert found his colossal figure too meager to represent her reign, so he increased its symbols. On the orb he placed a winged Victory, as if the traditional symbols of orb, scepter, and crown required supplementing in order to convey queenly authority. A personification of triumph, the willowy, graceful female Victory is also an alter ego of the queen, as their echoing names suggest. The great disparity in scale between the two female figures increases the impression of queenly massiveness.[24] Erect, wings unfurled, waving a palm, Victory hovers on Victoria's capacious lap, where so many royal babies had also perched.

To further proliferate the symbols of authority, Gilbert hung above Victoria's head yet another crown, this one more vast and elaborate, sumptuously decorated with tendrils and lilies trailing in space. The lilies—opened and lush—offer themselves as a fecund counterpart to Mary's virginal flowers. Again, as if to reiterate the message, the fifty years of rule increase Victoria's maternal authority. Multiplication, as in Carroll, provides possibilities for paradoxical meaning. On the one hand, the little queen, seen as having influence but no longer real political power, requires the double crowns to reinforce her monarchical authority. On the other, two crowns, like three queens, betoken the queen's multiple meanings: literal and allegorical; maternal and monarchical; imperial and familial; the diminishment of power and expansion of significance.

The simple throne also became massive and sprouted decoration. On the back stands a heavily draped Britannia who wears a helmet with a tall plume. Over her head hangs a canopy surmounted by three immense golden feathers, acting as a counterpart to the overscaled crown hanging over Victoria's head. The personification of the land, Britannia stands spatially opposite the seated queen, symbolically at her back. Active, wearing a helmet as opposed to a crown, she rules the waves, symbolized by the small warship, the *Royal Harry*, which she cradles in her arms. By using the cradling metaphor I mean to suggest that even Britannia does not entirely escape maternal symbolism, if only as a subtext. The ship (conventionally gendered female), its name, and its positioning suggest maternity—its hold, at least since the time of Virgil, has been traditionally likened to a uterus. By bestowing a baby ship on the military Britannia, Gilbert has thus multiplied the symbolic meanings of maternity.

In addition to Britannia, Gilbert surrounded the queen with two more sets of allegorical figures in two different scales, making three scales of allegory in all. Above and on either side of the queen stand Science and History; in canopied niches are Faith, Hope, Charity, and Law. Calling the portrait of Queen Victoria "a mixture of extreme realism and gross exaggeration," Richard Dorment attributes the statue's "glacial dignity and commanding presence" to its "huge proportions." A "seductive" illusion persuades the viewer about Victoria's temporal authority. The viewer believes that this massive figure must be a queen because she wears the Koh-i-noor diamond, for example, and because the allegorical figures body forth "Queen Victoria's position and virtues." Seeming to find Victoria herself an inadequate representation of queenship, Dorment explains her size as an effort to compensate for that inadequacy. "The artist convinces us that this giantess is the Queen by the device of seducing the viewer into admiring the gorgeous textured robes of state, the profusion of realistic details."[25] Since Dorment himself accepts the "tiny" queen's own body as insufficient to command regal authority, he believes that the sculptor needed to "seduce" the viewer by vesting her authority in optical magnification and figural multiplication.

Although George Gissing's *In the Year of Jubilee* (1894) alludes in its title to the Golden Jubilee, unlike Gilbert's proliferating Victoria Gissing's novel evokes the queen's presence by denying its importance. Gissing thus varies the central hyperbolic trope traced in this chapter by first evoking the queen in his title but then replacing what Gilbert saw as her massiveness with the masses of her subjects. He sets one scene in the midst of the London Jubilee festivities, with some of the main characters pushing their way toward the Jubilee throngs. In the middle of the immense celebration, the novel's most pompous character, Samuel Bennett Barmby, dismisses Queen Victoria's importance:

> Now, *I* look at it in this way. It's to celebrate the fiftieth year
> of the reign of Queen Victoria,—yes: but at the same time,
> and far more, it's to celebrate the completion of fifty years of
> Progress. National Progress, without precedent in the history of mankind! One may say, indeed, Progress of the
> Human Race.[26]

Britannia on the Jubilee Monument. In an unusual pairing that separates the figures while also merging their meanings, Gilbert places Britannia in back of Victoria, as if she were a counterpart. *Courtesy of the Conway Library, Courtauld Institute of Art.*

Barmby cannot be seduced by the pomp into believing that Queen Victoria matters much in the sweep of progress, but Gissing portrays him as a self-important narrow man who can only speak in platitudes and only voices truisms, some obviously questionable. So while the reader is left to imagine what other than technological advances and imperial conquest Mr. Barmby might consider to be "progress," the novel presents its possible answer in the rise of formerly marginal classes. *In the Year of Jubilee* struggles with the implications of gender issues as the crux of a struggling and proliferating middle class.

Set mainly in the suburban, middle-class suburb of Camberwell, the novel follows some characters—both women and men—in their attempt to raise themselves through entrepreneurship while others struggle to maintain their respectability. Class and gender issues intertwine. Queen Victoria, associated in sentiment and representation with the very suburbs in which the novel is set, presides invisibly over this realm.

On Jubilee night, Nancy Lord walks toward Pall Mall with a woman friend and an ambitious young suitor from Tooting Common, Luckworth Crewe, who grants the queen some place in the 1887 celebration: "I caught a glimpse of the procession. In its way it was imposing—yes, really. After all, the Monarchy is a great *fact.* I like to keep my mind open to facts" (61). Later Nancy reflects that the tramping populace is the greater fact, more significant than the monarchy. Crewe, in his striving for personal wealth, and Lord, in her striving for autonomy, represent what the Jubilee celebration stands for. Both striving masses and aspiring women looked to the queen, despite herself.

Nancy wishes for independence but finds herself forced to marry. Gissing allows women sexual desire, but his romance plot cannot quite rearrange conventional gender arrangements in order to produce a happy ending. Gissing suggests a sort of bisexual authorship of his novel that reflects his struggle to reformulate power relations between the sexes. Thinking herself either abandoned or widowed with a son to raise, Nancy Lord decides that she can become a novelist and write the melodrama of her life, a plot that is also the plot of *In the Year of Jubilee.* Lionel Tarrant, Nancy Lord's reluctant husband, suppresses this shadow novel. His own expectations of inheritance foiled, he, like Gissing, becomes a hack journalist but returns to his abandoned wife in time to render judgment on her novel. Though publishable, he claims the novel is not "literature." He holds her writing to a higher literary standard than his own:

> I am writing because I must do something to live by. . . .
> Whatever trash I turned out, I should be justified; as a man,
> it's my duty to join in the rough-and-tumble for more or less
> dirty ha'pence. You, as a woman, have no such duty; nay, it's
> your positive duty to keep out of the beastly scrimmage.
>
> *(391)*

Gissing's novel denies both female authorship and female sovereignty as worthy or noticeable activities in the world of necessity. Gissing ultimately enshrines his independent heroine in a queen's garden, yet it is a garden whose walls offer a vista of a larger world.

In the Year of Jubilee attempts to keep the queen somehow in the novel as what Luckworth Crewe calls "a fact" yet to rid it of her influential presence. Given the centrality of the gender debate in the novel, Victoria unavoidably presides over it, lending her paradoxical authority to its efforts to redraw Victorian gender lines. She cannot be banished, much as one would wish in a country whose "tramping populace" seems to be celebrating its accomplishments in her name. She presides over the growing struggle of voices from new quarters, which must be acknowledged. She presides in Nancy Lord's "woman's" novel, the novel that is and is not *In the Year of Jubilee.* She figures its gender instability where one mother—Nancy Lord's—abandons her children to follow her own desire.

Victoria's own views about what women could do in the world conflicted with what she actually did. She disavowed her own desire—she had no choice but to rule, she claimed but she could not give up her throne to a foolish son. Despite anyone's effort to deny her representational force (including her own disclaimers), there she was—a fact that even she seemed to have trouble grappling with. "I should like to retire quietly to a cottage in the hills and rest and see almost no one," she maintained.[27] Victoria presides in the very attempt to deny her power. In Gissing's novel, which proclaims itself to be not about Victoria but about her Jubilee year, the queen reigns as an image by being relegated to a fact or perhaps as being a great media event, a mere factitiousness.

In their different ways these examples of regal representation attempt to comprehend the queen's maternal meanings as at once contradictory, nonsensical, massive, and inconsequential. She herself knew the confusion her reign stimulated. Recognizing the anomaly she embodied, she occasionally tried to exploit it. On the occasion of her daughter Helena's wedding, she inquired indirectly if she might perform the traditional duty of a father. Helena wrote to Lady Augusta Stanley, wife of the dean of Windsor:

> Mama is anxious if there is not *actual* bar against it to give me away at my wedding—. . . Mama will walk with me to the Altar on that eventful day and is anxious to give me away—She says as she is the Sovereign and does the work of man and is in a peculiar position now, that she does not see why she cd. not do it as well as she sits on a throne and does so many things wh. a man does, why she cd. not do this also—[28]

On July 5, 1866, Helena was given as a bride to Prince Christian of Schleswig-Holstein-Sonderberg-Augustenberg by her mother. Victoria's struggles to rationalize her desire to act as father as well as mother reveal her in a rare explicit effort to embrace contradiction and to exploit its masculine advantages. Mother of her peoples, she became their mother in ways as multiple and excessive as the combination of individual meaning intersecting with cultural possibilities allows.

At her death the metaphor of motherhood seemed to many not only appropriate for the sovereign but also an accurate description of a mental construct in many subjects' unconscious life. And although the maternal imago had a common embodiment in Victoria's corporeal lineaments, each subject also imbued it with unique meaning, often independent of anyone's actual mother. When Victoria died, Arthur Munby inserted into the national anthem "God Save the Queen," verses demonstrating his own version of a national mother. The middle-class Munby, whose clandestine marriage to the domestic servant Hannah Cullwick is only in this century being explored (using his photographs and Cullwick's diary, written at his behest), enjoyed having the servants describe in detail the jobs requiring the most intimate encounters with dirt and the manipulations required to clean it. He enjoyed photographing his wife, maid-of-all-work, in blackened body, collar around her neck. Yet he wrote verses about his mother-queen that could only be considered conventional in their sentiments and in their embracing of the maternal imago.

By placing his memorial tribute into the national anthem, Munby makes her into an allegorical motherhood figure for the nation. Glossing the verses sung to all English monarchs, he glorifies this mother-monarch as unique. He associates the child's position to its mother with the subject's relation to the nation:

> Henceforth no Englishman now living, whether British or Colonial, can recollect without a sob in his throat that he will never again sing or hear "God Save the Queen." . . . In the highest and most intimate sense Queen Victoria is not, and never will be, the *late* queen to those who have grown up under her influence, have been stimulated by her example, and have all their lives felt for her a filial and passionate devotion such as no other English Sovereign has enjoyed. . . . Our Queen was no Rex; her great charm was that she was always and emphatically Regina, a queenly woman, and a mother.

If the spirit of the prince consort could have read Munby's tribute, he might have recognized the fruit of his strategy in promoting certain advantages that accrue to a female monarch. Passionate loyalty inspired by maternal idealization grafted to loyalty to nation becomes a new figuration—"matriatism." Munby's rhetoric assumes that matriatism inspires unambivalent and eternal devotion. He concludes his tribute with his added stanzas to the national anthem:

> Yes! though her reign be o'er,
> Still she for evermore
>   Rules us, unseen:
> Rules in all hearts that move
> True to that world above,
> True to her lasting love—
>   True to the Queen.

> She is our Mother still—
> Always in good or ill,
>   Faithful, serene:
> So, we will sing it yet—
> We, though our eyes are wet,
> We, who can ne'er forget—
>   God save the Queen![29]

Yet despite overflowing emotions and great sense of loss, Munby does not forget that one's mother presides over "ill" as well as "good." To be ruled "unseen," as Munby would have it, signifies in part that one is ruled secretly, in unknown ways that one therefore cannot control.

To conceptualize one's queen as if she were a mother bestows upon her eternal sovereignty, for if a queen's reign ends with her death, a mother extends her rule to the death of her children. One's mother is one's mother forever. In fact, one could argue that the dead mother rules even more powerfully for being disembodied. Victoria's death, according to Marie Corelli, novelist of the supernatural, diffused her spirit into a ubiquitous influence. Corelli's eulogy to the nation's mother links Victoria conceptually with Haggard's *She*:

> War and rumours of war,—nation rising against nation,—
> these fulfilled and yet threatening disasters have culminated
> in the worst disaster of all, the "passing" of the greatest,
> purest, best and most blameless Monarch in our history.

England's Queen is dead! The words sound as heavily as though one should say, "The sun is no longer in the sky!" Strange indeed it is to think of England without the Mother-Queen of the great British people:— to realize that she, the gentle and beneficent Lady of the Land, has left us for ever! We had grown to think of her as almost immortal.[30]

The adventurers in *She*, a novel about the ends of empire, explore an uncharted land ruled by a woman who does not die but evolves backwards into a simian form. So Corelli, but more positively, connects her mother-monarch with the fecundity of an evolving empire.

At the hour of Victoria's death, Corelli evokes benevolent elements of an eternal imperial mother:

Thither she has gone, the great Mother of a great people; a people growing out like their own English oaks, far and wide, taking broad root and spreading mighty branches in all lands—just as her new Empire of the South has been affixed like another jewel to her crown, she has put off the earthly diadem and robes of earthly state and has "passed" into that higher condition of being.[31]

Corelli's doctrines blended Christian faith with science to convince her that "there is no such thing as Death," but in life as she knew it, the queen lived in her empire, infinitely expanding, upward into the heavens and outward in mighty branches of the English oak. Released into its essence, Victoria's maternal body diffused infinitely, "free to an eternity of endless joy, work and wisdom,"[32] while her peoples grieved the loss of its material shell.

The mother figure emerged in full flower at the Golden Jubilee; at Victoria's death, fourteen years later, her subjects attached to that maternal imago an aura that outshone her faults. Victoria's unique kind of excess, leaving a tension within representation sometimes figured as absence, provokes a sense of endless mystery, of multiplied treasures, of adventures into a world imagined in terms of superfluity and empire, endless reproduction, production, fecundity, diffusion, absolute absence, and simultaneous total presence.

EPILOGUE: VICTORIA AMAZONICA

Army and Navy shall lead the way
For that wonderful coach of the Queen today
Kings and Princes and Lords of the land
Shall ride behind her, a humble band;
And over the city and over the world
Shall the flags of all nations be half-mast furled
For the silent lady of royal birth
Who is riding away from the courts of the earth
—Ella Wheeler Wilcox

By the end of her sixty-three year reign, Victoria's legend joined other legendary women whose stories were often disseminated in popular compendia of the ten best of a category. Her sexual passion singled her out as one the world's famous lovers, comparable to Cleopatra, Helen of Troy, and George Sand.[1] As "founder of the Victorian age," and with such religious luminaries as "the Blessed Virgin Mary, mother of Jesus, The great Queen Hatshepsut, foster mother of Moses, Saint Teresa, reformer of the Carmelites, and Mary Baker Eddy, founder of Christian Science," she approached canonization in *Women Who Influenced the World*.[2] She qualified as one of ten girls from history with Joan of Arc, Jenny Lind, and Cofachiqui, an Indian princess.[3] A contemporary history of the first Opium War (1840–1842), in which the Treaty of Nanking ceded Hong Kong to England, concludes: "China has been conquered by a Woman."[4]

That last sentence could not have meaning in reference to a king. Victoria's womanhood allied her with the mythical Amazons on the one hand and with allegorical personifications on the other. Powerful beyond human possibility, her presence reminded the less reverential—such writers as Rudyard Kipling and Wilfrid Scawan Blunt, for instance—of the carnage performed in her name. No simple synec-

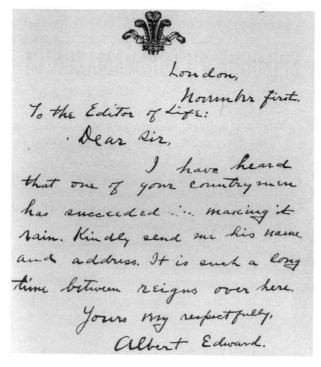

London,
November first.
To the Editor of Life:

· Dear Sir,

        I have heard
that one of your countrymen
has succeeded in making it
rain. Kindly send me his name
and address. It is such a long
time between reigns over here.
        Yours very respectfully,
        Albert Edward.

Ten years before the end of Victoria's reign, *Life*, vol. 18, November 5, 1891, imagined a wistful Albert Edward trying to influence nature.

doche, Victoria stood for her nation and for the weaker sex grown impossibly strong. That this allegory actually walked about seemed wondrous to many, while to others, such as the writer Laurence Housman, history used a passive queen ("It was not she who 'took occasion by the hand'—occasion took hers") simply as a tutelary deity. She lived too long, thought Housman; for her heir as well as for her subjects, "an everlasting Mother . . . was too much of a good thing."[5] Yet her admirers loved her because she gave the lie to notions of remote regality by remembering minute details of a cottager's or a servant's life, by spinning yarn, and by weeping for strangers.

Given the mid-Victorian craze for plant collecting with an imperialist cast, it is not surprising that the Victoria legend should colonize the vegetable world. Botanists scoured remote corners of the earth for unique specimens, only the most astonishing of which bore royal names. The story of missions to sight, propagate, and name a fabulous water lily growing in the depths of the Amazon rain forest assumes allegorical outlines, a wondrous yet true story characterizing both the age and its monarch. In the year of Victoria's accession, an amazing lily with an eighteen-inch flower floating on the Amazon was described by a plant scout, Sir Robert Schomburgk, as "a vegetable wonder!": "gigantic leaves, five to six feet across, flat, with a deep rim, light green above and a vivid crimson below, . . . while in keeping with this astonishing foliage I beheld luxuriant flowers . . . [of many petals passing] from pure white to rose pink . . . [with] sweet scent. . . . As I rowed from one to another, I always found something new to examine."[6]

Another plant adventurer, Thomas Bridges, described the lily with an amazement similar to that of Hatshepsut beholding baby Moses in his rush basket on the Nile: "Fain would I have plunged into the lake to obtain specimens of the splendid flowers and foliage but the knowledge that these waters abounded with alligators . . . deterred me."[7] Protected by dangers, the lily inspires both intense fear and desire. With geographic alteration, Mrs. Malaprop's allusion to Cleopatra, "She's as restless as an allegory on the banks of the Nile," could apply to both plant and queen.

To name the lily reenacted in the plant world power a controversy similar to the one involved in naming the princess at her birth. She was christened "Alexandrina Victoria," as a courtesy to Czar Alexander of Russia, one of her godfathers, and not christened "Georgiana" after her other godfather, the prince regent, or "Charlotte," after his daughter, because he refused both honors. The lily, incorrectly named *Nymphaea victoria* by Schomburgk, did not belong to that genus. Linguists debating between *Victoria regia* or *Victoria regina* decided in favor of the former, when, adding further confusion, a plantsman discovered that the lily had already been named *Euryale amazonica*. However, since that genus was no more scientifically appropriate than *Nymphaea*, the lily ultimately occupied a unique genus, *Victoria*. In the flower kingdom as in world history, experts acknowledged that Victoria was one of a kind. Ponsonby's awe at Victoria's singularity, quoted in chapter 1 ("Queen Victoria did not belong to any conceivable category of monarchs or of women") unites the royal lily to its namesake.

The species name, *amazonica*, remained a delicate problem. Once named, it could not be changed. Referring to the river, the name nonetheless seemed to ally the queen with aggressive female warriors, a breast lopped off, the better to hold a shield. "Victoria, queen of the Amazons," sounded like an indecorous honor. Perhaps a sense that the label might be all too appropriate intensified the stakes in suppressing it. The flower of femininity, sometimes referred to in verse and image alike as "the Rose of England,"[8] should not also be related to an ancient myth about women who refused to marry and bear children and assumed male prerogatives.[9] The controversy raged in botanical circles during the late

Victoria regia Fully Expanded, engraving by Rosemary Clark. Many contemporary books about Queen Victoria use the *Victoria regia* as a visual motif. In Clark's rendering, the lily looks like a crowned queen, translated to a vegetable idiom.

1840s, under the sway of Victoria and Albert's idylls of domesticity. The myth of Amazon queens contributed a spectral fear of ruling women, one the Ideal Couple vigorously countered. Consequently, for fifty years, until the queen died, the lily was known as *Victoria regia* and has only recently been known under its proper name, *Victoria amazonica.*[10]

As if to reinforce allegorical possibilities, the race to propagate the lily in captivity narrowed down to three great botanical rivals; but Joseph Paxton, a gardener employed by the Duke of Devonshire, created a special greenhouse sixty-one feet by forty-six feet, with a water tank of over thirty feet in diameter for the lily's propagation and ultimately won the contest. In November 1849 the first bud—pure white with a strong fruity smell, some thought like a pineapple—appeared. By the next day the petals had fully expanded to a foot and a half, the center was tinged with pink; by evening the pink center stood erect, but it had lost its scent. Then, all the petals changing to pink, it turned to its side and slowly sank beneath the water. At its first anniversary the lily's generative power produced one hundred twenty-six flowers.

Those who had traveled down the Amazon had noted the Indians resting their children on the leaves. Paxton's employer encouraged him to perch his eight-year-old daughter, dressed as a fairy, in the center of a leaf. Seated on a fifteen-pound copper lid to distribute her weight, the forty-two pound fairy-girl floated on the water in her father's glorious conservatory. *Victoria amazonica*'s leaves, so delicate

The *Victoria regia* in the greenhouse at Cherkeley Court, *The Gardeners' Chronicle*, February 28, 1885. These illustrations indicate that Paxton's daughter, the first English child to float on a *Victoria regia* leaf, inspired many imitators. *The Library of the New York Botanical Garden, Bronx, New York.*

that a straw dropped on them would pierce them, were found to be so strong in their structure—resembling a complex spiderweb—that they could support all fifty-seven pounds. Others imitated the feat, showing young girls and boys standing or sitting on *Victoria amazonica* leaves.

Adapting the principles he learned from studying the leaves' phenomenal structure, Paxton recast his glass house built for the royal lily and won the competition for the structure housing the Great Exhibition of 1851, called the Crystal Palace. To demonstrate the ingenuity of his design to the Fine Arts Commission headed by the prince consort, Paxton brought along a *Victoria amazonica* leaf. What was it about the queen that seemed to turn so many spectacular adventures into allegories of her selfhood?

Mark Twain asked himself a similar question in the year of the Diamond Jubilee. Viewing the great procession of June 22, 1897, he reported on it "both in the light of history and as a spectacle." Twain's American sensibility, though impressed, tried not to succumb to statistical Anglophilia:

> When the Queen was born there were not more than
> 25,000,000 English-speaking people in the world, there are

"Under-surface of Leaf of Victoria Regia," *The Gardeners' Chronicle*, February 28, 1885. One cannot see from the illustration that the veining is covered with thorny spines. *The Library of the New York Botanical Garden, Bronx, New York*.

about 120,000,000 now. The other long-reigned Queen, Elizabeth ruled over a short 100,000 square miles of territory and perhaps 5,000,000 subjects. Victoria reigns over more territory than any other sovereign in the world's history ever reigned over, her estate covers a quarter part of the habitable globe and her subjects number about 400,000,000. It is indeed a mighty estate and I perceive now that the English are mentioned in the Bible: Blessed are the meek for they shall inherit the earth.[11]

Despite himself, Twain was stunned by the spectacle: "All the nations seemed to be filing by," he reported; "it was a sort of allegorical suggestion of the Last Day."[12] In that biblical reference to the apocalypse,

Twain captures some of the awe and dread Victoria inspired. The queen recalled images of the prime source of all peoples of the earth, the earth mother. First they all came to pay homage to their progenitor. But the queen herself finally eclipsed the "human race on exhibition." The American humorist seemed almost stripped of irony at the sight of Victoria: "The Queen Empress was come. She was received with great enthusiasm. It was realizable that she was the procession herself; that all the rest of it was mere embroidery; that in her the public saw the British Empire itself. She was a symbol, an allegory of England's grandeur and the might of the British name."[13] By that time, not only could Victoria be invoked as the imperial muse, she also embodied and named it victorious. Caught up in ceremonial, Twain augments Gissing's observation in *In the Year of Jubilee* that the tramping masses represent a great historical significance given prominence in relation to the queen as their unlikely national symbol.

Twain and Gissing represent two intertwining aspects of Victoria's image. In 1861, the year of Victoria's great sorrows, *The Victoria Regia*, a volume of verse and prose, appeared, published by "Emily Faithfull and Company," printed by the "Victoria Press (for the Employment of Women)," and dedicated to the queen. Faithfull explains the volume's genesis, the result of various social committees, inquiries, studies, and reports into the "miserable condition" of women who needed but could not find respectable employment. Finally constituted as the "Society for Promoting the Industrial Employment of Women," the committee found that the printing trade would benefit from women's "quick eye, ready hand, and steady application to work" without exposing them to unfeminine indignities.

Under encouragement and with appropriate underwriting, in 1860 Bessie R. Parkes and Emily Faithfull learned the printing trade and set up the Victoria Press. In its first year it published *The English Woman's Journal* and the transactions of the Association for the Promotion of Social Science, the organization originating the inquiry into women's employment. In the second year *The Victoria Regia* appeared, edited by one of Queen Victoria's favorite poets, Adelaide A. Procter, and intended to demonstrate the skills of the newly trained women compositors.[14] A thick and elaborate volume, it was dedicated to Victoria, "whose royal approval had already signified to the undertaking which bears Her name." Faithfull closed her account with homage to her sovereign: "I trust that the *Victoria Regia* will be found a not unworthy record of the literature adorning the rule of a Sovereign who has known how to unite the dignified discharge of public duties with a constant regard for the cares of domestic life; and who has thus borne a noble and enduring testimony to the value of woman's intellect and heart."[15] Because Faithfull reveres the queen's mental capability, she adds "intellect" to the "heart" that is the Victorian woman's quintessential attribute. Whatever the queen's actual intellectual limitations, Faithfull's evaluation of Victoria's mental acuity extends women's proper sphere to include more than mindless, though tender, or even "instinctual" emotions. And, although Victoria has not earned a reputation as a woman of intellect, it may be a limited definition of intellect rather than her particular failings that has allowed her intense kind of thinking, what Housman characterized as "an obstinate and impetuous mind" to be discounted as thought.

W. T. Stead claimed more than the feminist Faithfull on the issue of what Victoria had done for women. Three decades later, along with Twain and countless others, Stead tallied Victoria's significance. He argued that the very fact of Victoria's successful reign promoted women's right to be part of the political process:

> The fortunate accident, if I may use such a word, that for sixty years the Throne has been occupied by a female sovereign, has been of inestimable advantage to the cause with which the future progress of the race is most closely bound up. The arrival of women on the stage of citizenship may possibly be regarded by the future historian as the greatest social and political event of the Victorian era. And in promoting and facilitating the advent of women as a political factor, the Queen's influence has been simply incalculable. . . . No one could pretend that it was unwomanly to take a serious interest in State affairs. And with the . . . volume of testimony as to the supreme ability, the keen sagacity, and the shrewd common-sense with which the Queen bore herself . . . no one of her subjects could honestly repeat the old rubbish about the natural incapacity of women. What the Queen's own views are upon the subject of Woman's Suffrage is comparatively immaterial. By the patient and punctilious discharge of all the complex and multifarious duties of her political and social position, the Queen has vindicated the capacity of her sex to perform political and social duties, and has dispelled as the sun dissipates the mist the foggy notions entertained by many as to political incapacity being one of the natural disabilities of her sex.[16]

Republican in leaning, Stead almost reluctantly made an argument in favor of monarchy because it gave women an opportunity to prove their worth. "All existing Republican systems have carefully provided against the possibility of any woman ever having any such chance, by denying to all women any right even to stand as candidate for supreme office."[17] Stead's overstatement ignores how the queen, with Albert's training, also defended the prevailing views about gender. But it is true that she at the same time disrupted them. Her "heat" allowed certain foggy notions to be, if not dispelled, at least questioned, challenged, and made into a proposition rather than Almighty or natural will.

Thus the name *Victoria amazonica* suits the lily standing for her, floating now in Kew Gardens and on the Amazon.[18] Like that other holy mother whose flower is the lily, the queen apparently circumvented physical laws. Standing for both fierce warrior and sheltering mother, she exceeded any single myth of her virtues. Parkes, cofounder of the Victoria Press, paid tribute to the queen and her lily, conveying some of the queen's imaginative power, not yet at its mythic crescendo:

Victoria Regia

When on the shining waters of the west
An English traveller saw the queen of Flowers,
He sought a name whereby might be exprest
The chiefest glory of this world of ours.
Victoria Regia!—Never Happier Name
A Flower, a woman, or a queen could claim![19]

Its dated rhetoric a part of its message, the paean captures a Victorian wonder at her female presence, found and appropriated in a Western rain forest. Even its misnomer and the cause of its suppression fits Victoria's ambiguous position, in relation to the Woman Question.

Victoria's death at the beginning of a new century felt like an omen, signaling the end of an era that rationally could have concluded earlier. That the queen lingered to see her millions of subjects through whatever anxieties arise at the turning of a century befits her reign's allegory. Ella Wheeler Wilcox, an American reporter and poet traveling in Europe when Victoria died on January 22, 1901, was asked by her editor to view the queen's funeral procession. Wilcox wired back the poem (her most well known) from which the epigraph to this chapter is taken, only one of the thousands of verses in many languages written on the occasion. While not the best (or the worst), the poem conveys the sense, echoed in the verses of Munby and Corelli quoted in the previous chapter, of grown people thrown back on the cadences and needs of childhood. Wilcox's poem revises Arthurian

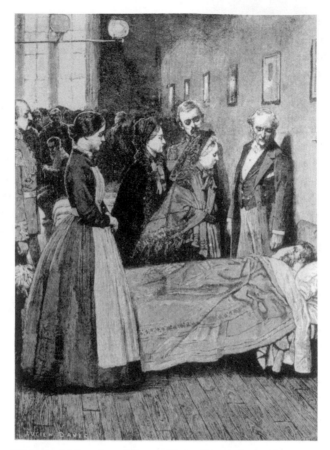

Victoria visiting the soldiers at Netley Hospital; wood engraving by Lucien Davis. Victoria had laid the foundation stone of
the military hospital at Netley, with Prince Albert at her side,
dedicating herself to the soldiers: "Loving my dear brave army
as I do, and having seen so many of my poor sick and wounded
soldiers, I shall watch over them with maternal anxiety."

legend to evoke a great ruler conveyed to another kingdom, leaving
behind nostalgia for a time when a code of behavior could be elicited
by a monarch's name. Many people found themselves surprised by
their mourning for Victoria. "I felt her death much more than I had
expected," wrote Henry James. "She was a sustaining symbol and the
wild waters are upon us now." [20] Death, arriving none too soon for
many eager for modernity, swept away a figurehead of a stable ship
of state.

Rather than conclude with an allegory of death, however, it may be
better to end with one about Victoria's birthright, told by Margaret

Oliphant in her personal sketch of Victoria, published the year before the queen died. Oliphant, author of over ninety novels, also lived in Windsor as a widow and more and more began to identify with Victoria, whom she knew and visited at Windsor Castle. "I also work hard, Mrs Oliphant," she reported the queen as saying to her during one of their meetings.[21] Although Oliphant doubts the veracity of the story, she tells it because, like many other such tales, it seems emblematic of Victoria's mandate: "The first man privileged to hold the little Princess in his arms was Robert Owen, the founder of that curious colony of New Lanark, in which the theory of co-operation between master and man was first put into practice. . . . If anything, it must have been a blessing the visionary left upon the little head, which was to think so much and so long in its day upon the condition of the people, and to preside over so many changes tending to their advantage."[22] As many biographers point out, Victoria actually missed many opportunities to better the workers' conditions. Yet she seemed their champion, made in their image, with blessings like a happy peasant to Elizabeth Barrett [Browning] or the queen of the people to T. Mullet Ellis. The year before Victoria died she visited every soldier in two hospitals, passing out medals and expressing her personal thanks for their sacrifices during the Boer War, a war that for many represented a useless waste in the name of Victoria's imperialist ambitions. Paradoxically for a person of immense privilege, she became the symbol of the hope of marginalized people. She performed monarchy, her performances and meanings transgressing not merely gender but race and class, genus and species.

Victoria came into the world as already an allegory, but one whose meanings changed over time. Soon after her death most post-Victorians saw her as Amy Lowell's "bat-eyed narrow-minded Queen":

> Confound Victoria, and the slimy inhibitions
> She loosed on all us Anglo-Saxon creatures![23]

The American Lowell's New England envy of what she conceived as less inhibited races echoes in her accusation, a charge that nonetheless imparts great powers to a dominating queen. For the contemporary Canadian poet and popular songwriter Leonard Cohen, Victoria dominates a nostalgic imagination that desires limits and takes pleasure in sexual spanking. Cohen invokes the queen in his heart by connecting his lost lover with hers and sees Victoria's meanings in "all her forms":

> the slim unlovely virgin anyone would lay
> the white figure floating among German beards

the mean governess of the huge pink maps
the solitary mourner of a prince.[24]

As the many conflicting images of the monarch demonstrate, Queen
Victoria's secrets depended upon the imaginative life of her subjects.
Displayed at her white funeral for all to see, her secrets rode away with
her "from the courts of the earth," but, like the myth of her "ancestor"
King Arthur, they return in our own century packaged in different,
sometimes astonishing guises.[25]

NOTES

✦ 1. Elements of Power ✦

1. Gosse, "Character of Queen Victoria," p. 302.

2. In his study of royal ceremonials, "The Context, Performance, and Meaning of Ritual," Cannadine echoes other historians when he observes that "the deliberate, ceremonial presentation of an impotent but venerated monarch as a unifying symbol of permanence and national community became both possible and necessary" (122). How politically impotent Queen Victoria was is debatable, but her imaginative power reigns to our own day, sometimes eclipsing that of her living descendants. Cannadine's recent projects promise to stimulate reassessments of Victoria.

3. Bagehot, *The English Constitution*, p. 88.

4. Ibid., p. 100

5. Turner, "Frame, Flow, and Reflection," p. 33.

6. Turner, *Anthropology of Performance*, p. 22.

7. In " 'To the Queen's Private Apartments,' " Homans focuses on Victoria's construction as a wife-queen, a useful role that occupied one-third of her reign. For the delineation of middle-class values that depended on setting up a (fictional) distinction between public and private, see Davidoff and Hall, *Family Fortunes*, and for challenges to their work, see Wahrman, " 'Middle-Class' Domesticity Goes Public."

8. Some studies describing women's place in defining the Victorian sense of the social order inform my thinking: Armstrong, *Desire and Domestic Fiction*; Auerbach, *Woman and the Demon*; Barickman, MacDonald, and Stark, *Corrupt Relations*; Poovey, *Uneven Developments*; Sedgwick, *Between Men*; and Walkowitz, *City of Dreadful Delight.*

9. Sunday, April 10, 1836; *Girlhood of Queen Victoria*, vol. 1, pp. 154–55.

10. *Letters of Queen Victoria*, 1st ser., vol. 1, p. 134. Henceforth this nine-volume series will be cited as *Letters*.

11. Albert had a photographic studio installed in Windsor Castle. See Gernsheim and Gernsheim, *Victoria R.*

12. Martin, *Life*, p. 256.

13. Windsor Castle, April 6, 1850. Martin, *Life*, pp. 259–60.

14. Martin, *Life*, p. 225.

15. Ames, *Prince Albert*, pp. 26–27.

16. Gladden, Sermon, pp. 22–23.

17. St. Aubyn, in *Queen Victoria*, explains Victoria's many-sided personality without trying to reconcile its different facets. According to St. Aubyn, Victoria never presented a consistent identity. "The Queen not only simultaneously held incompatible beliefs," he notes, but "in the very depth of her being" were "lodged contrary qualities which might have caused another personality to split into fragments" (58).

18. Gosse, "Character of Queen Victoria," p. 303.

19. Ponsonby, *Henry Ponsonby*, p. 70.

20. Gosse, "Character of Queen Victoria," pp. 302–3.

21. Hibbert, ed., *Queen Victoria in Her Letters and Journals*, p. 23. Subsequent references to this volume will be cited as *Letters and Journals*.

22. Barrett Browning, "The Young Queen" and "Victoria's Tears," in *Poems*, pp. 54–56.

23. Tuesday, January 25, 1820; *Private Letters of Princess Lieven*, p. 6.

24. For interpretations of their remarkable relationship, see Duff, *Victoria and Albert*; Aronson, *Heart of a Queen*; and Longford, *Queen Victoria*.

25. Woodham-Smith, *Queen Victoria*, quotes Lord Albemarle's recollection: "One of my occupations of a morning, while waiting for the Duke, was to watch from the window the movements of a bright pretty little girl, seven years of age. It was amusing to see how she divided the contents of the watering pot between the flowers and her own little feet" (61).

26. July 22, 1837, to Miss Mitford; *The Brownings' Correspondence*, vol. 3, p. 261.

27. In "The Powers of Powerlessness," Homans argues that Victoria "gives power away in order to keep it" and analyzes Barrett's queen poems as representing these negotiations.

28. Tooley, *Personal Life of Queen Victoria*, p. 119.

29. Ruskin, "Of Queen's Gardens," p. 132.

30. Ibid., p. 135.

✦ 2. Genealogies in Her Closet ✦

1. Grey, ed., *Early Years*, p. 72.

2. *Queen Victoria to the King of the Belgians*, April 19, 1842. *Letters*, 1st ser., vol. 1, p. 493.

3. In my use of the word *race*, I follow Victorian ethnographic practice, which considered what we would usually call "ethnicity" to be biologically determined and used *race* to describe differences among groups of people.

4. Kennedy, *Natural History of Man*, p. 12. Kennedy quotes Bishop William Paley, an influential proponent of natural theology, to explain the human colonizing propensity.

5. Ibid., pp. 17, 18.

6. Beddoe, *Races of Britain*, p. 4.

7. Longford, *Queen Victoria.*

8. Vanantetzie, *Discent of Her Majesty Victoria.*

9. Smith, *Coronation Stone.*

10. Tooley, *Personal Life*, pp. 155–56.

11. Ibid., p. 168.

12. *Times* (London), May 13, 1842.

13. *Ladies Magazine and Museum* 11 (July 1837): 79.

14. Thompson, *Chartists*, provides a useful Chartist context for the Plantagenet Ball.

15. Hovel, *Chartist Movement*, p. 254.

16. Ibid., pp. 254–55.

17. *Times* (London) May 11, 1842.

18. Tooley, *Personal Life*, p. 128.

19. See, for example, Longford, *Queen Victoria*, p. 197.

20. Ormond, *Sir Edwin Landseer*, p. 156.

21. In "Royal Family Portraiture," pp. 155–85, Schama argues that in Landseer's portrait "a bourgeois marital idyll . . . is at its controlling center." Schama's article emphasizes family portraiture as a strategy royalty employed in order to participate in the bourgeois hegemony.

22. Flanagan, *Spitalfields Silks*, p. 22.

23. Jerrold, *Married Life of Queen Victoria*, p. 149.

24. May 15, 1842; *Letters*, 1st ser., vol. 1, p. 495.

25. Weintraub, *Queen Victoria*, p. 166.

26. *The Queen's Masque*, pp. 7–9.

27. Nairn, in *The Break-Up of Britain*, argues that the British form of empire building depended upon hierarchy and a symbiosis of a capitalist system with "maritime and conquering adventures" (20). Victoria and Albert, I suggest, played out a pattern laid down by centuries of imperialism, a pattern Nairn calls "absorption" (12).

28. Queen Victoria, *Leaves*, p. 34. Subsequent references to this edition will be cited in parentheses in the text.

29. Geertz, "Centers, Kings, and Charisma," p. 125.

30. Howie, *The Queen in Scotland.* Subsequent references to this pamphlet will be cited in parentheses in the text.

31. Oliphant, *Queen Victoria*, p. 14.

32. Brown, *Balmoral*, pp. 64–66.

33. "The Queen in the Islands and Highlands," p. 31.

34. Hardie, in *The Political Influence of Queen Victoria*, describes the surprise felt when the queen's letters revealed the extent of her political power. Victoria's representation of herself as simply a family woman, exemplified in the *Leaves*, was effective.

35. Cumming, *Royal Dress*, p. 109.

36. Colley, *Britons*, p. 121.

37. Colley, *Britons*, p. 395.

38. Joseph Kestner, personal communication.

39. See in particular, Trevor-Roper, "The Invention of Tradition," pp. 15–42.

40. "Some Talk," p. 703.

41. "Scottish Characteristics," p. 452.

42. "Some Talk," p. 704.

43. Brown, p. 67. The adoption of the "laird" posture was conscious. The concept of the place of a laird rather than the castle of a monarch governed the interior dec-

oration of Balmoral: while the outside looked like a castle, the inside was to resemble a "seat" (63).

44. A phrase used by Brown in his sympathetic portrayal of the royal uses of Scotland.

45. The Neiman Marcus Christmas catalog for 1993 delineates a journey made imaginable, even created, by Queen Victoria's "Balmorality," an indication that the retail trade has inherited the role of ethnic patron:

> The welcoming of the New Year remains the greatest of all annual festivals in Scotland, so we've created an itinerary . . . based at the elegant Balmoral Hotel in Edinburgh. . . . To ensure the exclusivity of Hogmanay 1993/94, we have arranged for one of the traditional designers and weavers of tartan to produce The Neiman Marcus Tartan. . . . A "Taste of Scotland" welcome dinner with actors entertaining you at your table. A special "Golfing Lunch," to celebrate 500 years of golf at the St. Andrews Old Course Hotel. . . . An evening with a themed tribute to Robert Burns, complete with Scottish folk musick, sword dancing, and a ceilidh. A chance to visit the Palace of Holyrood House . . . plus a special showing at the Balmoral of ancestral tartans, Stuart crystal, and malt whiskey. On New Year's Eve, it's off to Stirling Castle for a festive black tie Hogmanay dinner. . . . This magnificent castle, situated on a hill and specially floodlit for the evening. . . . Traditional Scottish attire will be provided for the male guests.
>
>   Highlights . . . include a ceremonial tree planting in dedication to Neiman Marcus on the grounds of Scone Palace and a "Haste Ye Back" . . . dinner full of entertainment, with the Reverend Howard Haslett—a true Scottish character—as the speaker. Throughout the trip, you'll be able to purchase items made in the exclusive NM tartan print.
>
> (33)

46. See, for example, "Scottish Characteristics," pp. 452–59; "The Scot at Home," pp. 735–52; "Scottish National Character," pp. 715–31.

47. Longford, *Queen Victoria*, p. 78.

48. Kingsley, *Life and Works*, vol. 11, p. 1.

49. Horsman, "Origins of Racial Anglo-Saxonism," p. 399.

50. Kennedy, *Races of Man*, p. 26.

51. For a summary of Anglo-Saxon racializing, see Stocking, *Victorian Anthropology*, particularly ch. 2 on ethnology, pp. 48ff.

52. Kingsley, *Roman and the Teuton*, p. 5.

53. Pearson, *Early and Middle Ages*, p. 68.

54. "The political constitution which we inherit, our common law, even our philosophy, bear the traces of medieval workmanship as plainly as the castles and churches that still testify to the past. The ideas that regulate the life of gentlemen were not derived from Greece and Rome, or invented by eighteenth-century *savants*. We cannot disclaim our father without being untrue to ourselves" (Pearson, *Early and Middle Ages*, p. vii).

55. Grey, ed. *Early Years*, p. 25.

56. Pearson, *Early and Middle Ages*, p. 207.

57. Besant, *The Rise of Empire*, pp. 13–14.

58. Kingsley, *Roman and the Teuton*, p. 54.

59. Quoted in Briggs, *Saxons*, p. 10.

60. "Land Occupancy in Scotland," p. 320.

61. Besant, *The Rise of Empire*, p. 17.

62. Ibid., p. 14.

63. Stanton, *The Aristocrat as Art*, p. 110.

64. Marx, "The Eighteenth Brumaire," p. 300.

65. Saturday, April 21, 1855; Queen Victoria, *Record of the Visit*, p. 67.

✦ 3. Dressing the Body Politic ✦

1. "Art of Dress," p. 375.

2. Bulwer-Lytton, *England and the English*, 2 vols., 1:87, quoted in Wahrman, "'Middle-Class' Domesticity Goes Public," p. 396.

3. Cunnington and Cunnington, *History of Underwear*, p. 8.

4. Roberts, "The Exquisite Slave," pp. 554–69.

5. Carlyle, *Sartor Resartus*, chap. 5, p. 26. Subsequent references to this edition will be cited in parentheses in the text.

6. Richards, *Commodity Culture*, pp. 73–118.

7. Norris and Curtis, *Costume and Fashion*, p. 40.

8. Strachey, *Queen Victoria*, p. 37.

9. Longford, *Queen Victoria*, p. 27,

10. Moers, *The Dandy*, pp. 13–14.

11. Tooley, *Personal Life*, p. 158.

12. "Fashions in Hair and Head-Dresses," p. 569.

13. Quoted in Fulford, *Prince Consort*, p. 50.

14. Crampton, *Collection of Broadside Ballads*, vol. 3, n.p.

15. Grey, ed., *Early Years* p. 319.

16. Although she accepts the idea that a man should manage his wife, Bennett's *King Without a Crown* provides evidence that Albert was given advice about how to control Victoria and that this was an issue for him to the end of his life.

17. March 24, 1958; Fulford, ed., *Dearest Child*, p. 77.

18. "The Queen's Marriage," Ashton, ed., *Modern Street Ballads*, p. 277.

19. Quoted in Wilson, *Queen Victoria*, p. 110.

20. Crampton, *Collection of Broadside Ballads*, vol. 7, n.p.

21. Williams, "Fetishism and Hard Core."

22. McDowell, *Dressed to Kill*, p. 55.

23. Steele, in *Fashion and Eroticism*, makes the point about Victorian women's clothes: "The Victorian woman was not supposed to be 'strong' and 'aggressive' but the sheer size of her dress and its stylized but definite silhouette might be interpreted as emphasizing the female presence in a way that male clothing singularly failed to do" (92). Auerbach's *Woman and the Demon* demonstrates how women came to dominate the cultural imagination, signified by depictions of their great size in relation to the men who supposedly dominated them.

24. "Raiment of Victorian Women," p. 424.

25. Thursday, August 9, 1832; Esher, *Girlhood*, vol. 1, p. 47.

26. Monday, April 16, 1855; Queen Victoria, *Record of the Visit*, pp. 28–30.

27. April 18, 1855, Queen Victoria, *Record of the Visit*, p. 42.

28. Fulford, ed., *Dearest Child*, pp. 32, 34–38.

29. In "The Love of Finery," pp. 169–88, Valverde explores the moral control of working class women by means of strictures regarding "finery."

30. Gernsheim, *Victoria R*, p. 15.

31. August 19, 1855; Queen Victoria, *Record of the Visit*, p. 82.

32. Tisdall, *Queen Victoria's Private Life*, pp. 34–35.

33. Cumming, *Royal Dress*, p. 112.

34. Tisdall, *Queen Victoria's Private Life*, p. 27.

35. Eliot, *Felix Holt*, p. 160. Subsequent references to this edition will be cited in parentheses in the text.

36. For a discussion of the mutual construction of discourses of fashion and taste, see Wahrman, "'Middle-Class' Domesticity Goes Public," pp. 396–97; 430–31.

37. Barrett, *The Queen*, p. 47.

38. Ponsonby, *Henry Ponsonby*, p. 79.

39. T. Mullet Ellis, *The Fairies' Favourite*, p. 30. Subsequent references to this edition will be cited in parentheses in the text.

40. April 19, 1858; Queen Victoria, *Record of the Visit*, pp. 32, 52, 95.

41. Ponsonby, *Henry Ponsonby*, p. 79.

42. One of Her Majesty's Servants, *Private Life*, p. 9.

43. Edel, ed., *Letters*, vol. 1, p. 184.

⇢ 4. Imperial Tears ⇠

1. *Baby's ABC.*

2. Grasse, April 10, 1891; Mallet, *Life with Queen Victoria*, p. 44.

3. Ponsonby, *Henry Ponsonby*, p. 50.

4. April 10, 1861; *Dearest Child*, p. 321.

5. Ibid., p. 320.

6. *Letters and Journals*, p. 193.

7. Bolitho, *Victoria*, p. 3.

8. Benson, *As We Were*, p. 8.

9. May 15, 1861; *Dearest Child*, p. 332.

10. Tennyson, "In Memoriam" 51, *Poems*, p. 907.

11. Dyson and Tennyson, eds., *Dear and Honoured Lady*, p. 70.

12. *Daily Telegraph*, December 24, 1861; Duff, *Victoria and Albert*, appendix 2, p. 269.

13. Longford, *Queen Victoria*, p. 297.

14. Queen Victoria to the King of the Belgians. Osborne House, October 17, 1844; *Letters*, 1st ser., vol. 2, p. 30.

15. Watson, *A Queen at Home*, p. 156.

16. Osborne, December 23, 1861; *Dearest Mama*, p. 27.

17. See Richards, p. 100, for a description of the objects in the Blue Room as "kitsch" and the devotion to them as a kind of religion.

18. December 14, 1862; *Letters and Journals*, p. 169.

19. Osborne, February 7, 1862; *Dearest Mama*, p. 46.

20. Herne the Hunter [pseud.], *A Fragment*. Subsequent references to this pamphlet will be cited in parentheses in the text.

21. Benson, *Queen Victoria*, p. 213.

22. *Letters and Journals*, p. 172.

23. *Letters and Journals*, p. 174.

24. Tennyson, "In Memoriam" 90, *Poems*, p. 942.

25. Procter, "The Angel of Death," in *Legends and Lyrics*, p. 86.

26. One of Her Majesty's Servants, *Private Life of the Queen*, p. 16.

27. Grey, ed., *The Early Years*, p. 289.

28. *Private Life of the Queen*, p. 69.

29. August 8, 1887; from a letter to Oliphant's publisher, Blackwell, quoted in Colby and Colby, *Equivocal Virtue*, p. 116.

30. W. R. Greg, "Why Are Women Redundant,"*National Review* 14 (1862): 434–60.

31. Garlick, in "The Staging of Death," pp. 59–76, refers to the Iron Duke's ceremony as one "produced . . . by the ruling class for political motives" (59). Victoria and Albert helped arrange the funeral. Garlick suggests that Victoria's sense of staging and performance guided her funeral plans.

32. See the opening pages of Benson's *As We Were* for one of the most memorable descriptions of Queen Victoria's visitations.

33. Benson, *Queen Victoria*, pp. 281, 283.

34. Kipling, "Ave Imperatrix," in *Kipling's Verse*.

⇨ 5. Queen of a Certain Age ⇦

1. Tilt, *Change of Life*, p. 6. Subsequent references to this edition will be cited in parentheses in the text. I thank Susan Walsh for giving me this reference; her paper on Mrs. Threadneedle and the climacteric women gave me further ideas about Queen Victoria. See Walsh, "Bodies of Capital."

2. W. Tyler Smith, "Climacteric Disease in Women," pp. 604–5. Subsequent references to this work will be cited in parentheses in the text.

3. Reid, *Ask Sir James*, p. 74.

4. Mallet, *Life with Queen Victoria*, p. 33.

5. Ibid., p. 36.

6. Ponsonby, *Henry Ponsonby*, p. 48.

7. Reid, *Ask Sir James*, p. 57.

8. As early as 1873, Gilbert had transformed an amorous theme to a political one by altering one of his own plays. He took his spoof of romantic love, *The Wicked World*, and changed its terms to politics, calling the burlesque version *The Happy Land*. In the comedy, the fairies, wishing to test their idealized notions of human love, are disillusioned; while in the burlesque, they are seized by an equally irrational curiosity about "popular government," with the same disappointing results. The ease with which the transformation from the individual emotional sphere to the larger political arena is made foreshadows the more subtle and complex transpositions in the Savoy Operas. See Lawrence, " 'The Happy Land,' " pp. 161–83.

9. Act 1; Gilbert, *Savoy Operas*, p. 74. Subsequent quotations from the operas are taken from this edition.

10. Davis, "Woman on Top," p. 130.

11. Stedman, "From Dame to Woman," pp. 27–46.

12. Davis, "Woman on Top," p. 127.

13. Some of the grim lustiness of the battle-ax derives from the contemporary burlesques, pantomime, and travesty from which Gilbert refined his work. The classical burlesque "The Best of Mothers with a Brute of a Husband" commented ironically upon the issue of sovereignty, as did "Alcestis, the Original Strong-Minded Woman." A favorite subject of travesty was the myth of Venus and Adonis, a story of the seduction of a young man by an experienced woman, a precursor, perhaps, of

Ruth and Lady Jane, Venuses of the Savoy. See, for example, Adams, ed., *A Book of Burlesque*, p. 44.

14. Havelock Ellis, *Studies*, vol.1, part 2, p. 75.

15. December 8, 1880; *Letters and Journals*, p. 264.

16. Chodorow, *Reproduction of Mothering*, and Dinnerstein, *Mermaid and Minotaur*, adapt object relations psychology and derive theories to explain the maternal force in culture. That force threatens to infantilize adults by means of a regressive pull. Hence, a ruling woman's perceived power mobilizes various forms of resistance, such as ridicule.

17. Goldberg, in "W. S. Gilbert's Topsy-turvydom," found the queen's image, but he refers to it only in passing: "As I have sat before one of the Savoy Operettas, with their recurrent types of the all-too-fleshly, all-too-unmarried predacious female, I have thought that I could see a malicious reference to the Queen" (140).

18. Keith Thomas, *Religion*, p. 460.

19. Gibson, *Breugel*, p. 108.

20. On pornographic propaganda for the French Revolution, see Chantal Thomas, *La Reine Scélérate*, and Hunt, "The Many Bodies of Marie Antoinette," in Hunt, ed., *Eroticism*.

21. Windsor Castle, February 11, 1840; *Letters*, 1st ser., vol. 1, p. 274.

22. Bargainner, "Ruddigore," p. 14.

23. Davis, p. 141.

24. April 19, 1862; *Dearest Mama*, pp. 55–56.

25. Osborne, December 30, 1884; *Beloved Mama*, p. 176.

26. Osborne, January 15, 1879; *Beloved Mama*, p. 34.

27. Freud, in *Totem and Taboo*, vol. 12, quotes Kaemfer on the totemic aspects of the Mikado (44–45). Freud's discussion of the underlying oedipal theme could be applied to this opera as well.

28. Weisinger, in "The Twisted Cue," finds that all Gilbert's ladies of misrule are archetypes of the great mother, but he ascribes the influence on Gilbert to Spenser's *Fairie Queen* (167), and ignores Elizabeth I's influence on Spenser's allegory.

29. In 1878, eight years before the opening of *The Mikado*, Gilbert himself was forcefully reminded of the queen's mourning customs and recorded the event in his diary: "Dressed for the Queen's Levee . . . I went to levee—turned back at Buckingham Palace, because no crape on arm—went to Gorringe's to repair this omission—crape sewn on in shop—then admitted." Quoted by Hesketh Pearson, *Gilbert*, p. 97. Possibly the crape was for Victoria's daughter Alice and Alice's baby, who had died on December 14 of that year.

30. *Letters and Journals*, p. 305.

→ 6. Domesticity; or, Her Life as a Dog ←

1. Turner, in *Reckoning with the Beast*, argues that the question of how one should treat animals arose at a time when people began to conceptualize themselves as akin to animals and when new notions about pain helped to transform the Anglo-American mind. Jean-Jacques Rousseau and Jeremy Bentham based their animal ethics on animals' ability to suffer.

2. Turner, *Reckoning with the Beast*, p. 44.

3. August 11, 1880; *Letters and Journals*, p. 265.

4. Secord, *Dog Painting, 1840–1940*, p. 236.

5. On animal immortality, see Keith Thomas, *Man*, p. 140.

6. Tooley, *Personal Life*, p. 256.

7. Thomas, *Man*, p. 98.

8. Ibid., p. 172.

9. Ritvo, in *Animal Estate*, arguing that animals became more under human control, presents one aspect of the change in the power relation between animals and the English. She claims that the English appropriated the power formerly given animals, thus excusing them from human punishment.

10. Turner and Ritvo explore this paradox.

11. *Letters and Journals*, p. 202.

12. Eliot, *Mill on the Floss*, book 1, ch. 11, p. 110.

13. Ibid., p. 122.

14. Dickens, *Our Mutual Friend*, p. 357.

15. Ibid., p. 501. When reporting on women's reproductive cycle, Victorian medical literature frequently lumped women with other mammals—typically dogs—under the rubric of "brutes." For example, Laqueur, in "Orgasm," quotes a *Lancet* article of 1843: "The menstrual period in women bears a strict physiological resemblance to the heat of brutes" (p. 27).

16. Dickens, *Our Mutual Friend*, p. 646.

17. The poisoned soup in the English folk song "Lord Randall."

18. Dickens, *Our Mutual Friend*, p. 631.

19. Stead, *Her Majesty the Queen*, p. 8.

20. Walter Deverell's coyly named painting, *A Pet* (1852–53), provides a precedent for associating images of women with other pets. It shows a young woman on tiptoes peeking at a caged bird, while a dog rests on the floor near her skirts.

21. On canine classifications, see Ritvo, *Animal Estate*, p. 93.

22. Dickens, *Our Mutual Friend*, p. 229.

23. Ormond, *Landseer*, p. 5.

24. Landseer's romantic conception of Highlands history contributes to the "invention of tradition" discussed by authors in the collection edited by Hobsbawm. The mythology, conservative in nature, appealed mainly to the aristocracy—for example, Landseer's patrons for his pictures of Highland life, the dukes of Atholl, Bedford, Northumberland, Gordon, and Wellington. See Ormond, *Landseer*, p. 6.

25. Markree Castle, Sligo, July 4, 1860. Kingsley, *Life and Works*, vol. 3, p. 111.

26. Lodge, Phoenix Park, August 6, 1849; Queen Victoria to the king of the Belgians, *Letters*, 1st ser., vol. 2, p. 268.

27. *Letters*, 2d ser., vol. 3, p. 162.

28. The Victoria Memorial in Pall Mall shows a maternal queen surrounded by symbols of the four continents under her care, as part of a domesticated globe.

29. I thank Peter Funnell, curator at the National Portrait Gallery, London, for information about the Belfast exhibition, at which the painting was entitled *The Secret of Her Greatness*.

30. Stead, *Her Majesty the Queen*, p. 20.

31. Ibid., p. 19.

32. An unidentified print in the National Portrait Gallery shows a youngish Victoria handing a Bible to a dark-skinned man wearing a feather headdress and earrings while uniformed white-skinned dignitaries attend the cermony. I am grateful to Peter Funnell for showing me this image.

33. Mallet, *Life with Queen Victoria*, p. 70.

34. Murphy, *Price of Stone*, p. 49.

35. The paintings discussed here as representing a colonizing attitude present

the outer reaches of the British Isles as victims of colonization. As I pointed out in chapter 2, many Scots were also part of the imperializing mission. So, too, were many Irish. Ronald Hyam considers the Irish presence in the Bengal Indian army of almost 50 percent before 1850 as an example of their "dynamic contribution" to their role in empire building (8).

36. See Hyam, p. 32: "India was the one piece of genuine imperial real-estate possessed by the British, and thus validated her claims to be a world power. India functioned chiefly as a symbol."

37. Balmoral Castle, September 10, 1891; *Letters*, 3d ser., vol. 2.

38. Preface to Razzak, *Native Officer's Diary*, n.p. Subsequent references will be cited in parentheses in the text.

39. June 23, 1887; *Letters and Journals*, p. 308.

40. Reid, *Ask Sir James*, p. 129.

41. *Letters and Journals*, p. 313.

42. *Letters*, 3d ser., vol. 3, p. 73.

43. To Ponsonby, *Letters and Journals*, p. 328.

44. Reid, *Ask Doctor Reid*, p. 142.

45. Balmoral, November 5, 1896; Mallet, *Life with Queen Victoria*, pp. 95–96.

46. Blunt, *My Diaries*, part 2, p. 2. The Pomeranian, Turi, stayed briefly and unwillingly on her bed the last day of her life. Longford states that Victoria's last word was "Bertie" as she opened her arms to the Prince of Wales (561), and St. Aubyn—more melodramatically—describes a scene: "Just before the end, the Queen suddenly raised herself and gazed towards the window. There was a look of joy and recognition in her eyes. 'Oh Albert . . .' she cried, and sank back on her pillow" (596).

⇢ 7. Petticoat Rule; or, Victoria in Furs ⇠

Casey Finch's generosity in sharing his interest in the cultural meanings of underwear and his knowledge of Victorian pornography provided inspiration and bibliographical material for my initial study of this topic. See his " 'Hooked and Buttoned Together.' "

1. Strachey, *Queen Victoria*, p. 49.

2. Despite the popular image of a dour Victoria, some studies, and not simply the most recent, acknowledge her sexuality and her subjects' recognition of it. See particularly Aronson's, *Heart of a Queen*, and Duff's *Victoria Travels* and *Victoria and Albert*.

3. For a sample of jokes, see Pearsall, *Worm in the Bud*, pp. 25ff.

4. Biographers quote Greville's diary as the source.

5. Tuesday, October 8, 1861; *Leaves*, p. 207.

6. September 8, 1862; *Dearest Mama*, pp. 105–6.

7. The political acquisitions under Disraeli, the Royal Titles Bill whereby Victoria gained the title Empress of India, and the prime minister's special relationship with Victoria were controversial. The complex role of a Semitic wooer to the monarch aroused virulent chauvinism. Nonetheless, the relationship was generally regarded as "productive," in the sense that Dizzy seemed to get his way with the queen where others (Gladstone, in particular) had spectacularly failed.

8. Trevor Turner, "Erotomania," p. 226.

9. Dorothy Thompson, *Queen Victoria*, p. 74.

10. Dorothy Thompson, who believes there might well have been an affair between Brown and the queen, points out the disparity between the tolerance for kings' sexual comforts and the fuss raised by the relationship between Victoria and

Brown. She downplays disturbances in protocol, however; Brown's authority superseded those in whom authority was officially placed (61).

11. According to the self-edited memoirs of James Reid, her personal physician at Balmoral, the queen left instructions about the souvenirs to be placed in her coffin. In went mementoes, including the plaster cast of Albert's hands and his dressing gown, covered with a cushion "so that it looked as if nothing had been put in"; then he asked the family to leave the room. "Then I . . . put in the Queen's left hand the photo of Brown and his hair in a case (according to her private instructions), which I wrapped in tissue paper, and covered with Queen Alexandra's flowers." Reid, *Ask Sir James*, pp. 216–17.

12. Dimond and Taylor, *Crown and Camera*, p. 23.

13. Kirwan, *Palace and Hovel*, p. 52.

14. Ibid., p. 53.

15. Ibid., p. 55.

16. Pearsall, in *Worm in the Bud*, quotes an earlier version on this theme:

> "You have not seen all the *beauties of England* yet," observed Lord
> Paget to the Prince, after he had *dismounted* from a *riding* excursion with the Queen; "there are some counties remarkable for
> their scenery. I dare say your highness will *like hunts!*"
>
> "Vare much! Vare much!" replied Albert, "I have been in several, and do like them all vare much!"
>
> (31)

17. K. T. [pseud.], *John Brown*, p. 5. I thank Dorothy Thompson for lending me this pamphlet.

18. *Brown on the Throne*, p. 1. I thank Dorothy Thompson for lending me this pamphlet. Subsequent references to it will be cited in parentheses in the text.

19. These lyrics are the closest Dorothy Thompson's student could remember, with a possible euphemism corrected by Professor Thompson.

20. *Letters*, 2d ser., vol. 2, p. 19.

21. Ponsonby, *Henry Ponsonby*, p. 98.

22. Savory and Marks, *Smiling Muse*, p. 33.

23. Longford, in *Queen Victoria*, quotes the "legend" in the context of the queen's great emotional energies and large appetites, p. 78.

24. Siegel, in the introduction to *Male Masochism*, explores some of the masochistic dimensions of the love story.

25. *Whippingham Papers*, n.p.

26. Esher, ed., *Girlhood of Queen Victoria*, vol. 1, p. 25.

27. Havelock Ellis, *Studies*, vol. 1, p. 76.

28. Ibid., vol. 1, p. 89.

29. The earliest date of this novel is 1896. Kearney, in *The Private Case*, attributes the work to John S. Farmer, a well-known writer of pornographic fiction. See also Lansbury, *Old Brown Dog*.

30. It may be a coincidence, but Queen Victoria's softly modulated voice was commented on from the moment she read her first declaration to her councillors on the famous morning of her accession.

31. Quoted in Lansbury, *Old Brown Dog*, p. 102.

32. October 10, 1839; *Letters and Journals*, p. 55.

33. Jerrold, *Married Life*, p. 42.

34. Charlot, *Victoria*, pp. 189ff. See also Duff, *Victoria and Albert*, p. 229.

35. Duff, *Victoria and Albert*, p. 28.

36. Esher, ed., *Girlhood of Queen Victoria*, vol. 2, pp. 135–36.

37. Grey, ed., *Early Years*, p. 183.

38. Ward, *Marcella*, intro. by Watters, p. vii.

39. Robert Stoller, in *Perversion*, points out that many kinds of pornography portray the male protagonist suffering humiliation against his will.

40. Swinburne, *Poems*.

41. Lang, ed., *New Writings by Swinburne*, p. 229.

42. Ibid., p. 105.

43. Havelock Ellis, *Studies*, vol. 1, p. 131.

44. Ashbee, *Forbidden Books*, p. 22.

45. Ibid., p. 178.

46. *Romance of Chastisement*, quoted in Ashbee, *Forbidden Books*, p. 66.

47. Recent scholarship, however, attributes the novel to a London lawyer, Stanislas Matthew de Rhodes. See the introduction by Michael R. Goss to *The Petticoat Dominant*, a "sequel" to *Gynecocracy*. No one has done a stylistic analysis, but *Gynecocracy* seems to me better written, more sophisticated, *The Petticoat Dominant* a crude imitation.

48. Robinson [pseud.], *Gynecocracy*, p. 2. Subsequent references to this edition will be cited in parentheses in the text.

49. *Venus School-Mistress*, p. xi.

50. Ashbee, *Forbidden Books*, p. 28.

51. Hand-kissing rituals in flagellation scenes are common. Martinet's beating inspires the gesture as does Severin's recounting his initiation into masochistic desire by a sexy aunt:

> One day when my parents had gone to town, my aunt decided to take advantage of their absence to administer justice to me. Wearing her kazabaika, her fur-lined jacket, she burst into my room, followed by the cook, the kitchen-maid and the little kitten whom I had spurned. . . . they seized me and in spite of my resistance, bound me hand and foot. Then with a wicked smile my aunt rolled up her sleeve and began to beat me with a long switch. . . . She had me unbound but I then had to go down on my knees to her, thank her for the punishment and kiss her hand.
>
> (*Venus in Furs*, pp. 174–75.)

52. Esher, ed., *The Girlhood*, intro., p. 40.

53. Hawthorne, *Knickers*.

54. Cunnington and Cunnington, *History of Underwear*, pp. 105, 106.

55. Ibid., p. 72.

56. "Fetishism, as defined by the process of disavowal and suspension of belief, belongs essentially to masochism." Deleuze, "Coldness and Cruelty," p. 32.

57. Stoller, *Sexual Excitement*, p. 21.

58. Chantal Thomas, *La Reine Scélérate*, p. 16.

→ 8. Motherhood, Excess, and Empire ←

1. For a discussion of the formation of the state as a military entity and women's roles within that model, see Elshtain, *Women and War*.

2. Benson, *Queen Victoria*, p. 382.

3. "Life's Gallery," p. 17.

4. Warner, in *Alone of All Her Sex*, examines the myth of the Virgin Mary. Victoria takes on different attributes and imagery of the Virgin, such as lilies, and is sometimes venerated as if she were an English Protestant adaptation of Mary.

5. Hardie, *Political Influence*, pp. 14–15.

6. Ibid., pp. 24–26.

7. Kingsley, *Life and Works: Hypatia*, vol. 9, p. xiii.

8. Queen Victoria, *Record of the Visit*, p. 13.

9. E. Ann Kaplan, in *Motherhood and Representation*, traces from 1762 the motherhood ideology that limits the mother's function (pp. 17–26).

10. *Letters and Journals*, p. 152.

11. Osborne, March 1, 1858; *Dearest Child*, p. 67.

12. Aix-les-Bains, April 15, 1885; *Dearest Mama*, p. 186.

13. April 30, 1887; *Letters and Journals*, p. 303.

14. Craik, "Dedicatory Verses," in *Fifty Golden Years*, n.p.

15. For this reason, I suggest, many histories have found it possible to ignore her. In addition, until recently, histories of motherhood and the family have not considered the mother's point of view. For a notable exception, see Ross, *Love and Toil*. Although she does not mention the queen as a mother, her penetrating study suggests to me that Victoria's mother image signified differently to the working classes, many of whom worked for their own mothers.

16. Carroll, *Through the Looking-Glass*, p. 187. Subsequent references to this edition will be cited in parentheses in the text.

17. Weintraub, in *Victoria*, notes that exchanges in writing in which Victoria used *I* were extremely rare: "Only personal matters, on very rare occasions, could elicit a royal first-person-singular pronoun from the Queen" (431).

18. Ponsonby, *Henry Ponsonby*, pp. 134–35.

19. Ibid., p. 115.

20. Ibid., pp. 115–16.

21. In *Woman and the Demon*, Auerbach calls Ayesha "a suprahuman absolute monarch, a galvanized and transfigured Victoria" (37).

22. Haggard, *She*, p. 19. Subsequent references to this edition will be cited in parentheses in the text.

23. Dorment, *Alfred Gilbert*, p. 72.

24. Marina Warner, in *Monuments and Maidens*, considers how the female form represents authority as a powerful allegory.

25. Dorment, "The Jubilee Memorial to Queen Victoria," in *Alfred Gilbert: Sculptor and Goldsmith*, n.p.

26. Gissing, *In the Year*, p. 51. Subsequent references to this edition will be cited in parentheses in the text.

27. Balmoral, June 5, 1872; *Darling Child*, p. 47.

28. Lady Augusta Stanley, *Later Letters*, p. 51.

29. Munby, "The Queen's Best Monument," pp. 59–60.

30. Corelli, *The Passing*, p. 5.

31. Ibid., p. 6.

32. Ibid., p. 7.

→ Epilogue: Victoria Amazonica ←

1. Lionel, *Historic Lovers*.

2. D'Humy, *Women Who Influenced the World.*

3. Sweetser, *Ten Girls from History.*

4. Bingham, *Narrative of the Expedition to China*, vol. 2, p. 372.

5. Housman, *Victoria Regina*, p. 13.

6. Scourse, *Victorians and Their Flowers*, p. 1.

7. Ibid., p. 105.

8. See Stein, *Victoria's Year*, fig. 2.3, for an illustration of Victoria's face within a rose, surrounded by a rose garland.

9. Tyrell, *Amazons.*

10. Scourse, *Victorians and Their Flowers*, p. 109.

11. Clemens, "The Great Procession," p. 17.

12. Ibid., p. 18.

13. Ibid., p. 20.

14. Faithfull, preface, *The Victoria Regia*, pp. v–viii.

15. Ibid., p. viii.

16. Stead, *Her Majesty the Queen*, p. 24.

17. Ibid., p. 25.

18. The struggle to propagate the lily in England is a story equally susceptible to allegorical interpretation. See Scourse, *Victorians and Their Flowers.*

19. Faithfull, "Dedication," *The Victoria Regia*, p. iii.

20. James, *Letters*, vol. 1, p. 184.

21. Colby and Colby, *Equivocal Virtue*, p. 237. Longford, *Queen Victoria*, p. 24, states that the duke died before he could execute his plan to take Victoria to New Lanark Mills to meet Owen.

22. Oliphant, *Queen Victoria*, p. 8.

23. Lowell, "The Sisters."

24. Cohen, "Queen Victoria and Me."

25. As this book goes to press, Queen Victoria has returned as a possible bastard, according to Malcolm Potts and William Potts in their book, *Queen Victoria's Gene.*

WORKS CITED

Queen Victoria: Letters, Journals, Memoirs

Advice to a Grand-daughter: Letters from Queen Victoria to Princess Victoria of Hesse. Edited by Richard Hough. London: Heinemann, 1975.

Beloved Mama: Private Correspondence of Queen Victoria and the German Crown Princess, 1878–1885. Edited by Roger Fulford. London: Evans, 1976.

Darling Child: Private Correspondence of Queen Victoria and the German Crown Princess, 1871–1878. Edited by Roger Fulford. London: Evans, 1976.

Dear and Honoured Lady: The Correspondence Between Queen Victoria and Alfred Tennyson. Edited by Hope Dyson and Charles Tennyson. Rutherford, New Jersey: Fairleigh Dickinson University Press, 1971.

Dearest Child: Private Correspondence of Queen Victoria and the Crown Princess of Prussia, 1858–1861. Edited by Roger Fulford. London: Evans, 1964.

Dearest Mama: Private Correspondence of Queen Victoria and the Crown Princess of Prussia, 1861–1864. Edited by Roger Fulford. London: Evans, 1968.

The Girlhood of Queen Victoria: A Selection from Her Majesty's Diaries Between the Years 1832 and 1840. 2 vols. Edited by Viscount Esher. London: John Murray, 1912.

Leaves from the Journal of Our Life in the Highlands from 1848 to 1861. Edited by Arthur Helps. New York: Harper and Brothers, 1868.

Letters of Queen Victoria. 9 vols. Edited by Arthur Christopher Benson and Viscount Esher (1st ser.) and George Earle Buckle (2d and 3d ser.) London: John Murray, 1907–1931.

Letters of Queen Victoria from the Archives of the House of Brandenburg-Prussia. Edited by Hector Bolitho. New Haven: Yale University Press, 1938.

Queen Victoria: Leaves from a Journal: A Record of the Visit of the Emperor and Empress of the French to the Queen, and of the Visit of the Queen and H. R. H. The Prince Consort to the Emperor of the French. Edited by Raymond Mortimer. New York: Farrar, Straus and Cudahy, 1961.

Queen Victoria in Her Letters and Journals. Edited by Christopher Hibbert. New York: Viking, 1985.

Victoria in the Highlands: The Personal Journal of Her Majesty Queen Victoria. Edited by David Duff. London: Frederick Muller, 1968.

Your Dear Letter: Private Correspondence of Queen Victoria and the Crown Princess of Prussia, 1865–1871. Edited by Roger Fulford. London: Evans, 1971.

Other Memoirs, Memorials, Biographies, and Material About the Queen

Ames, Winslow. *Prince Albert and Victorian Taste.* New York: Viking, 1968.

The Argosy: The Reign of Woman Under Queen Victoria. London: George Allen, 1901.

Aronson, Theo. *Heart of a Queen: Queen Victoria's Romantic Attachments.* London: John Murray, 1991.

Barrett, Richard. *The Queen and Albert the Good.* London: privately printed, 1862.

Bennett, Daphne. *King Without a Crown: Albert, Prince Consort of England, 1819–1861.* New York: Lippincott, 1977.

Benson, E. F. *As We Were: A Victorian Peep-Show.* 1930. Reprint, London: Hogarth, 1985.

——. *Queen Victoria.* London: Longmans, Green, 1935.

Bolitho, Hector. *Victoria the Widow and Her Son.* London: Cobden-Sanderson, 1934.

——. *The Reign of Queen Victoria.* New York: Macmillan, 1948.

Brown, Ivor. *Balmoral: The History of a Home.* London: Collins, 1955.

Brown on the Throne. London: Montague, Smith, Chapman, Lee, and Co., 1871.

Browning, Elizabeth Barrett. "The Young Queen," "Victoria's Tears," and "Crowned and Wedded." *Poems of Elizabeth Barrett Browning.* Edited by Ruth Adams. Boston: Houghton Mifflin, 1974.

——. *The Brownings' Correspondence.* Vol. 3. Edited by Philip Kelley and Ronald Hudson. Winfield, Kansas: Wedgestone, 1985.

Charlot, Monica. *Victoria, the Young Queen.* Oxford: Basil Blackwell, 1991.

Clemens, Samuel. [Mark Twain]. "The great procession of June 22, 1897, in the Queen's honor, reported both in the light of history, and as a spectacle by Mark Twain." Privately printed, 1897.

Cohen, Leonard. "Queen Victoria and Me." In *Flowers for Hitler.* Toronto: McClelland and Stewart, 1964.

Corelli, Marie. *The Passing of the Great Queen: A Tribute to Queen Victoria.* London: Methuen, 1901.

Craik, Dinah Maria Mulock. *Fifty Golden Years: Incidents in the Queen's Reign.* London: Raphael Tuck and Sons, 1887.

D'Humy, Fernand Emile. *Women Who Influenced the World.* New York: Library Publishers, 1955.

Dimond, Frances and Roger Taylor. *Crown and Camera: The Royal Family and Photography, 1842–1920.* Harmondworth: Penguin, 1987.

Duff, David. *Victoria and Albert.* New York: Taplinger, 1972.

——. *Victoria Travels.* New York: Taplinger, 1971.

Ellis, T. Mullet. *The Fairies' Favourite, or The Story of Queen Victoria Told for Children.* London: Ash Partners, 1897.

French, George Russell. *The Ancestry of Her Majesty Queen Victoria and of His Royal Highness Prince Albert.* London: William Pickering, 1841.

Fulford, Roger. *The Prince Consort.* London: Macmillan, 1949.

Gersheim, Helmut and Alison Gernsheim. *Victoria R.: A Biography with Four Hundred Illustrations Based on Her Personal Photograph Album.* New York: G. Putnam's Sons, 1959.

Gladden, Washington. "Sermon in Columbus, Ohio, First Congregational Church, January 27, 1901." Columbus: Chaucer, 1901.

Gosse, Edmund. "The Character of Queen Victoria." *The Quarterly Review* 193 (January-April 1901): 301–37.

Grey, General C., ed. *The Early Years of His Royal Highness The Prince Consort.* Compiled under the direction of Her Majesty, The Queen. New York: Harper and Brothers, 1867.

Hardie, Frank. *The Political Influence of Queen Victoria.* London: Oxford University Press, 1935.

Herne the Hunter [pseud.]. *A Fragment from the Fine Art Follies of Frogmore, or the Secrets of the Belgian Mystery Unveiled.* Windsor Home Park: privately printed, 1869.

Housman, Laurence. *Victoria Regina: A Dramatic Biography.* New York: Charles Scribners' Sons, n.d.

Howie, James, M.D. *The Queen in Scotland: A Descriptive Poem.* Edinburgh: Q. Dalrymple, 1842.

Jerrold, Clare. *The Married Life of Queen Victoria.* New York: G. P. Putnam's Sons, 1913.

Kipling, Rudyard. "Ave Imperatrix." *A Choice of Kipling's Verse.* Edited by T. S. Eliot. London: Faber and Faber, 1941.

K. T. [pseud.]. *John Brown: A Correspondence with the Lord Chancellor, Regarding a Charge of Fraud and Embezzlement, Preferred against His Grace the Duke of Athole.* London: Alexander Robertson, 1873.

Ladies Magazine and Museum: A Family Journal. Vol. 11 (July 1837).

Lieven, Princess Darya Khristoforovna (Benchendorff). *The Private Letters of Princess Lieven to Prince Metternich, 1820–1826.* Edited by Peter Quenell. London: John Murray, 1937.

"Life's Gallery of Beauties, Number 26." *Life* 15 (October 17, 1889): 17.

Lionel, George Walter. *Historic Lovers.* London: Huchinson, 1926.

Longford, Elizabeth. *Queen Victoria: Born to Succeed.* New York: Harper and Row, 1964.

Mallet, Marie. *Life with Queen Victoria: Marie Mallet's Letters from Court, 1887–1901.* Edited by Victor Mallet. London: John Murray, 1968.

Martin, Theodore. *Life of the Prince Consort.* 6 vols. 7th ed. London: Smith, Elder, 1880.

Oliphant, Margaret. *Queen Victoria: A Personal Sketch.* London: Cassell, 1900.

One of Her Majesty's Servants. *The Private Life of the Queen.* London: C. Arthur Pearson, 1897.

Ponsonby, Arthur. *Henry Ponsonby: His Life From His Letters.* London: Macmillan, 1942.

"The Queen in the Islands and Highlands." *London Quarterly Review* (January 1868): 27–43.

"The Queen's Best Monument," and Other Articles, Poems, and Letters on the Queen. London: The Spectator, 1901.

The Queen's Masque: A Satirical Sketch. By the author of "The Palace Martyr," &c. &c. London: W. Gilling, 1842.

Razzak, Jemadar Abdur. *The Native Officer's Diary.* Madras: Higgenbotham, 1894.

Reid, Michaela. *Ask Sir James.* New York: Penguin, 1990.

St. Aubyn, Giles. *Queen Victoria: A Portrait.* New York: Atheneum, 1992.

Smith, Shirley. *Coronation Stone: Pedigree of Her Most Gracious Majesty Queen Victoria.* Manuscript. Christmas, 1884.

Stanley, Lady Augusta. *Later Letters of Lady Augusta Stanley, 1864–1876.* Edited by the Dean of Windsor and Hector Bolitho. New York: Jonathan Cape and Harrison Smith, 1929.

Stead, William. T. *Her Majesty the Queen: Studies of the Sovereign and the Reign.* London: Review of Reviews Office, 1887.

Strachey, Lytton. *Queen Victoria.* New York: Harcourt Brace, 1921.

Sweetser, Kate Dickinson. *Ten Girls from History.* New York: Duffield, 1919.

Thompson, Dorothy. *Queen Victoria: The Woman, the Monarchy, and the People.* New York: Pantheon, 1990.

Tisdall, E. E. P. *Queen Victoria's Private Life, 1837–1901.* London: Jarrolds, 1861.

Tooley, Sarah A. *The Personal Life of Queen Victoria.* New York: Dodd Mead, 1897.

Vanantetzie, S. Mirza. *Discent of Her Majesty Victoria Queen of England from the Arsacid Kings of Armenia.* Smyrna: H. Dedeyam, 1866.

Watson, Vera. *A Queen at Home: An Intimate Account of the Social and Domestic Life of Queen Victoria's Court.* London: W. H. Allen, 1952.

Weintraub, Stanley. *Queen Victoria: An Intimate Biography.* New York: Dutton, 1987.

Wilson, Mona. *Queen Victoria.* Edinburgh: Peter Davis, 1933.

Woodham-Smith, Cecil. *Queen Victoria: From Her Birth to the Death of the Prince Consort.* New York: Knopf, 1972.

Other Sources

Adams, William Davenport, ed. *A Book of Burlesque.* London: Henry, 1891.

Anderson, Amanda. *Tainted Souls and Painted Faces: The Rhetoric of Falleness in Victorian Culture.* Ithaca: Cornell University Press, 1993.

Armstrong, Nancy. *Desire and Domestic Fiction: A Political History of the Novel.* New York: Oxford University Press, 1987.

"Art of Dress." *The Quarterly Review* 1, no. 79 (1847): 372–99.

Ashbee, Henry Spencer. *Forbidden Books of the Victorians.* Edited and abridged by Peter Fryer. London: Odyssey, 1970.

Ashton, John, ed. *Modern Street Ballads.* London: Chatto and Windus, 1888.

Auerbach, Nina. *Woman and the Demon.* Cambridge: Harvard University Press, 1982.

Baby's A.B.C. New York: McLoughlin Bro's, 1897.

Bagehot, Walter. *The English Constitution.* 1867. Reprint, Ithaca: Cornell University Press, 1963.

Bargainner, Earl F. "Ruddigore: Gilbert's Burlesque of Melodrama." In James Helyar, ed., *Gilbert and Sullivan: Papers Presented at the International Conference.* Lawrence, Kansas: University of Kansas Libraries, 1971.

Barickman, Richard, Susan MacDonald, and Myra Stark. *Corrupt Relations: Dickens,*

Thackeray, Trollope, Collins, and the Victorian Sexual System. New York: Columbia University Press, 1982.

Barthes, Roland. *The Fashion System*. New York: Hill and Wang, 1983. Viking, 1968.

Bayly, C. A. *Imperial Meridian: The British Empire and the World, 1780–1830*. London: Longman, 1989.

Beddoe, John. *The Races of Britain: A Contribution to the Anthropology of Western Europe*. Bristol: J. W. Arrowsmith, 1885.

Besant, Walter. *The Rise of the Empire*. New York: M. F. Mansfield, 1897.

Bingham, Elliot J. *Narrative of the Expedition to China from the Commencement of the War to Its Termination in 1842*. 2 vols. 1842. Reprint, Wilmington, Delaware: Scholarly Resources, 1972.

Blunt, Wilfrid Scawen. *My Diaries: Being a Personal Narrative of Events, 1888–1914*. Part 2. New York: Knopf, 1921.

Briggs, Asa. *Saxons, Normans, and Victorians*. Sussex: The Hastings and Bexhill Branch of the Historical Association, 1966.

——. *Victorian Things*. Chicago: University of Chicago Press, 1988.

Cannadine, David. "The Context, Performance, and Meaning of Ritual: The British Monarchy and the 'Invention of Tradition,' c. 1820–1977." In Eric Hobsbawm and Terence Ranger, eds., *The Invention of Tradition*, pp. 101–164. Cambridge: Cambridge University Press, 1982.

Carlyle, Thomas. *Sartor Resartus*. New York: Scribners, 1921.

Carroll, Lewis. *Alice in Wonderland*. 1866. Facsimile ed., New York: Knopf, 1985.

——. *Through the Looking-Glass and What Alice Found There*. 1872. Facsimile ed., New York: Knopf, 1985.

"The Character of Costume." *Chambers's Edinburgh Journal* 3, no. 9 (1848): 313–16.

Chodorow, Nancy. *The Reproduction of Mothering: Psychoanalysis and the Sociology of Gender*. Berkeley: University of California Press, 1978.

Colby, Vineta and Robert A. *The Equivocal Virtue: Mrs Oliphant*. Hamden, Connectictut: Archon, 1966.

Colley, Linda. *Britons: Forging the Nation, 1707–1837*. New Haven: Yale University Press, 1992.

Crampton, T. *A Collection of Broadside Ballads Printed in London*. 9 vols. Manuscript collection. n.d.

Cumming, Valerie. *Royal Dress: The Image and the Reality, 1580 to the Present Day*. London: Batsford, 1989.

Cunnington, C. Willet and Phillis Cunnington. *The History of Underwear*. London: Faber and Faber, 1951.

Curl, James Stevens. *A Celebration of Death*. London: Constable, 1980.

Darby, Elisabeth and Nicola Smith. *The Cult of the Prince Consort*. New Haven: Yale University Press, 1982.

Davidoff, Leonore and Catharine Hall. *Family Fortunes: Men and Women of the English Middle Class, 1780–1850*. Chicago: University of Chicago Press, 1987.

Davis, Natalie Zemon. "Woman on Top." In *Society and Culture in Early Modern France*. Stanford: Stanford University Press, 1975.

Deleuze, Gilles. *Masochism: Coldness and Cruelty*. New York: Zone, 1989.

Dickens, Charles. *Great Expectations*. 1861. Reprint, Harmondsworth: Penguin, 1965.

——. *Our Mutual Friend*. 1865. Reprint, London: J. M. Dent, 1907.

Dinnerstein, Dorothy. *The Mermaid and the Minotaur: Sexual Arrangements and Human Malaise*. New York: Harper and Row, 1976.

Dorment, Richard. *Alfred Gilbert.* New Haven: Yale University Press, 1985.
——. "The Jubilee Memorial to Queen Victoria." In *Alfred Gilbert: Sculptor and Goldsmith.* London: Royal Academy of Arts and Weidenfeld and Nicholson, 1986.
Eliot, George. *Felix Holt, the Radical.* 1866. Reprint, Harmondsworth: Penguin, 1972.
——. *The Mill on the Floss.* 1860. Reprint, New York: Oxford University Press, 1980.
Ellis, Havelock. *Studies in the Psychology of Sex.* 1898. Reprint, New York: Random House, 1936.
Elshtain, Jean Bethke. *Women and War.* New York: Basic Books, 1987.
"Fashions in Hair and Head-Dresses." *Eclectic Magazine* 85 (1870): 569–76.
Finch, Casey. "Hooked and Buttoned Together: Victorian Underwear and the Representation of the Female Body." *Victorian Studies* 32 (Spring 1991): 337–65.
Flanagan, J. F. *Spitalfields Silks of the Eighteenth and Nineteenth Centuries.* Leigh-on-Sea: F. Lewis, 1954.
Fredeman, William. "A Charivari for Queen Butterfly: *Punch* on Queen Victoria." *Victorian Poetry* 25 (1987): 47–73.
Freud, Sigmund. *Totem and Taboo.* Translated by James Strachey. *The Standard Edition of the Complete Psychological Works of Sigmund Freud.* Vol. 12. London: Hogarth, 1973.
Garlick, Harry. "The Staging of Death: Iconography and the State Funeral of the Duke of Wellington." *Australian Art Journal* 9 (1992): 59–76.
Geertz, Clifford. "Centers, Kings, and Charisma: Reflections on the Symbolics of Power." In *Local Knowledge: Further Essays in Interpretive Anthropology.* New York: Basic Books, 1983
Gibson, Walter. *Breugel.* New York: Oxford University Press, 1977.
Gilbert, Sandra and Susan Gubar. *The Madwoman in the Attic: The Woman Writer and the Nineteenth-Century Literary Imagination.* New Haven: Yale University Press, 1979.
Gilbert, William Schwenk. *The Savoy Operas.* London: Macmillan, 1926.
Gissing, George. *In the Year of Jubilee.* New York: D. Appleton, 1895.
——. *The Odd Women.* 1893. Reprint, New York: Norton, 1978.
Goldberg, Isaac. "W. S. Gilbert's Topsy-turvydom." In John Bush Jones, ed., *W. S. Gilbert: A Century of Scholarship and Commentary.* New York: New York University Press, 1970.
Haggard, H. Rider. *She.* 1887. Reprint edited by Norman Etherington, Bloomington: Indiana University Press, 1991.
Hawthorne, Rosemary. *Knickers: An Intimate Appraisal.* Rev. ed. London: Souvenir, 1991.
Hechter, Michael. *Internal Colonialism: The Celtic Fringe in British National Development, 1536–1966.* Berkeley: University of California Press, 1975.
Homans, Margaret. "The Powers of Powerlessness: The Courtships of Elizabeth Barrett and Queen Victoria." In Lynn Keller and Christanne Miller, eds., *Feminist Measures,* pp. 237–59. Ann Arbor: University of Michigan Press, 1994.
——. "To the Queen's Private Apartments: Royal Family Portraiture and the Construction of Victoria's Sovereign Obedience." *Victorian Studies* 38 (Autumn 1993): 1–41.
Horsman, Reginald. "Origins of Racial Anglo-Saxonism in Great Britain." *Journal of the History of Ideas* 37 (1976): 387–410.
Hovel, Mark. *The Chartist Movement.* Manchester: Manchester University Press, 1918.
Hunt, Lynn. "The Many Bodies of Marie Antoinette: Political Pornography and the

Problem of the Feminine in the French Revolution. In Hunt, ed., *Eroticism and the Body Politic*, pp. 108–30. Baltimore: Johns Hopkins University Press, 1991.

Hyam, Ronald. *Britain's Imperial Century, 1815–1914: A Study of Empire and Expansion.* 2d ed. New York: Barnes and Noble, 1993.

James, Henry. *Letters.* Edited by Leon Edel. Vol. 1. Cambridge: Harvard University Press, 1984.

Kaplan, E. Ann. *Motherhood and Representation: The Mother in Popular Culture and Melodrama.* London: Routledge, 1992.

Kearney, Patrick. *The Private Case: The Erotic Collection in the British Museum Library.* London: Jay Landesman, 1981.

Kennedy, John. *The Natural History of Man; or, Popular Chapters on Ethnography.* London: John Cassell, 1851.

Kingsley, Charles. *The Roman and the Teuton.* London: Macmillan, 1889.

——. *The Life and Works of Charles Kingsley.* Vols. 9 and 11. London: Macmillan, 1902.

Kirwan, Daniel Joseph. *Palace and Hovel or, Phases of London Life.* Hartford, Conn: Belknap and Bliss, 1870.

Knox, Robert, M.D. *The Races of Men: A Fragment.* Philadelphia: Lea and Blanchard, 1850.

"Land Occupancy in Scotland." *Chambers's Edinburgh Journal* 3 (1848): 317–320.

Lansbury, Coral. *The Old Brown Dog: Women, Workers, and Vivisection in Edwardian England.* Madison: University of Wisconsin Press, 1985.

Laqueur, Thomas. "Orgasm, Generation, and the Politics of Reproductive Biology." In Catharine Gallagher and Thomas Laqueur, eds., *The Making of the Modern Body: Sexuality and Society in the Nineteenth Century*, pp. 1–41. Berkeley: University California Press, 1987.

Lawrence, Elwood P. " 'The Happy Land': W. S. Gilbert as Political Satirist." *Victorian Studies* 15 (1971): 161–83.

Leach, William. *True and Perfect Union: The Feminist Reform of Sex and Society.* New York: Basic Books, 1980.

Lennie, Campbell. *Landseer: The Victorian Paragon.* London: Hamish Hamilton, 1976.

Lowell, Amy. "The Sisters." In *What's O'Clock*. Boston: Houghton Miflin, 1925.

McDowell, Colin. *Dressed to Kill: Sex, Power, and Clothes.* London: Hutchinson, 1992.

MacDougall, Hugh A. *Racial Myth in English History: Trojans, Teutons, and Anglo-Saxons.* Montreal: Harvest House, 1982.

Marcus, Steven. *The Other Victorians: A Study of Sexuality and Pornography in Nineteenth-Century England.* New York: Basic Books, 1966.

Marx, Karl. "The Eighteenth Brumaire of Louis Bonaparte." *Karl Marx: Selected Writings.* Edited by David McLellan. Oxford: Oxford University Press, 1977.

Moers, Ellen. *The Dandy: Brummell to Beerbohm.* New York: Viking, 1960.

Murphy, Richard. *The Price of Stone amd Earlier Poems.* Wake Forest, Ill.: Wake Forest University Press, 1975.

Nairn, Tom. *The Break-Up of Britain: Crisis and Neonationalism.* Manchester: NLB, 1977.

Norris, Herbert and Oswald Curtis. The Nineteenth Century. Vol. 6, *Costume and Fashion.* London: J. M. Dent, 1933.

Ormond, Richard. *Sir Edwin Landseer.* New York: Rizzoli, 1982.

Pearsall, Ronald. *The Worm in the Bud: The World of Victorian Sexuality.* Harmondsworth: Penguin, 1971.

Pearson, Charles H. *The Early and Middle Ages of England.* 1861. Reprint, Port Washington: Kennikat, 1971.

Pearson, Hesketh. *Gilbert: His Life and Strife.* London: Methuen, 1957.

Petticoat Dominant or, Woman's Revenge. 1898. Reprint, London: Delictus Books, 1994.

Pickering, Paul A. "Class Without Words: Symbolic Communication in the Chartist Movement." *Past and Present* 112 (August 1986): 144–62.

Poovey, Mary. *Uneven Developments: The Ideological Work of Gender in Mid-Victorian England.* Chicago: University of Chicago Press, 1988.

Procter, Adelaide Anne. *Legends and Lyrics.* 1st ser. London: George Bell, 1892.

———, ed. *The Victoria Regia: A Volume of Original Contributions in Poetry and Prose.* With a preface by Emily Faithfull. London: Victoria Press, 1861.

"The Raiment of Victorian Women." *English Illustrated Magazine* 17 (1897): 421–38.

Richards, Thomas. *The Commodity Culture of Victorian England: Advertising and Spectacle, 1851–1914.* Stanford: Stanford University Press, 1990.

Ritvo, Harriet. *The Animal Estate: The English and Other Creatures in the Victorian Age.* Cambridge: Harvard University Press, 1987.

Roberts, Helene E. "The Exquisite Slave: The Role of Clothes in the Making of the Victorian Woman." *Signs* 2 (Spring 1977): 554–69.

Robinson, Julian [pseud.]. *Gynecocracy: A narrative of the Adventures and Psychological Experiences of Julian Robinson (Afterwards Viscount Ladywood) Under Petticoat-Rule, Written by Himself.* Paris and Rotterdam, 1893.

Ross, Ellen. *Love and Toil: Motherhood in Outcast London.* New York: Oxford University Press, 1993.

Ruskin, John. "Of Queens' Gardens." In *Sesame and Lilies.* Revised and enlarged ed. New York: Thomas Crowell, 1871.

Sacher-Masoch, Leopold von. *Venus in Furs.* New York: Zone, 1989.

Savory, Jerold and Patricia Marks. *The Smiling Muse: Victoriana in the Comic Press.* Philadelphia: The Art Alliance Press; London and Toronto: Associated University Presses, 1985.

Schama, Simon. "Royal Family Portraiture." *Journal of Interdisciplinary History,* 17, no. 1 (Summer 1986): 155–85.

"The Scot at Home." *Blackwood's Magazine* (December 1875): 735–52.

Scott, Sir Walter. *The Poetical Works.* London: Henry Frowde, 1894.

"Scottish Characteristics: A Prelection." By a Scoto-Celt. *Fraser's Magazine* (April 1869): 451–465.

"Scottish National Character." *Blackwood's Magazine* (June 1860): 715–31.

Scourse, Nicolette. *The Victorians and Their Flowers.* London: Croom Helm, 1983.

Secord, William. *Dog Painting, 1840–1940: A Social History of the Dog in Art.* Woodbridge, Suffolk: Antique Collector's Club, 1992.

Sedgwick, Eve Kosovsky. *Between Men: English Literature and Male Homosocial Desire.* New York: Columbia University Press, 1985.

Siegel, Carol. *Male Masochism: Modern Revisions of the Story of Love.* Bloomington: Indiana University Press, 1995.

Smith, W. Tyler. "The Climacteric Disease in Women: A Paroxysmal Affection Occurring at the Decline of the Catamenia." *London Journal of Medicine* 7 (July 1849): 601–9

"Some Talk About Scotch Peculiarities." *Fraser's Magazine* 54 (December 1856): 702–14.

Stanton, Domna C. *The Aristocrat as Art: A Study of the Honnête Homme and the Dandy in Seventeenth- and Nineteenth-Century French Literature.* New York: Columbia University Press, 1980.

Stedman, Jane. "From Dame to Woman: W. S. Gilbert and Theatrical Transvestism." *Victorian Studies* 4 (1970): 27–46.

Steele, Valerie. *Fashion and Eroticism: Ideals of Feminine Beauty from the Victorian Era to the Jazz Age.* New York: Oxford University Press, 1985.

Stein, Richard L. *Victoria's Year: English Literature and Culture, 1837–1838.* New York: Oxford University Press, 1987.

Stocking, George W. *Victorian Anthropology.* New York: Free Press, 1987.

Stoller, Robert. *Observing the Erotic Imagination.* New Haven: Yale University Press, 1985.

——. *Perversion: The Erotic Form of Hatred.* New York: Random House, 1975.

——. *Sexual Excitement: Dynamics of Erotic Life.* New York: Pantheon, 1979.

Swinburne, Algernon Charles. *Poems and Ballads.* 1st ser. London: Chatto and Windus, 1912.

——. *New Writings by Swinburne.* Edited by Cecil Y. Lang. Syracuse: University of Syracuse Press, 1969.

Tennyson, Alfred. *The Poems of Tennyson.* Edited by Christopher Ricks. London: Longmans, 1969.

Thomas, Chantal. *La Reine scélérate: Marie-Antoinette dans les pamphlets.* Paris: Seuil, 1989.

Thomas, Keith. *Religion and the Decline of Magic.* London: Weidenfeld and Nicolson, 1971.

——. *Man and the Natural World.* New York: Pantheon, 1983.

Thompson, Dorothy. *The Chartists: Popular Politics in the Industrial Revolution.* New York: Pantheon, 1984.

Thompson, Francis. "Victorian Ode" 1897. Privately printed.

Tilt, Edward John, M.D. *The Change of Life in Health and Disease: A Practical Treatise on the Nervous and Other Affections Incidental to Women at the Decline of Life.* London: John Churchill, 1857.

Trevor-Roper, Hugh. "The Invention of Tradition: The Highland Tradition of Scotland." In Eric Hobsbawm and Terence Ranger, eds., *The Invention of Tradition,* pp. 15–42. Cambridge: Cambridge University Press, 1982.

Turner, James. *Reckoning with the Beast: Animals, Pain, and Humanity in the Victorian Mind.* Baltimore: Johns Hopkins University Press, 1980.

Turner, Trevor. "Erotomania and Queen Victoria: or Love Among the Assassins?" *Psychiatric Bulletin* 14 (1990): 224–27.

Turner, Victor. *The Ritual Process: Structure and Anti-Structure.* Ithaca, New York: Cornell University Press, 1969.

——. *The Anthropology of Performance.* New York: PAJ Publications, 1986.

——. "Frame, Flow and Reflection." In Michel Benamou and Charles Caramello, eds., *Performance in Postmodern Culture,* pp. 33–55. Milwaukee: Coda , 1977.

Tyrrell, William Blake. *Amazons: A Study in Athenian Mythmaking.* Baltimore: Johns Hopkins University Press, 1984.

Valverde, Mariana. "The Love of Finery: Fashion and the Fallen Woman in Nineteenth-Century Social Discourse." *Victorian Studies* 32 (Winter 1989): 169–88.

Venus School-Mistress, or Birchen Sports. Reprinted from the edition of 1788, with a preface by Mary Wilson, containing some account of the late Mrs. Berkeley. 1862 (?). Reprint, New York: Grove Press, 1984.

Wahrman, Dror. " 'Middle-Class' Domesticity Goes Public: Gender, Class, and Politics from Queen Caroline to Queen Victoria." *Journal of British Studies* 32 (October 1993): 396–432.

Walkowitz, Judith. *City of Dreadful Delight: Narratives of Sexual Danger in Late-Victorian London.* Chicago: University of Chicago Press, 1992.

Walsh, Susan. "Bodies of Capital: Great Expectations and the Climacteric Economy." *Victorian Studies* 37 (Autumn 1993): 73–88.

Ward, Mary Augusta [Mrs. Humphry]. *Marcella*. Introduction by Tamie Watters. London: Virago, 1984.

Warner, Marina. *Alone of All Her Sex: The Myth and the Cult of the Virgin Mary*. New York: Knopf, 1976.

———. *Monuments and Maidens: The Allegory of the Female Form*. New York: Atheneum, 1985.

Weisinger, Herbert. "The Twisted Cue." In *The Agony and the Triumph: Papers on the Use and Abuse of Myth*. East Lansing: Michigan State University Press, 1964.

Whippingham Papers, Chiefly by the Author of the Romance of Chastisement. London, 1888.

Williams, Linda. "Fetishism and Hard Core: Marx, Freud, and the 'Money Shot.'" In Susan Gubar and Joan Hoff, eds., *For Adult Users Only: The Dilemma of Violent Pornography*, pp. 198–217. Bloomington: Indiana University Press, 1989.

Williamson, Judith. "Royalty and Representation." In *Consuming Passion: The Dynamics of Popular Culture*, pp. 75–89. London: Marion Boyars, 1986.

Wilson, Elizabeth. *Adorned in Dreams: Fashion and Modernity*. Berkeley: University of California Press, 1985.

INDEX

Designer: María Giuliani
Text: New Baskerville
Compositor: Columbia University Press
Printer: Maple-Vail
Binder: Maple-Vail